Leadership
Communication

Leadership Communication

How Leaders Communicate and How Communicators Lead in Today's Global Enterprise

E. Bruce Harrison and Judith Mühlberg

First published in 2014 by
Business Expert Press, LLC
222 East 46th Street, New York, NY 10017
www.businessexpertpress.com

ISBN-13: 978-160649-808-8 (paperback)
ISBN-13: 978-160649-809-5 (e-book)

Business Expert Press Public Relations Collection

Collection ISSN: 2157-345X (print)
Collection ISSN: 2157-3476 (electronic)

Cover and interior design by Exeter Premedia Services Private Ltd., Chennai, India

First edition: 2014

10 9 8 7 6 5 4 3 2 1

Printed in the United States of America.

To CCOs and future CCOs: Knowing that it's about leading and communicating, in the realization that you can't do one without the other.

Abstract

The quality of leadership in any organization—business, social, military, and government—is enhanced or limited by the quality of its leadership communication. The authors of this book, both of whom are experienced in the practice and study of enterprise communication, assert that leadership is given force by strategic communication that produces results *required in competitive conditions.* For the professional in enterprise communication, this brings into focus two questions: (1) What is the relevance of communication in the leadership process of reaching *best achievable outcomes* (BAOs)? and (2) How does the primary communication professional attain expert influence and success in a leadership position? This book provides insights and guidance on functioning at the highest levels of the corporate communications profession. This function by an individual identified in many companies as the *chief communication officer* (CCO) has risen in importance in free-enterprise economies, coincident with the evolution of social media, journalism, data analytics, government engagement, change management, and other factors shaping enterprise strategies and success. The book examines the enterprise CCO at three levels: the communicator rising toward, or newly positioned in responsibility for, enterprise communication; the CCO as a collaborator in leadership with others (chief executive and chief financial officer are examples of those with whom leadership communication is structured and driven); and the developed, influential communication chief dealing with missions, strategies, and the execution of enterprise vision. A detailed guidance is given on information flow that takes advantage of stakeholder perception management and the productive, enabled employee culture. Crisis communication in modern contexts is explained, with emphasis on precrisis intelligence gathering through social conversation analysis, and procedures for crisis communication management are drawn from cases provided by CCOs in author interviews and lectures in the authors' graduate classes at Georgetown University.

Keywords

advocacy, Arthur W. Page, best achievable outcomes, business purpose, CCO, chief communication officer, chief executive officer, collaboration, communication consulting, corporate character, corporate communications, corporate governance, corporate reputation, crisis communication, C-suite communication, culture change, employee value proposition, enterprise culture, influence, information flow, leadership communication skills, leadership presentation, leadership traits, leading change, shared value deals, social media analysis, stakeholder perception management, strategic communications, strategic leadership, strategy execution, strategy implementation, transformational change, vision, WIIFM, workplace motivation

Contents

Advance Quotes for Leadership in Communication

Two of the greatest communication pros have taken on the biggest challenge of our field and of industry in general—the paradox of leading with no illusions of being in control. In *Leadership in Communications*, Bruce Harrison and Judith Mühlberg walk us through their experience, share insights and stories from fascinating leaders, and lay out a point of view that is rich, fresh—and thought-provoking.

—Maril Gagen MacDonald, CEO, Gagen MacDonald; Founder,
Let Go & Lead; Former Chief Communication Officer,
Navistar International and Pitman-Moore

My graduate students like this book's real-world focus on public relations as a strategic role in the C-suite.

—Ron Culp, professional director, Public Relations &
Advertising graduate program, DePaul University; former
Senior Vice President, Chief Communication Officer, Sears

Bruce Harrison and Judith Mühlberg's experience as CCOs, leadership counselors, and university faculty yields this book's immensely useful insight. Anyone—student or enterprise leader—seeking to understand the requirements of leadership communication can find the answers here.

—Roger Bolton, president, Arthur W. Page Society;
former Senior Vice President, Chief Communication Officer, Aetna

Leadership in Communication is a cogent, bright, easily readable definition of what corporate communicators do. More than that, it's an uncommonly careful look at how strategic communication defines, drives, and creates value for a commercial enterprise—its employees, its owners, and those whom they serve.

—James S. O'Rourke, IV, PhD, Professor of Management,
Mendoza College of Business, University of Notre Dame

Harrison and Mühlberg bring practical experiences to the Georgetown classroom, and here they share cases and frameworks that can guide many of us in the profession for years. In a world that is 24/7, more wired, more engaged and more contentious than ever before, communicators are provided ways to navigate these treacherous waters—and win.

—Mike Fernandez, Corporate Vice President/
Corporate Affairs, Cargill

Preface

Communicating to Create Communities

How do you keep producing?
"There's a four-part mantra: idea, vision, execution, follow-through. I do that over and over and over. I think it's important to distill things down to the simplest idea with the biggest impact and the most originality."

—Cynthia Rowley, American fashion designer, as told to Spencer Bailey, *New York Times* magazine, November 10, 2013

"Effective leaders put words to the formless longings and deeply felt needs of others. They create communities out of words."[1] When leadership analyst Warren Bennis made this observation in 1995, he touched on a basic goal of corporate life: communities of individuals and groups that, because of shared values, hold stakes in the business leaders' success.

Community creation certainly involves more than words, but Bennis points us to the essential reality that the source and sustenance of connectibility is communication. This book focuses on that reality. We position communication as the starting point, and the chief communicator as the active C-suite-level agent for understanding and connecting the mutual or shared interests of business leaders and their supporters.

This reality shivers in winds of uncertainty. We are moving through profound changes in how people communicate with each other and with

---

[1] See: Bennis (1995). See also by Bennis, *The Leader as Storyteller* (1996), *On Becoming a Leader* (1989), and *An Invented Life: Reflections on Leadership and Change* (1993). Warren Bennis is a professor at the University of Southern California in Los Angeles. He is the founding chairman of USC's Leadership Institute.

businesses, how technology enables, invades, and creates multiple channels in the flow of information, shaping how participants and would-be participants in shared-value communities form opinions and ultimately how they act. Data mining and analytics are now integrated as both a disconnecting disrupter and a facilitating connector in corporate communication. Companies are examining the constant stream of stakeholder opinions, experiences, and choices, as well as waves of resistance from critics, for insights that can shape future value-influencing decisions.

The good news, and the focus of this book, is that in the world of business in a free-enterprise environment, the situation is manageable and transforming. Disruption can stimulate new thinking and competitive opportunities. Corporate communication transformation is enabled by modern, 24/7 flow of news, social, macro- and micro-blogging platforms. And this dynamic has stimulated new ways of connecting inspiration and ideas, storytelling and freelance publication, creating conversations, and providing graphics in innovative ways. The force multiplier of Twitter, Yammer, Instagram, Pinterest, et al., enlarged possibilities to corporate connectivity—bridging cultures, continents, communities, and generations. As the Boston Consulting Group has observed of the forces for success in high-performing companies, "Digitization has played a part, and so too have the spectacular advances of engineering, which have bridged the seemingly unbridgeable. As a result, organizations now need to be connected in the broadest sense with employees, customers, suppliers, shareholders, and a wide range of stakeholders."[2]

Corporate communicators are creatively engaged in the current and future shape of corporate–stakeholder community. To align corporate communication to strategically advance, transformational business realities, the Arthur W. Page Society (an organization of executives—top-level

---

[2] See Richard Barrett's (2013) commentary, at http://www.the-decisionfactor.com/business-analytics-strategy/thrive-while-others-survive-with-epm-and-bi/ Barrett found that the most successful sustainably transformed organizations follow these four pillars of conscious capitalism: higher purpose (beyond making money) supported by employees linking them to the common good of society; equal dignified treatment of all stakeholders (employers, suppliers, customers, shareholders, local community, and society); conscientious leadership (self-aware leaders living their values); and conscientious (company) culture (that can be measured).

officers usually identified as *chief communication officers*—or *CCOs*—in companies with accountability for corporate communication) has worked over the past several years to document the driving trends and to propose approaches to C-suite strategies and execution that ensure effective connections among people and forces inside and outside the company. The *New Model* for corporate communication, as articulated in the Page Society's report, *Building Belief* (2012), captured the changes that leading edge CCOs have created to help enterprises build and protect brand and reputation within the realities of transformation and transparency. The *New Model*, unveiled in April 2012, set the stage for communication leaders in business to help their organizations succeed in a radically different 21st century environment. The model was introduced in the Georgetown University master's degree program by faculty (your authors in putting together this book) and supported by CCOs as visiting lecturers in the leadership communication classes.

We are indebted to corporate communication leaders who have assisted us in our classes, have provided input and guidance, and have tested the relevance and understanding level of some of this book with their peers, teams, and university students. As you will quickly see in this book, we leaned upon and tried to advance the work of the Arthur W. Page Society in creating understanding of the values shared among those in business and stakeholder communities. Page was a lodestar in our attempt to chart the course for developing a new generation of communicators to lead and to support a new crop of leaders to communicate. This is our purpose, our beginning with the end in mind.

E. Bruce Harrison and Judith A. Mühlberg
Washington, DC

PART I

The New Model CCO: Grasping the Opportunity

This book is organized into three parts, but expressing one unified point: At the highest levels of an enterprise, leadership success depends on influential communication. In Part I, we draw on our corporate communication experience to describe the typical scope, challenges, and opportunities of the expert communicator in the leadership ranks of a competitive business enterprise. In Chapter 1, we lay out the role of chief communication officers (CCOs) as counselors to corporate executives and connectors to their followers in free-enterprise pursuits. Chapter 2 draws on examples such as those of Arthur W. Page, a public relations pioneer who linked telephone company initiatives with stakeholder interests in the 1940s to examine the transformational significance of C-suite communication in free-enterprise conditions. Chapter 3 examines a "VICTORY" route for an enterprise and the traits or strengths of leadership. Chapter 4 explores the leadership role and Chapter 5 summarizes the basics with an analysis of influence and its role in the CCO's toolbox.

In other words, Part I sets the foundation for what the CCO has to become in order to be effective, to work as part of the team, and particularly to serve the chief executive as a sounding board on issues both in the company's internal culture and in the ecosystem of stakeholders outside.

The authors make the point that influential communication at the top of an organization provides a consistent basis for, and a rewarding focus on, best achievable outcomes.

CHAPTER 1

What's In It for You?

What can you get from this book? We start with two assumptions about you as a reader. One, you are a leader, a learner, or both. Two, you know that communication is the critical path in leadership. With you in mind, we take it from there.

As former chief communication officers (CCOs), as counselors to corporate executives, and as faculty in university studies in corporate communication leadership and crisis, we are engaged in the current dynamics and the new, transformational significance of C-suite communication.

Drawing on what we have learned, we wrote this book to help you become, *or escalate your odds for success as,* an expert communicator in today's business enterprise.

In this book, we zero in on two perspectives—the perspective of the person at the top of the corporation and the perspective of the person in charge of the corporation's internal and external communications (and now less frequently referred to as public relations). There is a rapidly emerging opportunity for productive enterprise leadership in a collaboration between the Chief Executive Officer (CEO) and the CCO.

We analyze this opportunity and with the help of other experts—including most importantly, CEOs and CCOs—explore two critical questions: How do leaders communicate? And, how do communicators lead? How do CEOs (as well as other top leaders) and CCOs focus on competence, shared-value dedication, and emotional intelligence to realize victory for all who have a stake in the company's success?

We are looking for best achievable outcomes.

The purpose of this book is to help you become a force of leadership communication in a business setting, as CCO or CEO—in the corporate C-suite and beyond.

That expresses rule one for us—and a rule we will encourage you to adopt in every leadership communication strategy.

Start with the end in mind. Focus on your purpose.

The focus of this book is how successful companies are led in corporations operating in free-enterprise economies, particularly in the United States, to achieve positive business growth, positive external reputation, and positive internal workplace cultures.

What is a leader? "My simple answer," said the four-star general and former Secretary of State Colin Powell, "(is) someone unafraid to take charge. Someone people respond to and are willing to follow." Powell answered the question as to whether leaders are born or made, with a tilt toward instincts at birth ("a natural connection and affinity to others") that are then encouraged by parents and teachers "and molded by training, experience, and mentoring" (Powell 2012). Natural talents, quotients of both intelligence and emotions, are arguably the basis of leadership. In a large, general sense, leadership means the creation of followers. Leaders in an enterprise have an idea—a vision, as we will subsequently explain—toward an achievable outcome, a goal worthy of enterprise effort. Individuals and groups—employees, customers, investors, and others—see in the goal the value to the enterprise as well as the *what's-in-it-for-me* motivation for striving to achieve the leader's envisioned outcome. This idea of vision is the initial step in what we believe every competing enterprise pursues: victory, wins for the enterprise, and wins for followers—who are, we emphasize, stakeholders in the success of the enterprise.

That is where leadership communication comes into play.

Purpose and shared values enable leaders to lead and followers to follow. If followers are not able to internalize, and thereby personally buy into the purpose of the leader's vision, there will be little or no enthusiasm for going there. The vision is both constant and subject to change if conditions—contexts, competitive, and otherwise—require adapting to gain an advantage.

Leading is learning, as Powell indicated. Focus on purpose requires knowledge of stakeholder interests and of contexts that challenge the enterprise's ability to deliver. This means that you not only start with the end in mind, but also are sensitive to challenges in your path. "You should be able to see the freight train coming out of the mist," said former Congressman Joe Scarborough (Scarborough 2012) on his talk show toward political leaders who are blindsided by disruptive events during an election campaign. Relating this to corporate vision, leaders—CEOs and CCOs—must ask: What if the prospect of best achievable outcome is compromised by uncontrollable forces? What if corporate vision veers off-course? What is our plan B? We will get into the matter of vision reset in our victory discussion. Through deeds and words, corporate leaders and their expert communicators (the CCOs) form, describe, and motivate achievement of strategies that beat the competition and deliver desired value to the company's stakeholders. If you are the CCO, the CEO will assuredly have the power to determine your status and role in the enterprise, but we emphasize that stakeholders—acting on their perceptions with regard to the company—are effectively the arbiters of your success. This is demonstrated in Figure 1.1 that outlines leadership communication as a function of three things: strategy, engagement, and execution. We discuss these elements throughout this book.

Strategy

- Establish vision: strategic focus
- Communicate current realities
- Point to best achievable outcomes
- Assure reliance shared values
- Provide hope path: basis for dealing with difficulty

Engagement

- Build teams with stakes in BAOs
- Communicate value-based missions
- Assure mastery: technical, practical and emotional competence
- Influence shared-value culture
- Lead stakeholder information flow

Execution

- Communicate plan toward BAOs
  Develop structures, systems and processes to execute and measure
  Encourage team autonomy initiative and collaboration
  Recognize benchmarks set and met
  Engage external stakeholders

Figure 1.1 Leadership communication (CEO, CCO, C-Suite collaboration)

A Stakeholder Is a Risk Taker

The word *stakeholder* derives from the time when Americans took a chance on habituating the rugged Western lands, incentivized by the Homestead Act of 1862 that made land available to those who would work and live on it. "A stake became a section of land marked off by stakes and claimed by the farmer," as the political communicator and popular linguist William Safire (1995) explained in a *New York Times* article. "By extension, a 'grub stake' was money advanced by the government for food—or *grub*—as an investment or loan."

Safire (1995) cited a current sense of the word in a British *Handbook for Managers* published in 1975: "The needs of our 'stakeholders'—*i.e.,* the persons and groups having a direct stake in our organization: the owners, employees...customers, suppliers, financiers, managers, the area in which the organization is established...." It is essentially this meaning your authors have in mind when we speak of stakeholders. In our view, a stakeholder is a person or a group of people that takes steps to connect with a business enterprise as an owner (investor), direct engager (leader, manager, worker), direct support or beneficiary (community, neighbor, customer), or collaborator (supplier, corporate partner). The connection is voluntary, a specific return on the connection is subject to circumstances that may be beyond either the enterprise or the stakeholder's control. The corporate stakeholder is—as was the settler staking a claim in the rugged West—a risk taker.

Michael Novak (1996), in one of his Pfizer lectures, brought the risk factor into current reality in describing the American "stakeholder society" as one in which private stakeholders secure the general welfare and the larger public interest. "The stakeholder society in this sense is the very foundation of the free society. Maintaining it entails investment, hard work, responsibility, risk, and earned reward or, often enough, personal failure." Novak concludes on a large and noble theme: "Freedom is tied to risk and responsibility."[1]

---

[1] Novak won the Templeton Prize for Progress in Religion, the Wilhelm Weber Prize, and the International Award of the Institution for World Capitalism. He served as a director of social and political studies at the American Enterprise Institute, and held the George Frederick Jewett Chair in Religion, Philosophy and Public Policy at AEI. He was cofounder and publisher of Crisis and columnist for Forbes and National Review.

Corporate communication is both the ear to the ground listening for risk to the enterprise and the purveyor of information that at least attempts to keep stakeholders aware of risks, immediate or incipient. CCOs are thus critical in the risk-management considerations of the C-suite and in conveying risk signals that appear in the monitored inflow of stakeholder data and perceptions.

Leadership Communication Involves Strategy, Engagement, and Execution

There is no leadership without communication. The CCO enables the leadership communication process through three interrelated phases: strategic focus or vision (strategy), building productive teams (engagement), and achieving outcomes (execution). The CCO is most effective when he or she is in the role described by Rosabeth Moss Kanter (2009), Harvard Business School, as the connector—a counselor to others in the C-suite in building an enduring culture that enables change and renewal.[2] CCO influence, collaborating with others in the C-suite, is felt throughout the organization.

At his best the CCO, with the communication team directed from the C-suite, is a daily, invaluable resource to managers and leaders throughout the organization in their connections with and influence on the attitudes and actions of others.

Collaborating with others in the C-suite, the CCO must address big goal questions. What does the company do? Why do we do what we do? How do we attract stakeholders, beginning with employees and investors? What does the company plan to be known for? What promise or strong intention can we put into words that will be achievable, believable, and influential to stakeholders, inside and outside the enterprise?

With CEO buy-in, the CCO can facilitate the process of discussing, deciding, and approving the shared values, big-goal communication. Behind a simplified statement, which will appear in various forms in leadership communication vehicles, from annual report to advertising, the vision statement is the tip of a well-planned, multifaceted business model.

---

[2] See her several books on leadership and "vanguard" company performance.

How does a company turn a business model into a winning reality? What is the believable, attractive intention of the enterprise that stimulates stakeholder buy-in as well as employee efforts to deliver? The enterprise must be able to answer these questions.

Messaging channels will convey more than mere slogans, more than image (see Chapter 4 on reputation); it is an expression of the company's strategic focus on a purpose, a destination, and a deliverable, which assures the company's reliance on shared values, provides an optimistic outlook (or hope based on reality), and is not so resolute or limited that it cannot be changed without confusion toward a new vision ("vision reset"). In conclusion, the CCO is a master of the beacon that lights the road for stakeholder connections and is alert to deal with difficulties and to identify new opportunities.

The CCO has a guiding, expert responsibility—within his work on the flow of information, on stakeholder engagement, and on cultural influence—to contribute to and to manage this ongoing process of strategic visionary communication.

CCO Accountabilities: Information, Stakeholder View, and Culture Influence

CCOs enable visions to be executed through the strength of *shared values*. In the C-suite and beyond, the chief communicator's accountabilities embrace three critical areas: (1) multichannel information flow, (2) critical stakeholder perceptions, and (3) the prevailing corporate culture.

CCOs and the communication team are influential at all levels of the company and especially in the C-suite, where vision is formed and strategies are pursued throughout the organization. The goal is always Best Achievable Outcomes (BAO)—where each word is a factor in success: *Best* means our efforts are on or very close to the intended target; *Achievable* is the reality check, to reach for winnable conditions and to focus all available energies and talent; *Outcomes* remind us that we are always aiming toward valued results, within competitive conditions and a timeframe that separate winners and losers. The company's expert, master communicators lead the BAO effort in the following:

1. The accuracy and timeliness of an ongoing, two-way, trust-building *flow of information* (which requires a deep knowledge of every channel of communication).
2. An accurate understanding of key *stakeholder perceptions* (again, expertly engaging in the relevant flow of information and opinion in such channels as social media).
3. And implementing the advocacy of a *workplace culture* that is informed, motivated, productive, open to change and, to the extent practicable, autonomous (employees enabling one another to do his or her individual best).

The CCO's eye is always on the "why?"—the shared-value deals that are formed and nourished through the relationships, communication strategies, and other needs of every management executive. As a collaborator with other C-suite executives, the CCO understands where each executive is charged to lead: The missions that move toward realizing the enterprise's overall purpose in creating value and the stakeholders who must be engaged to strengthen and achieve the values in their respective areas.

Each executive is focused on a particular category of stakeholders. The chief financial officer (CFO) is most concerned with bankers, analysts, and investors (also referred to as shareholders or stockholders). The chief marketing officer (CMO) engages regularly with customers and distribution channel leaders. Chief operations officers (COOs) focus on production, quality, and sales; purchasing officers, on suppliers; human resources, on employees; and government relations—officials and regulators at federal, state, and local levels where the business has an impact. Depending on the make-up, needs, and decisions of the CEO and board, certain other specialists (such as chief sustainability officer, chief compliance officer, risk management officer, and others) will have their aspects of interests and partnering within the overall stakeholder ecosystem.

Communication is vital in each of these value–equation relationship areas, and the CCO will look for opportunities to influence and partner with the executive in charge. This partnership can range from direct counseling with the executive to providing resources—professional staff help on in-house or offsite programs, executive presentations to specific stakeholder groups, follow-up including research to plan or evaluate communication effectiveness, and any other support useful in (1) focusing on the needs of the executive and stakeholder connection and (2) aligning these discrete executive efforts with the overall, current corporate communication strategies.

CEOs and CCOs Share the Assets of General Context Awareness

Although the CCO is a counselor, a collaborator, and when needed, a coach in the C-suite relationships, her competence in communication matters is accomplished with a distinctive perspective that aligns precisely with that of the CEO. Each has the perspective of a generalist. As noted, others at C-level have their specialized areas of competence, well-developed knowledge, and current relationships in vital corporate areas. They are specialists, and they know and work to achieve the best outcomes in their specialized accountabilities.

The CEO is, and must be, a generalist. He is responsible for the overall movement toward and achievement of goals, and must therefore survey the entire scope of opportunity and operations. We believe that only one other key player in the company most commonly shares this sort of big-picture perspective and that is the CCO. Although, of course, the CEO and the CCO will have personal and professional differences in areas of education, training, and competence, these two leaders at the top of the organization are similarly positioned to view the vision, the missions directed toward the vision, and the total stakeholder universe. They must be comfortable and analytical in viewing the broad scan of stakeholders, the internal structures (such as the company's culture), and the external conditions (both competitive sector developments and general developments that have potential impact on the company; for example, international or domestic cultural or political unrest). Together, they look at the path forward and have a general sense of how all the elements of people, planning, and effort are coordinated to reach the planned goal.

An analogy may be helpful to make the distinction of specialists and generalists. If the company were a group of C-level executives hiking along a trail, the specialists are those who each interested in some particular aspects of the route—the lay of the terrain, the flora and perhaps the fauna, the pace of the hike, the temperature, or the hours before darkness. For example, the COO in this hypothesis might be determining—as Jim Collins (Collins and Hansen 2011), the author of leadership books, does in the metaphor of the "20-mile march"—the best per-day mileage target, good weather or bad, to reach the destination with all hands active, delivering value on time, and in the allotted time frame.[3] The CFO might be focused on the costs per mile of the hike, calculating outlay, and expected return or reward when the destination is reached. The mindset of the human resources officer may be on the physical condition of the hikers, knowledge of the surrounding ambiance, and determination of the value of pre-hike preparation, training, and support. Anticipating risks could be the orientation of the risk management officer. And so each individual focused and delivered part of the whole required for the journey.

While these specialists hike on, collaborating as a team, the two generalists—the lead chief and the communicator chief—are mentally infused with the totality of this effort and its realization. They maintain the vision—the victory—of destination. CEOs and CCOs are particularly aware of reality. It is their habit to know where things stand, where the team is, and, very important, the contexts, current or developing, that affect the ability to reach goals. It is useful to recall the example of the generalist in a story told by management author (Peter Synge 1990). In this case, imagine that the generalist is the corporate CEO. He drops back from the band of followers and, possibly with a boost from fellow-generalist CCO, climbs a tree to view the forward horizon. The leader sees something no one else on the hike has thought of. He comes down from the visionary spot and (let's hope!) he confers with his expert communicator to deliver to his fellow hikers a significant leadership message: "Wrong trail."[4]

---

[3] For another treatment of the book, see How to Manage Through Chaos, from Fortune magazine, October 2011, by Collins and Hansen at http://www.jimcollins.com/article_topics/articles/how-to-manage-through-chaos.html. An excellent summary of other business strategies contained in Collins' books can be found at http://www.inc.com/kimberly-weisul/jim-collins-good-to-great-in-ten-steps.html

[4] We especially recommend Chapter 9, which deals with fostering "personal mastery in the organization."

Counseling to Leadership: CEOs and CCOs

If Carol Bartz, the former chief executive of Yahoo, could go back in time, she would have changed one thing about her relationship with the board that fired her, in a brief and unexpected phone call.

She would have spent more time understanding the relationships among the board members, what they shared with each other, what worried them—almost none of which she was privileged to know about.

The former CEO told a reporter, in an interview conducted at a "Most Powerful Women" conference conducted by the magazine *Fortune* (2012), "I didn't understand or take the time to understand the relationships they had between themselves."

"How could you have done that?" asked the reporter.

"Well," Bartz answered with a smile and an open-palm, what-can-you-do gesture, "I guess you follow them into the men's room."

And then she added, seriously, "I could have taken charge of the communication. I could have listened more. I should have arranged regular dinners with two board members at a time. I could have asked them what they thought I should be doing, and again, I guess I should have listened better."

CEOs, as with CCOs, have to listen "up" (to the boards to whom they report) and it benefits them greatly if they listen "out" (to those who report to them). Most executives are aware of this. The authors of *Talk, Inc.* (Groysberg and Slind 2012) make the point that executive communication with employees is essential to enterprise success. "The only way to engage employees is through communication," said William Hickey, president and CEO of Sealed Air Corporation, a global packaging manufacturer. "I count on *communication from employees* as part of my overall effort."

Communication experts, with their knowledge of the process of connection, can be internal counsels or coaches to others in the C-suite. The CCO treats the executive as a client. Counseling—or coaching—starts at any level with the dynamics of conversation. You need to learn as much as you can from the person who can benefit from your listening, and you need to ask questions that challenge the current condition and motivate toward change.

CCOs, including your authors, have no trouble recalling cases in which CEOs were in need of at least one closed-door session, one out-of-town plane, or in-town private car ride, for one of the famous "truth-to-power" conversations, frequently centered on the topic of leadership communication. The conversation can be initiated by either person. The chief asks the counselor a question. Or a courageous question is posed by the trusted CCO-as-coach.

In either event, before you, as a CCO, meet with the internal client, we favor a three-question mental exercise. You will have an open mind to determine: What's happening? So what? Now what?

Whether the chief or you are initiating the conversation, the dynamics of open-ended questions provide you with focus, while showing respect for the C-suite executive. An internal consultant at PCS Health Systems asks open-ended questions to help understand the need for assistance: How can I help you? What is happening now? What are the issues? How do your managers and employees view the issue(s)? What is your vision? What are the roadblocks? What do you see as possible solutions? What has been tried? Where do you want to go from here? (Scott 2003).

The best achievable outcome of the follower–leader conversation is affected by the nature of the follower's question:

- *Context.* Timing, events, and circumstances make the question no big surprise.
- *Content.* The question is relevant to the CEO's best interests, to best outcome options.
- *Tone.* The question flows with the caring, connecting, and non-challenging valve open.

Within this trio of forces that are influential in leadership communication, *contexts* are usually dominant. CEOs and CCOs must constantly understand the contexts in which their information will be received. External conditions, often uncontrollable, will shape what you are trying to control. What news, what competitive strategies, what stakeholder perceptions, what social media contexts have the potential to limit (or, in happy circumstances, enhance) the company's drive to succeed?

What does the CEO want to know?

The CEO is a competitor. She leads a team and enables leaders who augment her instincts, her experience, and her management perspective. Our emphasis is on the C-suite communicator's influence. The CCO's perspective enables the CEO to compare contextual risks and rewards—to handicap the odds for maximum intended benefit of decisions and announcements.

What does the CEO want to know? Ram Charan (2001), a leading adviser to CEOs and senior executives in Fortune 500 companies, author of numerous books and articles, and a professor at Harvard and Northwestern, says in his book, *What the CEO Wants You to Know:*

> The best CEOs use their business acumen to cut through the complexity of their business, their industry, and the broader business environment. They continually improve the fundamentals to money making, and by so doing consistently and relentlessly over time, they create a track record. The investment community tends to reward such CEOs and companies with higher P-E multiples, which creates tremendous wealth for shareholders. It creates job security and growth opportunities for employees, and wealth for those who receive stock options (p. 86).

What does the CEO need to make those decisions? In short, CEOs need input on the factors that influence victory, that reach best achievable outcomes. These may be trends that affect sales in different regions of the world and what the competitors are doing. Or, they may need detailed information about employee engagement and morale and how that is affecting performance metrics. And, they will certainly need up-to-date information on the stock market reaction to their company, their thinking about the securities, and what actions they should be considering.

Charan (2001, 86) further argues: "An edge in execution comes from having the right people in the right jobs, synchronizing their efforts, and releasing and channeling their energy toward the right set of business priorities. It takes insight into people and the organization to get the energy aligned."

This means that the C-suite must be aligned and their energies channeled on the critical business priorities, and *cannot be strategically focused on transactional matters*—for example, in the CCO's venue getting out the news release, responding to social media, planning the internal meetings, preparing physical materials such as Q&As—as those tasks and tactics are not primarily on the top of the mind of CEOs: "How does this relate to selling our product (or service)?" When one drills down to the core of success in a competitive enterprise environment, one finds the essential element: income production generated by delivered value.

The CEO and the company need C-suite connectors working together, informed together, moving always toward what Ram Charan calls "the edge of execution." No one in the circle of influence is more critical than the CCO who is plugged into social, analytical, formal, and informal information related to customers, competitors, employees, investors, and others. No one is in a better position to serve the CEO in what she "wants to know about;" the CCO is also able, on the basis of stakeholder sensing and feedback evaluation, to connect with and enable anticipatory management value among others who report to the CEO and to the board.

This book deals with the CCO's C-suite relationship of values exchanged in good times and bad. Difficulty and crisis must be part of anticipatory management, and CCO strategies for online engagement with stakeholders will most usefully include pre-crisis intelligence gathering and analysis.[5] Tracking stakeholder interests and opinions, company people are positioned to spot sparks of potential fire. CCOs and their teams are moving toward organized concepts on risk awareness, not unlike Nassim Nicholas Taleb's (2007) call in *The Black Swan* to "imagine the unimaginable."[6]

---

[5] Pre-crisis intelligence projects, developed by the authors in teaching the advanced studies course on corporate crisis communication at Georgetown, have proven useful as a teaching tool for C-level leadership communication, with cooperation from more than a dozen major corporations.

[6] For Taleb (2007), "black swans" underlie almost everything about our world, from the rise of religions to events in our own personal lives. He says a "highly improbable event" has three characteristics: it is unpredictable; it carries a massive impact; and, after the fact, we concoct an explanation that makes it appear less random, and more predictable, than it was. Examples are the astonishing success of Google; the events of 9/11/01. CCOs may be inspired to look for "black swans" by reading this book and thinking "improbable event" that risks corporate success and may lead to crisis.

Having learned either directly or from the experience of others the potential of misguided action, corporate executives are conditioned to realize that they have in the CCO a risk manager who is familiar with stakeholders' opinion. This means that the CCO needs to keep improving his means of evaluating and managing the stakeholder trust equation. Listening to stakeholders—normally including, if not based on, online monitoring and engagement—is commonly considered a critical (arguably, the most important) aspect of the CCO's stakeholder perception analysis. Corporations frequently turn to outside experts to gather specific stakeholder intelligence data.[7]

Communication is Imbedded in Transformative Leadership

Leadership studies describe two levels of enterprise leadership: transactional and transformative. The first level addresses daily, consequential transactions that keep the organization in motion, moving as steadily and competitively as practicable for best achievable outcomes. Management teacher Peter Drucker (1973, 1993) provided a transactional guide in his three-part daily directive to managers: identify customers who expect something from the company, match this expectation to the promised value, and do today what it takes to execute toward this expectation.[8] Change of course occurs, but the response is more conditional than systemic: adjustments are made with significant attention to minimizing disruption.

In a transformative leadership, disruption is expected and is used to advantage. The number one focus now in many C-suites is on innovation.

---

[7] CCOs often contract with professional firms that specialize in online monitoring. One such firm (known as Crowdverb, in the Washington, DC, area) describes itself as "a digital advocacy and mobilization firm that harnesses the power of web data to identify and recruit large numbers of advocates." We do not know and are certainly not recommending this particular firm (which aims at political "advocates") but the following description of data gathering is relevant to a CCO's interest in "listening"/engagement with business stakeholders: "Our proprietary technology platform and tool set allows us to listen, analyze and immediately take action on issues that could positively or negatively impact our clients. By analyzing and learning from this data, we have the ability to better strategize and target campaigns to improve cost effectiveness and overall results."

With greater access to big data—enabling them to dig into customer preference, market habits, and competitive information—company leaders understand that disruption is built into the reality of doing business. Customer attitudes and choices, for example, can swing quickly from one buying habit, product, or service value perception to another. Communication is geared to change and success, as marketing experts have observed, will focus more on relationships than on transactions. Marco Bertini, of the London Business School, and John T. Gourville, business professor at Harvard, have recognized that the way in which some companies make money is itself disrupted to the point of being self-destructive. "From insurance and financial services to telecommunications and air travel," they wrote in a 2012 *Harvard Business Review* article in 2012, "companies use pricing to extract what they can from every transaction." The result is often customer rejection. They gave the example of Net-Flix, which in 2011 implemented a 60 percent price increase for customers who both rented DVDs and streamed video. The reaction disrupted the company's money flow: some 800,000 users cancelled their service, stopped paying for service, with the secondary result of driving the company's stock-market capitalization down by more than 70 percent. They also note that pricing should communicate that the company values the customers "as people, not as wallets," creating shared values.

Drucker's daily directive still holds, but must be adjusted to shifting expectations, demands, and response requirements. C-suite leaders in a

---

[8] We draw on management giant Peter Drucker's (1973, 1993) principles and writings to summarize his three "transactional" directives describing the role of managers and productive workers in his mammoth book, Management: Tasks, Responsibilities, Practices, first published in 1973. The book is now available in a version published in 1993 by HarperCollins, New York. A .pdf of the entire book can be read and copied by accessing: http://www.google.com/url?sa=t&rct=j&q=&esrc=s&frm=1&source=web&cd=7&ved=0CFsQFjAG&url=http%3A%2F%2Fwww.civil.pdn.ac.lk%2Facstaff%2Fjayalath%2Fpages%2Fbooks%2FManagement%2520-%2520Tasks%2C%2520Responsibilities%2C%2520Practices%2520by%2520Peter%2520Drucker.pdf&ei=e56nUvO_A8S1sASqi4CQAQ&usg=AFQjCNGM46lsRciGmhgIM0Rjv6l80pgCfQ&bvm=bv.57799294,d.cWc. In addition, we recommend The Practice of Management (Drucker 1954, 1984), which created the discipline of modern management practices.

successful company in today's consumer-active contexts, will look ahead, be ready to deal with, and plan to *drive change*.

What does transformational leadership imply for corporate communication as a function in current free-enterprise environments?

As the Corporate Communication International (CCI) group at Baruch College, CUNY has observed, the corporate communication discipline is in a period of intense consolidation of internal and external functions—marketing, public relations, employee relations, and financial and investor relations—greater relevance in the C-suite, supported by greater budgets (Goodman 2011). Even during the recent difficult economic downturn, CCI reported in a 2011 study that communication executives were optimistic that their budgets were not among the earliest targets for reduction, which reflect the value of the CCO function.

CCO Function Rose with Leaders like Arthur W. Page

CCOs have not always had this high C-level relationship or respect—and therefore the opportunities of substantial leadership. We source the breakthrough of the corporate communicator as counselor to senior management and contributor to best corporate outcomes to the period between America's two world wars.

In 1927, Arthur W. Page, the son of a publisher and diplomat, became vice president of public relations for the American Telephone and Telegraph Company. He was the first person in a public relations position to serve as a corporate officer and subsequently as a member of the board of directors of a major public corporation.

Page's speeches, writings, and actions during his years at AT&T[9] are the basis for corporate relationship guidelines (famously including the statement that "all business in a democratic country begins with public

---

[9] See Griese (2001), as well as books and writings available from the Arthur W. Page Society at www.awpagesociety.com. Page left the company in 1946 and became counselor to national government leaders, including Presidential cabinet member Henry L. Stimson; he is credited with writing, at Stimson's request, President Harry S. Truman's announcement of the dropping of the atomic bomb on Japan, effectively ending World War II.

permission and exists by public approval") and principles such as those on which the professional corporate leadership communication group—the Arthur W. Page Society—was founded and now functions.

The principles—beginning with "tell the truth" and "prove it with action"—reflect on the importance of transparency to the public. We weave this condition of open, responsible engagement with stakeholders into the basic communication leadership practice and aspirations that we explore in this book.[10]

As we wrote this book, extolling the stakeholder-valued necessity of transparency in corporate communication, we dealt with an anomaly. The biggest news in public journalism of 2013 (and of decades previous) was breaking. Amazon CEO Jeff Bezos had bought the venerable, world-class newspaper, *The Washington Post,* but when *Post* reporters tried to reach him for a comment to use in their stories, Bezos was unavailable. An important point here is that Bezos bought the *Post* as a personal investment, not as an Amazon acquisition, meaning that Amazon corporate communication executives, who declined to take calls from the journalists, were actually outside the deal. That said, however, the appearance of media rejection was enough to ignite criticism from both *Post* and *New York Times* reporters who were working on a *Sunday Business* lead article and who teed off on Bezos about Amazon's corporate news relations (Streitfeld and Haughney 2013). Among other things, the *Times* described the quarterly phone and online hook-up with journalists and eager analysts from big investment firms—a test of transparency for most CEOs and CFOs, especially those heavily backed by large and small investors—as "festivals of vagueness."[11]

As with lawyers studying precedent cases for guidance, we professional communicators study ours. Our purpose in recalling the Bezos communication case is to underscore that *transparency* and *prevailing contexts* are controlling realities. Leadership communication begins at the starting

---

[10] The Page Principles are provided in Chapter 15.

[11] Quote: "Amazon's quarterly earnings calls with analysts and journalists are festivals of vagueness." See http://www.nytimes.com/2013/08/18/business/expecting-the-unexpected-from-jeff-bezos.html?pagewanted%253Dall

line, when you as a leader and as a communicator are most apt to have followers and potential stakeholders' open attention.[12]

In our graduate studies classes at Georgetown University—on corporate leadership and on corporate crisis communication—we emphasize the role of relevance to stakeholders and to surrounding conditions. Communicators who are effective learn to use the vocabulary and access routes that fit the time and place where and when they wish to connect. Rosanna Fiske (2009), a former communication instructor at Florida International University, has said her teaching aim is to develop "cultural anthropologists" who understand the nuances within the culture in which the communication attempt either scores or fails to score.[13] We teach that context is a particularly powerful factor in influencing communication impact. Communicators must decide on the timing, content, and tone of messages within the contexts of what's going on that will surround, reinforce, or weaken what we are trying to get across to stakeholders. We ask you to consider, as you read this book, that leaders successfully communicate and communicators successfully lead to the extent that they understand prevailing contexts.

Our purpose in writing this book is to help you become a force of success in a business enterprise. We bear down on competent performance. We have also kept in mind that leadership hinges on very human, personal considerations. The ability, style, and personal value proposition of the leader with whom a CCO counsels and collaborates will inevitably apply in best achievable outcomes for the enterprise. As for the BAO for this book, we eagerly associate with the summing up what James M. Kouzes and Barry Z. Posner (2012) used in one of their books:

---

[12] Bezos and, by association, the company he leads seem to have regained the ground lost by a leader's reticence to communicate when the time seemed ideal, and when stakeholders were all ears.

[13] Fiske says, "Today a student must leave a PR program with the basics, but also with a clear understanding of social, economic, and lifestyle preferences and how these affect communication, consumer behavior, culture, and technology usage.

Leadership is about "[giving] courage, [spreading] joy, and [caring] about people, product and process all along the way."[14] We hope that you will find some of that kind of personal inspiration along with the professional instruction in this book.

---

[14] Kouzes and Posner (2012) say that a leader's value is not only determined by a set of guiding beliefs (vision), but also by his or her ability to act on these beliefs. Embedded in these, they say, are behaviors, which they call these "ten commitments of leadership":

- Find your voice by clarifying your personal values.
- Set the example by aligning actions with shared values.
- Envision the future by imagining, exciting, and ennobling possibilities.
- Enlist others in a common vision by appealing to shared aspirations.
- Search for opportunities by seeking innovative ways to change, grow, and improve.
- Experiment and take risks by constantly generating small wins and learning from mistakes.
- Foster collaboration by promoting cooperative goals and building trust.
- Strengthen others by sharing power and discretion.
- Recognize contributions by showing appreciation for individual excellence.
- Celebrate the values and victories.
- Summarized in a 2008 review: http://bookreviewsummaries.wordpress.com/2008/03/24/the-leadership-challenge-by-james-m-kouzen-and-barry-z-posner/

CHAPTER 2

Leadership Is Communication

Leadership communication in the business setting is the process through which corporate leaders connect with and influence stakeholders.

More than half a century ago, a corporate public relations leader, Arthur W. Page of AT&T, observed that in democratic societies, a company exists only if it has the permission of what he called the public and what we know as stakeholders.[1] *Corporate communication is the link.* Page advanced the idea that effective information is required to gain this permission.

What is effective information at the corporate business level? We define it as the flow of strategic interactions that inform and influence corporate–stakeholder relationships. Communication strategies are executed through *engagement* among teams and individuals who understand, and have a stake in best achievable outcomes (BAOs) reaching and enhancing stakeholder interests and mutuality. The exchange of information is clear, constant, open, honest, two-way, and caring. Content, context, and tone are the structural elements of effective communication. To achieve maximum effectiveness among recipients (followers, stakeholders) communication originating in the company should pass through three strategic screens (Figure 2.1).

- **CONTENT:** Ask, "What?"

    This is where the company has maximum control over transmission. What is our news or information? What is the best (or required) timeframe for making it known?

---

[1] Page was AT&T vice president, 1926–1941, acknowledged as one of the earliest, highly placed executives in a corporate public relations role; his principles are the basis for the Arthur W. Page Society.

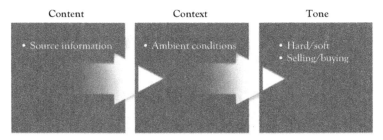

Figure 2.1 Leadership communication: source strategies

- **CONTEXT:** Ask, "Where, When, Why now, What now, What next, Who?"

  This is where external, ambient factors limit our control of the reception. Where will this be seen, read, and heard? In the communication channels and their respective and combined followers, what are the conditions surrounding the release of our information? Is this information expected, required? How will this release relate to or be influenced by existing information, opinion, or conditioning?

- **TONE:** Ask, "How?"

  This is where we can control the style or manner in which we connect best. What can we do with the decided CONTENT of our information, and with a good understanding of prevailing CONTEXTS, to reach our followers or stakeholders in the best achievable manner—language, reassurance, optimism, reality, openness? Does our "TONE" of writing, stating, and delivering information—or in our conversations with stakeholders—connect emotionally and intelligently to engender better understanding and support?

In short, we believe the purpose of leadership communication is to create and sustain stakeholders in the company. As described in Chapter 1, we see stakeholders as the employees, investors, customers, and others who make some level of commitment to a values-based deal with the company. Although each individual or group has its own motivations or drivers, they come to work, they buy the stock, and they buy the services and products, or otherwise enter into the deal with the company.[2] In some manner or at some level, each of these followers (employee, investor, customer, community supporter, and advocate) assumes a stake in the company's success. And, to achieve its own best outcomes—from support to advocacy, the company has stakes in the satisfaction and followership of one, more, or all of its stakeholders. The aim is toward a win-win relationship, or, as we introduced it in Chapter 1, a value-delivering BAOs.

We will acknowledge various levels of followership (a subject very usefully explored by Barbara Kellerman (2010) of Harvard in *Followership: How Followers Are Creating Change and Changing Leaders*) and compare this concept with what we see as the advanced level of followers, to believers and advocates (a subject of study by the Arthur W. Page Society), to our focus on stakeholders (who are in fact the arbiters and enablers of victory in the success quest of corporations).[3]

Followership is neither automatic nor specifically sustainable. That is to say that followers—groups or individuals who have a stake in the leader's success—(1) must be attracted, convinced, and in some manner satisfied or rewarded, and (2) cannot be assumed to stay committed to the company's deal or the values inherent in the relationship.

One Lesson is Clear: Communication *Is* Two-Way.

The company is less a conveyer of messages than a convener of *interests*. It is the company's responsibility—lodged in every level of corporate control or authority—to engage with stakeholders in order to understand what the company must deliver to create and deliver the deal of stakeholder support. We will examine the vital impact of *stakeholder perceptions*, affected by leadership communication, in the rise and the fall of presumptive leaders—and how this has been changed dramatically by the nature of communicating in the digital decades. In publicly

---

[2] Drive: The surprising truth about what motivates us, by Daniel H. Pink (2009), is a recommended source for understanding employee, customer and other stakeholder motivations. An interview with Pink, by Maril MacDonald, is available at www.letgoandlead.com.

[3] See Kellerman (2010), for a guide to leaders from all walks of life—from Lao Tsu and Confucius to Sigmund Freud and Nelson Mandela.

owned companies, stakeholders are the arbiters of the company's—and its leadership's—level of success.

Take Away: Leadership Is Communication

To execute strategies, a business leader must communicate persuasively. The most capable chief executive officers benefit from collaboration with an expert communicator, who knows, believes in, and can engage with followers to help the CEO move toward execution of missions and strategies.

In this hierarchical view of followership, it is clear that Leadership Communication requires different approaches to engage effectively with followers or stakeholders. Figure 2.2 demonstrates the different approaches.

ALL IN: This includes the group of C-suite executive leaders, top 100 managers, motivated by money, power, and succession who are buying heavily into the deal, accessible to leadership.

PLAYERS: This goes beyond the C-suite to others (investors, analysts, and many of the company's employees) who are motivated by income, security, and opportunity to substantial commitment to the company's deal, but they have options, to leave, to put other deals into play.

BETTORS: This gets into conditional—call them "fair-weather friends"—who have a stake in followership and the company's deal, but can be swayed to stay with their bet or to get out, if the odds change; business partners, suppliers, customers, even some government regulators or politicians depend (or essentially bet) on the company's commitment to them.

HOLD 'EMS: These players or bettors are more passive than active. Customers, for example, buy the brand because they always have been longtime investors and typically hold the stock with little or no activity

Figure 2.2 Followership: A view for leadership communication

(maybe following their parents clipping coupons). They trust the deal—the product does what it has always done, the company keeps paying dividends, the employee is locked into the promise of income. Call them "followers by hopeful habit," more comfortable not changing than changing, more inclined toward staying the course, and not betting on a competing deal.

Scattered through these categories is another clique of followers: individuals including investment advisers, who are enamored with the product "genius" (e.g., Steven Jobs) or "icon" (e.g., Warren Buffett). They follow the leader's record of seemingly enduring success. Call them "business model addicts."

Communication Leadership

John Baldoni, a leadership adviser following a corporate career, was told by a chief executive of the leadership advice he got from his father when the son was 26 years old and had just received his first promotion in a company. "His father told him that from now on his son was the most important person in his employees' lives. It was he who would decide their jobs, their schedules, and their futures." Baldoni (2012) commented: "This was a heady lesson for a young man but one that guided his life and should guide the thinking of anyone who aspires to lead. Purpose is the inner compass that holds a leader on course, but more importantly provides a lodestone for others to follow, too."

Leading is embedded with serious obligations. Max De Pree (1989), the former CEO of the Herman Miller office furniture company, has called leadership stewardship—with accountability to owners and followers in terms of relationships "of assets and legacy, of momentum and effectiveness, of civility and values." Communication enables this process.

The purpose of leadership communication in a corporate setting is to support the serious obligations of positive business growth, positive external reputation, and positive workplace culture. It is, to draw on Baldoni's analysis, the manifestation of lodestone: a constant, free-flowing, freely available source of inspiration and enablement for reaching BAOs. In the modern American corporation the job of counseling and collaborating toward this realization begins with the CCO's trustworthy, often confidential, business-centered relationship with the CEO. As we observe in this book, the distinctive ability shared by CEO and CCO is the broad perspective.

As an illustrative analogy, we use the tale of the three specialists attempting to describe an elephant by assumptions based on their grasp of a tail, a trunk, or a leg. Each executive in the upper ranks of any organization knows, understands, and is considered an expert in a specific area—finance, law, risk, operations—while the chief executive and chief communicator reach beyond their specialty strengths to see the big picture.

The generalist pair considers contexts affecting all the special masteries in the C-suite. In the enterprise march forward, CEO and CCO together view the trail ahead, to see what entanglement and opportunity (enemy in the bush or favorable clearing) will be encountered. This (eye of the elephant) seeing and (ear of the elephant) hearing what critics and stakeholders perceive are a vital element in the assortment of impact and effectiveness of leadership communication.

In democracies, corporate executives understand that (1) their effectiveness requires them to be very good communicators and (2) they must rely on experts in effective communication—verbal, visual, written, or in person—to create content and connect with stakeholders.

CCO "New Model" Leadership: "Looks Like, Thinks, Performs Like" Collaboration

Use the New Model introduced in Preface to improve your C-suite connections. The model says a winning company *looks like, thinks like, and performs like its stated character*. This means two-way (active, reactive, interactive) communication at all management levels. How can you, as Chief Communication Officer, use this framework to find more ways in which to collaborate with C-suite peers?

Selling the Vision: The AIDA Rule

Leadership communication is about selling. It is the process of selling to stakeholders the value of achieving a mutually rewarding outcome. In this sense, the leader is a sales person with an imperative need to generate buy-in from followers.

There is an honored method in sales success. Created by E. St. Louis Elmo (1898), it is the AIDA rule. Communicating toward the buy-in at the corporate level can, and often does, follow the salesperson's AIDA strategy: Align with the prospective customer, stakeholder, or follower, and successively create Attention, Interest, Desire, and Action.

Here is a story that may get your attention, and possibly lead to your action as expert communicator near the top of your organization:

In 2011, the chief executive of Nokia decided, possibly with input from his communication adviser, that he needed to get the attention of employees and investment analysts. Having recently joined Nokia from an executive job at Microsoft, Stephen Elop concluded that radical change was needed to save the company from its disadvantaged market position. It was time to shake things up before the investor briefing in two weeks.

He opens the 1,300 word letter casually. "Hello, there," he writes—attempting to ease the tension that comes with any memo from the boss—and immediately tells a story.

It is the tale of a man working on an oil platform. It is night. The platform, in the North Sea, stands 30 meters high, with dark and icy waters far below. Suddenly there is an explosion. A horrible fire breaks out. The worker retreats to the edge of the platform. He is trapped, facing deathly fire. The man hesitates. The imperatives are both perilous: Stay and be burned. Or jump and risk freezing. Desperate, the frightened worker jumps. And, the way that CEO Elop concludes his story, the worker survives.

Elop concluded his burning platform on that note: risk, opportunity, survival.

"We have multiple points of scorching heat that are fueling a blazing fire around us," said Elop, making his point: the company found itself in an untenable position, facing economic perils, and a seeming desperate move was required, in hopes of renewed, rescued business life.[4]

---

[4] Origin of the "burning platform" story is said to be that of the 1988 Piper Alpha oil-drilling platform in the North Sea.

The CEO's letter was leaked, as no doubt the Nokia leadership team had intended. Writers and stakeholders paid attention.

A *New York Times* "Deal Book" piece speculated, obviously correctly, that Elop's burning platform allusion had set the stage for management's strategy to pursue one or more potential deals, with Nokia as either buyer or seller, to transform a desperate situation into a leap of rescue and success.

The AIDA rule was in play. CEO Elop needed to sell an urgent idea. He not only got the attention of Nokia employees. His leak to the outside brought attention from many stakeholders, and positioned him and the company toward action leading to the vision of new opportunity with an established, successful business partner.[5]

Few situations are this hot, and few executives and their expert communicators are likely to engage in what might seem to be unorthodox message delivery. Contexts vary, content follows, and style or tone of delivery need to resonate with well-known stakeholders.

The lesson is that visions must be brought into performance. Visions and missions do not execute themselves. They must be conveyed, accepted, believed in, and, if truly realized, not only adopted but advocated by stakeholders.

Our cool point about this is that leadership communication is no different from any other attempt to generate buy-in from followers. Chief communicators and chief executives can start their strategy plans with consideration of the AIDA rule.

Information, Stakeholders, and Culture: CCO Accountabilities

How do expert communicators, through their C-level company counsel with the leaders of companies, do their jobs and, in best-case circumstances, become leaders in the organization? How does the CCO become a substantial catalyst for leading a company's success?

---

[5] Subsequently, Nokia would enter into a partner arrangement with Microsoft, as CEO Elop moved toward company survival and success. And, two years thereafter, Elop would rejoin Microsoft, responsible for the Nokia business.

Figure 2.3 CCO accountability

Expert communication performance in the corporate C-suite involves three direct accountabilities for the chief communication officer: *Information flow, stakeholder perception and cultural influence.* (See Figure 2.3)

Information Flow

Stakeholders inside and outside the company are the day-to-day and ulti- mate arbiters of the company's ability to win in competitive, free-market conditions. Information is the influence factor. The effective CCO con- ceives and manages the content and flow of information, internal and external, to engage with the company's stakeholders. Content, context, and tone determine the impact of information flow.

Here is the goal of the CCO's team: the *content* of company messages— starting with leadership communication—will be consistently timely, open, and honest; *contexts*—external factors that can compete with or confuse reception of company message content—will be used to advan- tage; and the *tone* or style of every piece of company information will be managed to the company's advantage. In the C-suite, the CCO will assist, coach, or counsel company spokespersons in the appropriate language, words, pace, and presentation to connect best with specific stakeholders. (In an end note, we provide a critical example, how the tone of leadership communication impacts investors and journalists in an earnings call that connects the enterprise C-suite with financial investment advisers, usually at the end of each calendar quarter).[6]

We make one point here to underscore the CCO's opportunity related to C-suite collaboration: the corporate communication wheel-

---

[6] For a transcript of a 2012 earnings call involving investment analysts and General Motors executives go to: http://seekingalpha.com/article/775021-general-motors-management-discusses-q2-2012-results-earnings-call-transcript

house should continue to be a go-to place for social media information counsel and practice. We say this while fully recognizing that in many companies strategies that involve institutional advertising are the purview of marketing. "Current best practices" for corporate communicators at a 2013 digital conference were use of digital and social media channels not only to build relationships with—and pitch story ideas to—journalists, but to engage customers and all other stakeholders in an influential exchange. However, in survey of marketing impact in the summer of 2014, Gallup Inc. told a *Wall Street Journal* reporter, "Social media are not the powerful and persuasive marketing force many companies hoped they would be," Gallup reported that 62 percent of the more than 18,000 U.S. consumers it polled said social media had no influence on their buying decisions. Another 30 percent said it had some influence. Companies in United States spent $5.1 billion on social-media advertising in 2013, but Gallup says "consumers are highly adept at tuning out brand-related Facebook and Twitter content." In a study in 2013, Nielsen Holdings NV found that global consumers trusted ads on television, print, radio, billboards, and movie trailers more than social-media ads.[7] Given this trend, the CCO and the chief marketing officer have related self-interest reasons to continue to collaborate on leadership communication—C-suite and corporate information that must align with marketing communication. While the individual leading the communication function within most enterprises many years ago began as the news media expert dealing with "the press," today's CCO continues to be positioned as the 360-degree connector of the C-suite to both social and traditional arbiters who influence competitive positioning and strategic success.

Stakeholder Perception

In Chapter 1, we recalled the origins, motivations and risks of enterprise stakeholders. Corporate communication leadership has no greater responsibility than that of connecting with stakeholders and influencing

---

[7] http://online.wsj.com/articles/companies-alter-social-media-strategies-1403499658?tesla=y&mg=reno64-wsj&url=http://online.wsj.com/article/SB10001424052702303773504579639550265288952.html

their support. The CCO executes strategies aimed at accurate, positive ecosystem perceptions, and advocates for stakeholders within the C-level leadership. The rationale of leadership communication is as a harmonizing force, assuring that the enterprise consistently relates to the values expected by stakeholders. Enterprise risk management, which is directly related to stakeholder perceptions (What do they fear? Believe? Advocate?), provides a greater opportunity—we think, in fact, an obligation—for CCO influence in C-suite management.

The CCO's competence depends on knowledge from the field of followers—inside and outside the organization—on the perceptions held and expressed about company leadership and performance. Within the C-suite, the CCO will provide insights gained through stakeholder listening strategies (e.g., engagement in social media conversations) and feedback data analysis. Before we turn to the vital matter of corporate culture, let us pause to emphasize here two critical factors that determine CCO effectiveness: (1) current understanding by corporate leaders of the various shared-value stakeholder deals that bind followers to the enterprise; (2) timely delivery of information that is understandable and relevant to stakeholders—news and opinion clearly related to their values, their reasons to favor the enterprise, its products, its services, its consistent sense of caring .

Culture Influence

As we emphasize throughout this study of CCO effectiveness and influence, the culture of the enterprise is a huge factor in competitive success. The CCO works with other C-suite leaders—linking closely with the head of human resources—to reach BAOs. Traditions (essentially, "the way it is always been done here") and leadership inspiration to change can be in conflict. Enterprise leaders rely on communication in almost every step of the process that unites and enables employees toward execution of vision and missions. The former chief executive of Intel, Andrew Grove as reported by Pandya and Shell (2006), considered culture the immune system in the company's fight to stay competitively healthy. Among the eight attributes of lasting leadership identified by business experts in a Wharton school analysis, "building a strong corporate culture" was ranked first.

Positive cultural traits—openness, teamwork, trust in management, trust in fellow workers, factors such as safety at all operational levels—are influenced through counsel, collaboration, and leadership communication. Negative factors and disconnects in the company's information flow have a deleterious impact on culture (e.g., operational accidents or faulty financial record-keeping).

Human resources experts tell us that while there is no universally good culture, there are *cultural ideals* that are universal. Employees are accountable for their actions; they are competent and care about their work. But, as the firm Boston Consulting Group (BCG) (2012) describes in the case of a West Coast-based not-for-profit organization, the basic cultural attributes do not in themselves constitute a high-performance culture.

Leaders of the organization, reported BCG, worked hard to cultivate employee morale and commitment. Their efforts paid off: surveys showed that employees were committed to the organization's vision, understood their contribution to its long-term success, and considered their career opportunities attractive. Still, performance suffered. Delivery delays were chronic because the different functions insisted on executing tasks in their own way, rather than following distribution processes designed to keep handoffs in sync and workflow on schedule. Employees may have been motivated to do a good job, but the behaviors necessary to fulfill the organization's strategic needs—in this case, following established processes to maintain on-time deliveries—were lacking. No amount of emphasis on engagement would resolve this problem.

Our focus is on the CCO's ability to understand the huge impact of *corporate culture* and to factor into leadership communication the strategies that lift (in fact, *transform*) the internal culture to the BAOs of productive engagement and performance. Through the power of C-suite collaboration and communication expertise, the CCO is a force for activating cultural support that enables transformational leadership. We explore the area of communication and corporate culture in detail in Part II, especially in Chapter 7.

Beyond These Competencies: CCO as Connector in the C-Suite

Although these core competencies—influencing the flow of information, the engagement of stakeholders, and the teamwork of culture—are essential in the CCO's role in the C-suite and beyond, there are other, often more nuanced, ways in which communicators lead in the corporate structure, as counselors, collaborators, and at times, coaches with others at the top of the enterprise.

Strategic communication counsel to the CEO and others leading the corporation has often been cited as the primary role for CCOs in the studies conducted by the Global Center for Corporate Communication and Information for more than a decade. Corporate Communication International surveys confirm that CCOs are most influential by incorporating communication strategies into the decision-making process to develop trust with stakeholders, as well as to create, maintain, and repair the company's reputation.[8]

Thought leadership today is implicit in the surging new communication model of the CCO, as advanced by leading CCOs and organizations such as the Arthur W. Page Society. As the value of strategic corporate communication has become better understood in a business environment with wide-open, virtually continuous attention, CCOs have taken on greater responsibility for adjustment to achievable outcomes with the contexts of transformational management, the impact of digital and data analytical technology, and the assertion of stakeholders to express themselves on formalized and decidedly informal (e.g., Facebook) platforms. The Page Society's namesake, Arthur W. Page, provided thought leadership at AT&T in the 1930s to 1940s during a time of elevated challenge to U.S. corporations. Counseling management on engaging with stakeholders, he went on to write a thought-provoking book that advanced the right and obligation of companies to engage their public (stakeholders) to protect their earned status and reputations.[9]

The special skill of CCOs is awareness of current realities specific to the corporation's condition and the prevailing contexts. Thought leadership that results in communication that is influential and relevant is now, and will continue to be, an evolving function in good times or times that are unusually difficult.

---

[8] Corporate Communication Practices and Trends 2013, Corporate Communication International, presented at Baruch College/DUNY, November 2013.

[9] Bell Telephone System, a book by Page (1941) dealt with the government investigation of AT&T and the Bell System, which ended in 1939 with a watered-down report to Congress that basically cleared the companies of unethical or illegal behavior.

Principles of Communicating in Difficult Times

"Life is difficult." That reality, as expressed by M. Scott Peck (2003), is a useful communication perspective. "If you accept life's road as inevitably rocky with challenges," the popular psychiatrist wrote, "you tend to grow physically, intellectually, and emotionally."

The alternative mindset, losing out to problems, as specialists in emotional intelligence have counseled, denies a person the experience of advancing along the scale of human and spiritual achievement. Corporate leaders understand that their roads to success are not unobstructed. The process of drawing energy from difficulty and forging ahead engages these five principles:

1. **Reality.** Leaders who want followers to believe in them and the mission must tell it like it is. When the road ahead is rocky, they must let followers know everything that they know about the current situation.
2. **Hope.** If the leader is honest about the reality of difficulty, followers will listen to the options needed to get back on the road to progress, to go through the difficulty, and enjoy the benefit of achieving the mission.
3. **Inspiration.** Reality plus hope moves toward trust, which is the primary inspiration of followership. Followers are inspired by leaders who care about them and will stay with them to get to where they need to be.
4. **Shared value.** Leadership is a deal that works if leaders and followers mutually believe there is personal and organizational value in the relationship. Communication is two-way and interactive, reaffirming the leader's dedication to the satisfaction of needs—values protected and received.
5. **Shared credit.** Leadership communication changes "I" to "we." Although that certainly applies to the ongoing, essential goal of sharing values, it also applies to a recognition that leaders do not do it alone. Leaders enable followers to share a stake in the leadership, vision, and outcomes. Leaders start the vision. Communicators make it clear that the vision is achievable. Followers make it a reality. The CEO and the CCO need to remember: Of all the messages that a leader can deliver, as progress is made, none is more powerful than this: "Thank you, you did it."

In successful companies, presumed weaknesses and threats to strategic aims are best treated as solvable difficulties. The rocky road of shifting

Strength	Weakness	Opportunity	Threat
Corporate Communications			
• Employee recognition • Strong global relationships • Brand recognition	• Tarnished reputation • Lack of transparency (internal 7 external) • Ongoing legal obligation	• Organic growth • Leverage company culture • Global relationships	• Government regulations • Current economy • Public outcry
Leadership			
• Led company during difficult times • Industry leader seen as an authority in the field	• Arrogance • Lack of transparency • Limited communication	• Restore and manage public perception • Leverage philanthropic endeavors	• Current communication and leadership style • Competitors • Public outcry

Figure 2.4 *Example of a Strength–Weakness–Opportunity–Threat (SWOT) analysis, addressing both executive leadership and communication leadership of a selected company*

contexts, miscalculations, and unmet competition is a call for C-suite management of leadership communication, connecting with company followers, learning from the difficulty and converting it to BAOs.

Analysis of the current reality can be facilitated by the communication team's focus on its own clear paths and rocky roads and those of the corporate leadership team. A reliable organizer of thoughts is a Strength–Weakness–Opportunity–Threat (SWOT) analysis—discussing and agreeing on the Strengths, Weaknesses, Opportunities, and Threats achieved and anticipated. Figure 2.4 presents a SWOT result for a company, done by a team in our Georgetown leadership communication class.

CCO "New Model" Leadership: Stakeholder Values Analysis

In any leadership communication effort, the CCO and C-suite team need to evaluate the connection with stakeholder values. How does this message focus area (program, activity, or action) connect with the interests and values (affirming or not) in each group of stakeholders? While our information flow must be consistent to all who receive it, directly and indirectly, what can we anticipate, and how can we make sure we are ready to engage in any conversation?

CHAPTER 3

Leadership Traits

"How'm I doing?" When he was mayor of New York, the adroitly political Ed Koch had the habit of asking this question to his stakeholders—voters and team members. An elected official, understandably, needs to know constantly how he or she is perceived on the prospects and values that voters expect to receive as part of their "deal" for support.

Somewhat similarly at least, the chief executive of your company may pose a similar question: "how are we doing?" in delivering the outcomes—expected "deal-binding values"—through the vision and missions to which he is committed. He knows that leading a company is a constant, competitive condition. It is a race to perform better than others in your field.

If you, as Chief Communication Officer, are the company's stakeholder pulse-taker, you are prepared to provide the chief executive and others in the C-suite with updates and proof points (such as benchmark data or stakeholder feedback analysis).

Wharton Study of 25 Business Leaders

Leaders are made, not born. That is generally agreed, but there is far less agreement on the question, *what "makes" them*? What skills, talents, instincts, or habits can be observed in proven leaders, traits that bring people to admire and follow them?

In 2004, the Wharton School at the University of Pennsylvania tackled that question. They identified influential leaders of the previous quarter century. The list ranged widely, from Lee Iacocca (Chrysler) to Steve Jobs (Apple); from Warren Buffett, the wizard of Berkshire Hathaway to Oprah Winfrey, the wonder woman running Harpo. Bill Gates (Microsoft), Sam Walton (Wal-Mart), Andy Grove (Intel), Herb Kelleher (Southwest Airlines), Jeff Bezos (Amazon), Jack Welch (GE), Alan Greenspan (Federal Reserve), and more than a dozen others were studied. Here is the Wharton study's summary of identified leadership traits as reported in *Lasting Leadership*:[1]

- An ability to build a strong corporate culture
- Being a truthful person
- Ability to discover and exploit underserved markets
- Being able to identify "invisible" behavior (in other words, seeing potential winners or trends before competitors discover them)
- Ability to use price as a competitive advantage
- Adept at managing organizational brand
- Being a fast learner
- Skillful at managing risk

Without arguing with this analysis (in fact, we highly recommend the study for reading), at least two assumptions can be made from this study. The first assumption is that *exemplary leadership traits are studied in business executives who have achieved competitive success*. Each of the leaders in this study engaged his or her leadership skills or traits to envision

---

[1] See http://knowledge.wharton.upenn.edu/article.cfm?articleid=1054. The winners were chosen by six Wharton judges from more than 700 names submitted by NBR viewers. They include, in alphabetical order: Mary Kay Ash, founder of Mary Kay Inc.; Jeff Bezos, CEO of Amazon.com; John Bogle, founder of The Vanguard Group; Richard Branson, CEO of Virgin Group; Warren Buffett, CEO of Berkshire Hathaway; James Burke, former CEO of Johnson & Johnson; Michael Dell, CEO of Dell Computers; Peter Drucker, the educator and author; William Gates, chairman of Microsoft; William George, former CEO of Medtronic; Louis Gerstner, former CEO of IBM; Alan Greenspan, Chairman, U.S. Federal Reserve; Andrew Grove, chairman of Intel; Lee Iacocca, former CEO of Chrysler; Steven Jobs, CEO of Apple Computer; Herbert Kelleher, chairman of Southwest Airlines; Peter Lynch, former manager of Fidelity's Magellan Fund; Charles Schwab, founder of The Charles Schwab Corp.; Frederick Smith, CEO of Federal Express; George Soros, founder and chairman of The Open Society Institute; Ted Turner, founder of CNN; Sam Walton, founder of Wal-Mart; Jack Welch, former CEO of General Electric; Oprah Winfrey, chairman of the Harpo group of companies; and Muhammad Yunus, founder of Grameen Bank. Intel's Grove headed the NBR/Wharton list, earning the title of most influential business leader of the previous 25 years.

and realize more business and more profitable outcomes than their rivals. Each exercised what the Boston Consulting Group calls "the competitive imperative" to gain access to opportunities for growth and value creation (*The Wall Street Journal* 2013).

The other assumption has to do with communication. We know that *leadership is communication*, for better or not. We can confidently assume that all these 25 leaders communicated well enough to take their companies to victory. This focus on leadership *communication* impels our offering a set of traits or skills that bind leaders to followers in the C-suite and beyond. We believe that there is an ideal flow of leadership. It starts at the top of the enterprise. It touches, informs, inspires, and enables the rise of more leaders and the attraction of more followers.

An authority on leadership development—Bill George, the former CEO of Medtronic—describes the process in another way. He says a leader seeks "true north" on the compass of personal performance, a destination that is fixed and empowering (*The Wall Street Journal* 2013).

We suggest that the "true north" in **enterprise leadership** (in effect, a way of describing authentic behavior) is fixed on values—values sought by followers, values that can be delivered to sustain a relationship.

Focus on Values in Leadership Communication

Is your company a world-leading innovator, or a profit-mongering exploiter of the poor? Is it progressive, innovative, and adjusting to new realities, or is it abandoning its core values and putting profits ahead of people?

These questions were addressed in CEO interviews for a 2007 study on "The Authentic Enterprise" (Arthur W. Page Society 2007). The research report concluded that a company's values are the fundamental basis for effective leadership and a special focus for an effective communication function.

Every enterprise must be grounded in a clear sense of itself," said the study report. "An enterprise that is sure of its purpose, mission, and values—and that takes those bedrock definitions seriously—is effectively compelled to behave in ways that are consistent with its core values (Arthur W. Page Society 2007, 16).

VICTORY: *Seven Leadership Strengths*

In his book, *Good to Great*, Jim Collins (2001) found the one–two winning combination for building a company's enduring greatness: a fierce, professional will and a comfortable, personal humility.[2]

For all leaders, whether or not they meet Collins' "level 5 executive" model, one outcome that must be pursued is what we can describe simply as victory: beating the competition, meeting stakeholder expectations, building a motivated team, and executing strategies that sustain an exemplary, authentic enterprise.

Effective leadership communication reinforces deal-binding values shared by the company and its followers (stakeholders, believers, and advocates). The company's dedication to win–win outcomes needs to be constantly communicated, proved, and protected. As the 2007 Page Society study noted, "(The) communicators' counsel to the corporation must encompass its fundamental business model, brand, culture, policies and, most importantly, values" (Arthur W. Page Society 2007, 2013).

The flow of enterprise leadership can be seen as a circular process that energizes others and regenerates itself. Our leadership VICTORY circle suggests the traits of the company leaders that enable winning in the competitive condition of running a successful business for a long term (Figure 3.1).

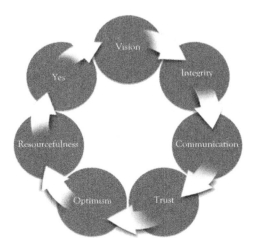

Figure 3.1 Leadership victory circle

---

[2] See Level 5 Leadership: Leaders who are humble, but driven to do what's best for the company. doi: http://en.wikipedia.org/wiki/Good_to_Great

We underscore the role of the chief communication officer leading and collaborating with other leaders, and especially with the chief executive, with whom there is the compatibility of leadership communication. The CCO and the CEO, acting, as we've established, as generalists in their perspective of leading toward the achievement of enterprise vision. Beginning with the end in mind (focusing on the central purpose: share a consistent effort to deliver stakeholder value), we believe that the evergreen goal of leadership is reaching "yes" with followers. For a leader—CEO, CCO, or others in the enterprise who influence the flow of success—the sought-after star of Bill George's "truth north" is to validate the agreement of followers that the enterprise is going in the right direction. Stakeholders are saying "yes" to whatever it is that they—as employee, customer, investor, or otherwise—value in their relationship with the company.

With the seven letters of the word "VICTORY" as a mnemonic, we can recognize seven qualities or personal traits of sustained leadership, with ongoing involvement of expert, winning communication. These traits typify the way in which CEOs and CCOs are able to collaborate.

Here then is our suggested *leadership VICTORY circle*: traits that help an individual in a position of responsibility to provide stakeholder-centered leadership.

Vision

A survey by Charles Farkas and Suzy Wetlaufer found relatively few CEOs describing themselves as the corporation's chief visionary (Farkas and Wetlaufer 1996, 115). However, how else to describe the leader who looks at the future of the company, and, from where he or she is standing, points to what is required, possible, and achievable? Leader A sees a path for a company recovering from a slip and rising to a front position. Leader B points toward product strategies that will engage with developing government market interests. Leader C envisions a trusting and productive sales method that will lift the company to success. Forward thinking—*thought leadership*—sets the course for the company. The rule that the CEO and CCO have to follow is that the best achievable outcome of enterprise leadership can occur only when a vision is clearly, consistently communicated. So, as the company's expert communicator, the CCO's leadership communication genesis is the leader's vision. The destination of enterprise effort must be translated into missions, strategies, and execution relevant to the values of the company and its stakeholders.

The vision statement can have a term limit, a BAO envisioned for a specific period of time, for a specific set of currently understood circumstances; for example, the vision for the year ahead, expressed in the CEO letter in the corporate annual report.[3] On the other hand, a vision statement can be stated broadly enough that it is sustainable over a great many years. One remarkable example is that of Hilton Worldwide, founded in 1919 by Conrad Hilton. His early 20th century beacon for employee guidance prevails. "To fill the earth with the light and warmth of hospitality" continued as the modern hotel corporation's vision statement in the 21st century (see http://www.hiltonworldwide.com/about/mission/).

In a current iteration, the online powerhouse Amazon has put its leadership vision into a broad, long-term perspective: "To be Earth's most customer-centric company where people can find and discover anything they want to buy online" (see http://phx.corporate-ir.net/phoenix.zhtml?c=176060&p=irol-factSheet).

Mary Parker Follett, one of the earliest authorities in the study of power, authority, and influence in private-sector business, observed in 1933, that among the essentials of leadership, the greatest importance is "the ability to grasp a total situation" (Graham 1995). In today's C-suite, the CEO and the CCO share that unique perspective: an overview of the entire company and where it is on the course toward realizing its vision, and delivering value to those who have a stake in it.

Leadership communication involves the task of keeping the vision relevant and alive. The former CEO of Starbucks, Howard Schultz, found his vision of the business threatened after he moved up to become its chairman in 2007. In a memo to employees, Schultz underscored the point that visions must be steeped in reality—"and that often begins by facing uncomfortable truths about the present." He returned to his role as chief executive basically to keep *his* vision alive (Schultz 2011). What is the lesson here? We see it reiterating our view that the CEO and CCO are locked together in the pursuit of "victory," and that any change in that partnership risks, if not always results in, skewed understanding among the players and diminished outcomes.

---

[3] See Chapter 8 on what we refer to as "leadership's cardinal communication."

Vision must be the guiding light of corporate communication and performance. Context can require vision reset. Holding onto a vision too long, neglecting or refusing to see the need to reset the BAO target, can discourage followers and encourage competitors. Consider the following as an example of using vision to demonstrate leadership (Isaacson 2011). Apple CEO Steve Jobs faced vision reset when competitive contexts caused the outlook for the iPod to blur. Jobs had convinced followers in the early 2000s that his vision of a pocket-size music device would be a winner. That envisioned goal was achieved. By 2005, the iPod was far outselling the Mac computer.

Jobs looked ahead again, and considered contextual clouds. What if phone companies figured out a way to play music on phones? What if other companies could make a quality product that is easy and fun to use? If a lot of people were carrying cell phones, would they continue to carry iPods?

The visionary executive took his concern to his board of directors. It was time to adjust the current vision, he told them. Although his profitable, pace-setting iPod was driving sales, creating value for stakeholders and energizing a culture of focus and momentum, something new was needed. Jobs' new vision, of course, was the iPhone, which was developed from concept to hand-held, in two years.

The leader in any field—military, corporate, nonprofit, and so forth—has to adjust to the reality of contexts he cannot control in order to maintain successful momentum. Something new—a method, a strategy, a weapon, or a product—may be required for victory in a combative environment.

CCOs use communication to light the path for vision achievement, illuminating the challenges and the inevitable, and sometimes surprising, changes that accompany all business strategies.

Integrity

A strong, modern influence on leadership, James MacGregor Burns (1979, 20) defined "transforming leadership" as collaboration with followers in a way that they "raise one another to higher levels of motivation and morality." Trust and ethics (morality) must flow from the top. As a leading public relations ethicist and professor, Shannon A. Bowen (2010, 3) of the University of South Carolina, notes:

> Trust as a relationship indicator spans the areas of ethics and moral philosophy, public relations, and stakeholder management. It also is a linchpin … because it touches upon the more elusive ideals of corporate citizenship and responsibility. Public relations and corporate social responsibility … are intertwined with the concerns of stakeholders because they revolve around common issues, and most of those issues have a component of values, principle, or ethics involved.

In successful, sustainable business relations, in all stakeholder relationships, integrity is a fundamental precept of modern, increasingly viewable corporate governance. A company's culture, its performance, and its leadership all can be said to rise or fall on the fact, as well as the perception, of its integrity.

The leader's first personal obligation is to assure that her personal word is a bond. Followers—beginning with those closest to her—look to the leader for direction as to what is acceptable and what is not. Bill George's "north star" benefit is that authentic leaders set the model for others by demonstrating their purpose, consistently practicing values of respect and honesty (George 1978). Personal integrity enables corporate integrity. "The genius of leadership," said James MacGregor Burns, "lies in the manner in which leaders see and act on their own and their followers' values and motivations" (Burns 1978, 20). As we will explain time and again in this book, followers and stakeholders essentially ask two questions about leaders: Do I believe her? Does she care about me or us? In an enterprise setting, uncertainty in response to these questions exposes and tests the integrity of the CEO and others at the top. Through their decisions, actions, and communication, C-suite leaders determine the public, and especially the stakeholder, belief in the *company's* integrity, which is communicated in decisions and messages flowing to followers inside and outside the company.

CCOs are action agents for integrity, the bedrock of authenticity, which enables stakeholder belief and trust.

Communication

To repeat the basic reality about enterprise leadership, there is no leadership without communication. Even the leader who tries not to communicate, not to show his hand in some situations, is communicating by that reticent strategy.[4] And yet, although every leader—and certainly every CEO of a public company—knows this, communication competence is not automatic; it does not come naturally to some who move toward leadership; and it can be mishandled or neglected, to the leader's and the organization's loss, especially in times of stress. There is more and more evidence in this wide-open age of communication that poor executive communication or gaffes are a significant factor in leadership change. CCOs help leaders to lead in the interplay and engagement with stakeholders. This creates greater demand for expert communicators, close to all leaders. This book is dedicated entirely to what it takes for chiefs in the C-suite of the modern American corporation—strongly focusing on chiefs of communication—to succeed in enterprise leadership.

CCOs are expert in the winning dynamics of content, contexts, and tones of the leader's communication obligations and opportunities.

Trust

This cannot be overstated: Of all the factors that connect leadership to followership and generate value sharing, trust is paramount. The leader must be trusted to act and deliver, to be as good as his word, to be worthy of followership. With management by CCOs, corporate leaders have a huge range of trust-building options: from interviews in print and broadcast media to strategic social media openness; as a writer on the corporate use of Twitter has observed, "it's amazing how one tweet can change the way thousands view your brand" (Capozzi and Ricci 2013). Corporate communicators need to bear down on the fact that this quintessential condition is a two-way street. The other direction is that in which the leader respects and trusts those she wishes to engage. Inside the company, the effective leader trusts—e.g., declines to micromanage—team members as they carry out their jobs focusing on visions, missions, and BAOs. Stakeholders, from colleagues to employees, from investors to customers,

---

[4] For more on this, see Moore, Hickson, and Stacks D. W. (2014).

are bound to leaders, in whatever their followership capacity, through trust. CEOs, old and new, know this. Warren Buffett strolls among visiting stockholders at his annual open-house event in Omaha, to engage in direct questions and conversations. Tony Hsieh builds his Zappos shoe and clothing business by trusting customers to buy or return products sent to them on inspection.

CCOs keep the flame of trust alive in the C-suite and in the stakeholder ecosystem through advocacy and the practice of open, two-way, positive, and authentic leadership communication—with a special emphasis on the feedback loop.[5]

Optimism

This is the emotional driver of confidence. We see optimism as the handmaiden of reality. The business leader describes current reality and provides hope or optimism about future achievement. Nobody follows a pessimist. Colin Powell, with a distinguished military and public-service career, summed it up in his book, *It Worked for Me* (Powell and Koltz 2012). "Optimism is a force multiplier," the former general and Secretary of State said; it brings greater energy and power to the force of followers to achieve goals." When things went wrong with a trusted executive, Warren Buffett accepted that reality; and he assured followers that one bad actor in his management team would not spoil the company's prospects. He is often quoted as having said to those managing Berkshire Hathaway properties: "If you lose dollars for the firm by bad decisions, I will understand. If you lose reputation for the firm, I will be ruthless" (Fuerbinger 1991, D1). Allan Mulally, CEO of Ford, reinforced statements about the future by consistently coupling them with "proof points," underscoring

---

[5] In a 2003 Corporatecomm.org report of a coalition of major public relations organizations, entitled Restoring Trust in Business: Models for Action, recommended that CCOs report to CEOs on trustworthiness in behavior and communication, and have access to boards of directors "to provide the broad perspective needed to balance conflicting interests" (p. 3) http://www.corporatecomm.org/pdf/PRCoalitionPaper_9_11Final.pdf

with a mantra:"The data will set you free" (Hoffman 2012).[6] Followers need to see in the leader the strength of belief in achievement. There is a caveat. As with all aspects of communication, optimism must be authentic. A CEO's overenthusiastic outlook, such as an inflated prospect of a financial result expressed on a quarterly call with investment analysts, can backfire. Phony optimism is a self-inflicted killer of trust. The expression of competitive, vision-centric reality plus a basis for BAOs is the formula for sustaining stakeholder optimism.

CCOs collaborate with leaders to describe current reality and provide an authentic case for optimistic outcomes.

Resourcefulness

This trait is not talked about much. Maybe it is because resourcefulness is frequently coupled with another "R"—risk taking. Effective corporate leaders are transformative leaders (long ago identified as the most effective kinds of leaders by author, teacher, and political leader James Mac-Gregor Burns).[7] Because they drive change, which is always necessary, and because change always involves risk, transformational leaders take calculated risks. In doing this, they are resourceful in redefining goals for competitive sustainability. Resourcefulness is the leader's ability to act effectively, even imaginatively, to keep the company on a victory path.

In her early studies of leadership, Follett said that the leader must do more than see and understand the situation as it is, to "see the evolving

---

[6] http://changethis.com/manifesto/93.01.AmericanIcon/pdf/93.01.AmericanIcon.pdf; http://www.cio.in/feature/how-analytics-helped-ford-turn-its-fortunes One of the authors knows Alan Mulally from their time as executives at Boeing. Judith Muhlberg remembers that Alan used his favorite saying, "the data will set you free" in their very first meeting in January 1999. She surmises that this was not his first utterance of the phrase, as she heard it consistently at various meetings and over a long period of time.

[7] In 1971, Burns won the Pulitzer Prize and the National Book Award for his biography, Roosevelt: Soldier of Freedom (1970). His book, Leadership, published in 1978, is considered the seminal work in the field of leadership studies. His theory of transactional and transformational leadership has been the basis of more than 400 doctoral dissertations.

situation…not on a situation that is stationary, but one that is changing all the time" (Graham 1995, 28).[8]

That point—that resourcefulness, developing a new approach, is rooted in an understanding of reality—was underscored as a trait for the success of Apple CEO Steve Jobs. Jonathan Rotenberg, president of Centriq Advisors, knew Jobs for more than 30 years. He was introduced by Jobs to meditation and Buddhism when he was 18 years old and Jobs was 25 years old. Writing in response to a *Harvard Business Review* article about Jobs, by biographer Walter Isaacson, Rotenberg (2012, 18) said: "What Steve meant by 'think different' is the source of all wisdom in Eastern traditions—mindfulness. Mindfulness means paying attention to your present-moment experience. 'Think different' means: Drop all your theories and preconceived ideas. Pay attention to the raw reality coming in through your five senses and your mind. This is where you will find insight and wisdom."

Effective CEOs and CCOs stay close to the business, attuned to conditions and to stakeholder values and attitudes; to understand hard reality; and to anticipate—or certainly be early to recognize—the need for strategic change, and to execute transformative communication.

Yes

Harvard professors Roger Fisher and William Ury (1981, 1893, 1991, 2011) wrote a negotiation guide entitled, *Getting to Yes*, which supports win–win outcomes. "Yes"—reaching equitable, value-based agreement with all desired stakeholders—needs to be the money shot for business leaders. Management experts such as Ram Charan (2012, 11) remind us that the leader who steps up and says "yes, we can do this" is one who can push colleagues to do things that some might consider impractical—or even impossible. Although the management style of Apple's Steve Jobs may have personified the possible limits of the management-prodding approach, there is no doubt that a leader's persistent drive for results that excite (or, to

---

[8] In this observation, Follett underscored that leadership shifts from one person to another, drawing on whoever has the knowledge and experience to "show the way."

use author Guy Kawasaki's (2011) phrase, *enchant*) stakeholders, providing them with the joy of realized values, is a compelling leadership factor.

Getting to yes on the circle of leadership fulfills what an accomplished industrial leader, Max De Pree, calls the leader's "debt to the future"—and that is to provide momentum. "Momentum in a vital company is palpable," De Pree (2010, 17) said in *Leadership is an Art*. "It is the feeling among a group of people that their lives and work are intertwined and moving toward a recognized and legitimate goal. It begins with competent leadership and a management team strongly dedicated to aggressive managerial development and opportunities." The momentum of yes—renewed commitment by the company and its stakeholders to the deal of delivered values—is effectively the proof of the "flywheel" power that Jim Collins (2001) identified in his study of sustainable success by *Good to Great* companies and their leaders.

Leaders need to keep in mind the truth that the win–win, realized-value deal is constantly in play. Both companies and stakeholders are always negotiating the proposition that can be simplified into the question: *"what's in it for me?"*

A four-step process for satisfying challenges to whether "yes" exists was suggested by Kenneth R. Feinberg (2012), who has engaged in stakeholder negotiations in corporate matters as serious as the BP oil leak crisis in 2010 and the General Motors automobile ignition crisis in 2014. He recommends to leaders: "One, know the facts. Two, be dogged (persistent). Three, keep an open mind. Next, be creative in getting to yes." This is not a bad recipe for leadership as chief executive or connecting with stakeholders as chief communicator. Feinberg ends his summary with the tell: "Finally, a very important basic proposition: (In negotiating,) put yourself in the other person's shoes" (Feinberg 2012, 9).

Dick Martin (2012), author and former CCO of AT&T, makes the win–win point in the title of his book, *OtherWise*. Leaders of companies—executives and communicators—will be "wise" to engage, understand, and respect the "others" who influence and define the victory of leadership touched on here.

CCOs, experts in information flow, stakeholder perception, and culture, will keep leaders aware that the "other" person is an active agent in the corporate success. The CCO has an ongoing responsibility to ask the question, how does the deal, as stated and proven, feel to others?

No leader has all these traits, and certainly not in the same measure. The lesson reinforced by our VICTORY mnemonic is that enterprise leaders are enabled for victory shared with stakeholders when qualities like these are activated. Our point, obvious by now, is the role of leadership communication and the forefront opportunity for the CCO.

CCO "New Model" Leadership: Corporate Character

Initiate a cross-C-suite effort to define your company's "corporate character." Try to answer this question: Does the company's internal culture and its external reputation reflect (and help move forward) the company's differentiating purpose, mission, and values?

CHAPTER 4

How Communicators Lead in the C-Suite

High-performance companies, those that meet challenges, drive change, and defeat competitors, add value and grow to peak levels of success on the strength of stakeholder confidence. In a five-year study of corporate performance reported in 2013, the international consultant firm Ernst & Young confirmed that successful firms excel in their ability to convince stakeholders—internal and external—to apply their talents and resources to achieving the firms' strategies.[1] The study found that high-performance companies understand that future success is global and value the ability to lead effectively in a global business environment. The studied companies emphasize individual treatment, linking pay with performance and providing customized employee development. They push decision making down as far as they can and they refine roles and job descriptions to make them more flexible.

We can summarize this fact demonstrated in the Ernst study: *Winning, high-performance companies excel in making the value they create visible to their stakeholders and thereby significantly increasing the talent, energy, and support of market-place victory.*

This puts leadership communication onto the field of influence in the extraordinary, growing battle for stakeholder commitment. This chapter concentrates on the CCO role in the process of converting thoughts or ideas into execution toward best achievable outcomes, with emphasis on stakeholder deals.

---

[1] Growing Beyond: How high performers are accelerating ahead, the 2013 Ernst & Young report, is accessible via Google search.

Winston Churchill, who eased his leadership stress by painting, once said to the British Parliament during a debate on the status of the war, "It is a good thing to stand away from the canvas from time to time and take a full view of the picture" (Haywood 1997).[2]

Look before you leap. That adage simplifies what we, other teachers, and communication leadership organizations have given serious study: the thought process that determines the influence of leadership communication. Thought leadership is the stand-back-and-view perspective. In our study, it refers to concepts generated by external thinkers as well as those leading inside the organization. Academics and management consultants are now common contributors to strategic communication and successful performance.

We see this as a positive continuum—thought leaders generate management vision and ideas that drive change and successful corporate action. We also see this as a considerable influence in the growing effectiveness of leadership communication. Enterprise executives, in charge of agenda setting, try to motivate followers through vision and mission statements (Hammer 2001).[3] We respect the observation that too often when the leader talks about vision, followers' eyes glaze over. One wag commented that "visions" without execution—moving toward a desired outcome—are actually "hallucinations" (Kanter 2009).[4] In this chapter, we delve into the role of a vital chief communication officer in vision relevance and value in the win–win deals with stakeholders. The point here is that communication strategies keep overarching visions alive in enterprise high performance.

CCO Role in Influencing Values

Relevance and value define everybody's job in any enterprise. Do CCOs influence or do they in effect own this function in today's corporate C-suite? Tom Martin, former CCO, teaching advanced studies at the

---

[2] Quoted in "Churchill on Leadership: Executive Success in the Face of Adversity" by Steven F. Hayward (1997).

[3] A preeminent management thinker of the 1990s, Dr. Michael Hammer, former MIT professor, spurred business leaders to set The Agenda to "dominate the decade."

[4] In her book "Supercorp," Kanter (2009) describes the way in which corporate leaders—in companies such as IBM—engage employees in bringing visions down to earth, putting them to work as missions.

College of Charleston, led a discussion among corporate communicators and college professors exploring these questions (Martin 2008).[5] It came as no surprise that the group's consensus was that everyone in the C-suite, and ultimately the chief executive officer has a hand in defining the enterprise values and behaving in value-based ways.

"[However]," said Martin (2008), "most agreed that the CCO has a major stake in influencing this behavior, and that we should take this responsibility very seriously. In this regard, those [of us] who teach, question the degree to which we are teaching students about the importance of instilling a value system within a corporation and the role of corporate communications in implementing and managing these values." Martin said the distinctive role of the CCO is serving as the voice of stakeholders not in the room when decisions are made that form or impact cultural values.

The flaw in this communication contribution by chief communicators, of course, is transmission loss. Visions and values shaped at the top of a company may dissipate or change at the outer reaches of operations. Expert communicators at the top of the organization customarily use their skills and influence to shape the values chain. And when something goes wrong in the last links of the value chain, the culture question snaps back to the top, where the CCO works. General Motors' ignition issue in 2014 as well as BP's Gulf of Mexico disaster in 2010 exemplify the problem of distance and disconnected communication between C-suite strategy and performance execution.

We see no way to relax communication vigilance in the vision-to-stakeholder value chain, no limit to the constant connection needed to understand, and address threats to the deals that sustain support and advocacy of the enterprise. The CEO of the file-sharing cloud service Hightail (formerly known as YouSendIt) told a *New York Times* interviewer that transparent, authentic communication is the key to culture and operational success. "You almost can't over-communicate," he said. "You can

---

[5] Martin, executive in residence, Department of Communication, The College of Charleston, Charleston, SC, served as an officer of ITT. This discussion was at the Tuck School of Business, Dartmouth College, Hanover, NH, academic symposium sponsored by Arthur W. Page Society and the Institute for Public Relations, May 2008; see www.awpagesociety.com/2008/05/the-authentic-enterprise-provides-basis-for rich discussion/ commentary by Tom Martin.

try, and you might think, 'oh, do I really have to say that again?' And the answer is yes." Continuous collaboration among all enterprise leaders and the top-level communication team is essential (Bryant 2013). Former CCO Tom Martin's colloquial discussion of C-suite ownership of enterprise value protection and behavior leaves no doubt that corporate communicators strongly feel that responsibility. Your authors, having also served as CCOs and having learned from peers in the profession, suggest that the following behaviors and achievements define the best achievable levels of CCO influence in the pipeline of from vision to win-win outcomes:

- Establish communication leadership expertise
- Become *the* reliable source of stakeholder perception
- Consistently "talk truth to power"
- Know the business, with focus on financial factors
- Inform the risk management process
- Become a long-term strategist
- Be a vision hawk, and an execution supporter
- Contribute from the top as a thought leader.

In the following paragraphs, we discuss the significance of attributes such as these in the level of CCO influence and success.

CCOs Establish Leadership Expertise

CCOs are—and confidently act as—masters of information flow, stakeholder perceptions, and culture-shaping aspects affecting fellow leaders.

These three areas of required accountability track the four areas—priorities and skills—identified in the Page Society "new model" narrative in which CCOs are uniquely positioned to assume strong leadership roles:[6]

- **Corporate culture**—defining and instilling company values;
- **Stakeholders**—building and managing multi-stakeholder relationships;

---

[6] See www.awpagesociety.com for development of the "new model" and discussion among CCO leaders on the state of corporate communication leadership.

- **Communication channels**—enabling the enterprise with "new media" skills and tools; and
- **Trust creation and maintenance**—building and managing the trust a successful company must have, in every dimension of that quality.

CCOs Become the Reliable Source of Stakeholder Perception

Larry Foster had been the night editor of the *Newark (NJ) News* before he was hired to head up corporate communication at Johnson & Johnson in 1957. Because he had been in the news business, he had a keen, current sense of what the media of that period were saying and thinking. When he sat with other C-suite executives, he not only had their respect for how J&J news would play, he was the reliable source on what questions could be anticipated. "I was used to expressing myself and asking the tough questions," Foster told an interviewer in 2003. "The chairman and the other guys would go along for a while and then they would turn to me and say, 'okay, Foster, tell us why we shouldn't do what we're considering'."[7]

If you are the company's expert in the constant flow of information relevant to your company, you are the "go to" C-suite source on current stakeholder perception, competitor communication, and knowhow for media, bloggers, and all other putative stakeholders and influencers who could react to newsworthy actions and decisions.

CCOs "Talk Truth to Power"

As a counselor, specialist in communication, attuned to stakeholder values and probable reactions to management decisions that can affect those values, the CCO is qualified, and must earn and keep the right, to be of confidential counsel to the CEO, listening, initiating, and "telling the

---

[7] From "Page Principles in Action," a collection of recorded interviews of Arthur W. Page Society leaders, conducted by Dick Martin of AT&T, edited by Mark Block, Ignite Technologies, inquiries to Susan S. Chin, www .awpagesociety.com

truth," as Arthur W. Page encouraged and CCOs from the days of Larry Foster forward have demonstrated.[8]

A leader needs a few special and trusted people around him who will react privately and honestly to his ideas and actions-in-the-making. Not everyone is capable of being available, open, and honest with the CEO and other C-suite leaders, to listen, to bring up issues, to address truly tough and confidential questions directly (e.g., CEO standing, compensation, viability), completely and with respect—and with options for best achievable outcomes.

Counseling is a special kind of power sharing. From the earliest years of conceiving corporate management as an art that could be developed, there has been a drive toward jointly developed or co-active "power" in leadership. Mary Parker Follett, writing in the 1920s, urged business leaders to see the advantage of "power-with" rather than "power-over" (Graham 1955).

CCOs Know "The Business"

In publicly held companies, CCOs work alongside the chief financial officer, and work with (in fact, may in some companies *direct*) the company's investor relations team in enterprise relationships with shareowners, investment advisers, and financial journalists. Daily monitoring of stock-related news and quarterly earnings reports and analyst phone and online conversations will keep "the business" at the top of the CCO engagement job.

Others in the C-suite consider it a given that the CCO is an expert communicator; they look for evidence that this expert is focused on, and intimately understands, how the company makes money. It is absolutely essential to understand what other leaders in the C-suite understand about the business "victory or loss" factors—with emphasis on the *performance*

---

[8] The "Page Principles" include: Tell the truth; Prove it with action; Listen to the customer; Manage for tomorrow; Conduct public relations as if the entire company depends on it; Realize a company's true character is expressed by its people; and Remain calm, patient, and good-humored. Your authors and series editors believe that these principles should drive public relations and corporate communication. For more, see: www.awpagesociety.com

metrics (Michaelson and Stacks 2011, 2014; Michaelson, Wright, and Stacks 2012; Stacks 2011). Business financial knowledge and economics studies will assuredly benefit the chief communicator, but however she achieves it, well-focused business and financial knowledge is a requirement for respect and a foundation for influence in the C-suite. A best practices survey of leading CCOs concluded that successful communicators in a business are in fact business leaders. "Our job when we come in every day is, how do we sell more (products and services) as competitively and at the highest margins possible?," one CCO said (Institute for Public Relations 2013).

In our Georgetown University "leadership communication" class, Navistar Senior Vice President Greg Elliott talked about one's "personal brand"—the reputation a person creates to make him or her trustworthy and attractive. He applied this to business. Executives and co-workers know you for something. Make it something they can depend upon, your true, authentic self. Elliott said CCOs are influential when they are competent, reliable, engaged, and "easy to do business with."[9] With leadership communication experience at General Motors and as a senior C-suite executive at the truck manufacturer, Elliott provided the class with a set of questions (Table 4.1) that can confront the C-suite communicator with regard to customers and other stakeholders.

Leadership communication in a modern American corporation means knowing the business. If you are interested in a job in a for-profit product or services business, asking and finding answers to the kind of questions posed by Elliott will help you move toward the top of any enterprise and to gain respect from peers when you are there.

CCOs Become Contributors to Enterprise Risk Management

Increasingly, corporate boards are establishing risk management committees to elevate the risk issues identified within companies that may require early mitigation attention and resolution. In 2013, a survey of

---

[9] John W. Gardner, who founded Common Cause, and whose ideas and actions have inspired national leaders and his university students for many years, wrote an article about "personal brand" (although he did not call it that) following a talk at a McKinsey conference in 1995. We recommend your reading it if you are pursuing your own "personal brand" development: http://www.pbs.org/john-gardner/sections/writings_speech_1.html

Table 4.1 Business questions every CCO needs to be able to answer

Business Questions Every CCO Needs to Be Able to Answer
Who are your company's top 10 customers?
What motivates them to buy your product or service?
When you lose customers, why do you lose them?
When you conquest customers, what was the value proposition you offered that compelled them to make the change?
How are the demographics and psychographics of your customers changing?
How is your investment base composed?
How many are retail investors versus institutional investors?
What motivates investors to own your stock?
When an investor takes a big position in your company, is it because they see growth opportunities, margin expansion, or a potential sale?
Who are your top suppliers?
What are the criteria by which your company chooses the suppliers?
Which unions represent your employees?
How many belong to each union?
What is each union's agenda—membership, growth, healthcare, retirement?
Which government agencies are having the biggest impact on regulating your business?
What are they saying about future regulation?
How do the communities perceive your company in the major markets you serve?
Are your retailers/dealers profitable?
Who are your best retailers/dealers, and why are they producing more results than others? Is it geography, management, or risk-taking?
With which universities and professional organizations has your company developed a partnership?
When the company successfully recruits from these schools and organizations, what are the reasons the candidate cites for joining your company versus a competitor or other company—pay, benefits, and flex-time; or career growth?
When an employee, especially a high-potential employee, leaves your company, what are the reasons the employee cites for jumping ship?

Source: Courtesy, Gregory Elliott, Navistar, 2014

446 companies found that 98 percent had designated C-level officers as chief risk officers (about 9 percent of whom were also chief financial officers), reporting to the CEO (*CFO Magazine* 2013, 43). The role of CCOs in enterprise risk management is increasingly important, as other officers take advantage of corporate communication's broad line-of-sight capability to probe stakeholder perceptions, and incipient risk situations.

As CCO, you are an expert in the specific values within each stakeholder group that bind them to the shared-purpose "deal" with the company—whether as employees, customers, or investors—and you can gauge the levels of perceived risks in these communities. In your ongoing aim toward a C-suite reputation as a trusted adviser, understand how risks are evaluated by others (CFO, COO, CEO, chief legal counsel) in the C-suite.[10] Connect with your peers by sharing insights on what your professional intelligence gathering in the stakeholder ecosystem reveals about perceptions that can escalate into risks to the corporation.

CCOs are Long-Term Strategists

C-suite players focus on the *direction* and *scope* of the enterprise over the *long term*. Ok, if you are the enterprise chief communicator, you certainly respond to alarms and help to put out "fires," but you are far more than "the fire department." Your expertise, your knowledge of values and expectations of stakeholders, your grasp of your company's business and its market competition, and your leadership in providing resources (skills, facilities) make you a *strategic player* at the highest levels of management. You understand the long-term vision. You have a corporate communication plan that is strategically tied to achieving missions. You grasp the reality of contexts—competition, risk factors—that favor or disfavor initiatives toward best outcomes. Overall, you are the business-intelligent collaborator, qualified and regularly engaged with C-suite peers in execution of long-range strategies.

In Chapter 14, we explore the dynamics that engage CCOs in three strategic performance circles: financial, social, and civic or political. Chief among these is financial performance. We underscore especially the collaborative relationship of the effective CCO with the chief financial officer and the investor relations executive. Communication is the pipeline to investors, analysts, media, and others (certainly including

---

[10] For risk management information on any public corporation you are studying, obtain the annual report 10-K, submitted annually to the Securities & Exchange Commission, and communicated to stakeholders. Risks to intended results are explained, often in detail.

the two-way pipeline with employees), making the CCO a high-value contributor to financial performance strategies and reporting. CCOs in public companies help to originate and communicate themes, benchmarks, and progress toward achieving business targets. Internal business unit strategy sessions benefit from facilitation provided by corporate communications. Communications strategies are at the forefront in preparing for annual and quarterly investor and analyst meetings, obtaining leadership speaking platforms, arranging interviews for top executives on corporate strategies, and producing the annual report. *We describe in Chapter 8 the CEO letter, engaging the communication and financial team in producing the most important strategy document available to stakeholders.*

CCOs Help Shape and Sustain Corporate Vision

The sustainable basis for leadership communication is being faithful to the promises in the company's vision statement. CCOs are charged with producing the enterprise's "this we believe" documents (codes of conduct, credos, mission statements, the annual report, and CEO letters) and keeping the vision active and viable. (see Figure 4.1 for the Johnson & Johnson *Credo*). The professional integrity of management is continuously on the line. The formula for sustaining belief in and advocacy of the vision and its values boils down to constancy. Stakeholders and critics are quick to detect inconsistency between *words* that are as close to "sacred" as an enterprise can get, and *deeds* that the leaders of the enterprise perform or permit to be performed. We humbly recognize the power of contexts in disrupting plans, and we counsel C-level communicators to stay strong on the things that can be controlled: the content of information and the tone in which it is conveyed. Within the CCO's mandate is the difficult "control" of allegiance to corporate codes or vision statements. Johnson & Johnson's credo has become the exemplar for company commitments. CCOs at J&J have been engaged in keeping it alive, taking actions to preserve—and when it is challenged, to restore—respect and support since the 1930s.

Our general advice to you, as CCO in the modern enterprise, is to be *vision sensitive*, a C-suite stalwart for its trustworthiness inside the company and in the domains of stakeholders.

Johnson & Johnson
Credo

We believe our first responsibility is to the doctors, nurses, and patients, to mothers and fathers, and all others who use our products and services. In meeting their needs, everything we do must be of high quality. We must constantly strive to reduce our costs in order to maintain reasonable prices. Customers' orders must be serviced promptly and accurately. Our suppliers and distributors must have an opportunity to make a fair profit.

We are responsible to our employees, the men and women who work with us throughout the world. Everyone must be considered as an individual. We must respect their dignity and recognize their merit. They must have a sense of security in their jobs. Compensation must be fair and adequate, working conditions clean, orderly, and safe. We must be mindful of ways to help our employees fulfill their family responsibilities. Employees must feel free to make suggestion and complaints. There must be equal opportunity for employment, development, and advancement for those qualified. We must provide competent management, and their actions must be just and ethical.

We are responsible to the communities in which we live and work and to the world community as well. We must be good citizens—support good works and charities and bear our fair share of taxes. We must encourage civic improvements and better health and education. We must maintain in good order the property we are privileged to use, protecting the environment and natural resources.

Our final responsibility is to our stockholders. Business must make a sound profit. We must experiment with new ideas. Research must be carried on, innovative programs developed, and mistakes paid for. New equipment must be purchased, new facilities provided, and new products launched. Reserves must be created to provide for adverse times. When we operate according to these principles, the stockholders should realize a fair return.

Figure 4.1 —Courtesy, Johnson & Johnson 2014

J&J put its corporate values out front. The code, intended to endure, is literally chiseled into stone. As CCO, you may not advocate putting your company's code of values onto the headquarters building face or a marble wall in the lobby; however, you can help your communication team and your leadership peers to be faithful to your company's competitive, orienting leadership vision. Vision awareness needs to encourage enabling communication. We have a suggestion: A printout of your company's vision statement to hang in your office where you see it constantly.

CCOs Advocate and Work to Achieve Vision and Missions

Communicating the company *vision* is the first step in communicating toward the various *missions* that various leaders (e.g., chief operations officer, chief financial officer, and many other leaders) form and execute. The process of achievement engages the CCO in maximizing *each* leader's communication skill. This can require a certain level of CCO assertiveness in defense of the vision's viability. Let us give you an example: When he was honored with the Arthur W. Page Society's "Hall of Fame Award" Larry Foster (1994), a former Johnson & Johnson chief communicator, described the critical role the CCO plays in the enterprise:

> It is one thing (for the chief communicator) to be invited to the company board room to participate, it is another to make an important contribution to the deliberations. We have learned to play the role of "loyal opposition" when important decisions are being discussed and debated—a voice that helps others focus on what is in the public's or the customer's best interest, as opposed to what may be seen as a more expedient course of action. As we have come to learn, what is in the best interest of the public and customer is ultimately in the best interest of the company.
>
> It takes courage to take a stand against the rising tide of management opinion, and we will not always be right. But presenting an opposite view often opens the door to alternative solutions, and that is an important contribution to the process and to the result.

Foster underscored that personal skill, based on knowledge of the business and confidence in stakeholder reactions, will influence C-suite decisions. The CCO's job includes high-level message shaping. Under the notion of "controlling what one can," the CCO's contribution begins with exploring the intention and content of information. With regard to any significant company situation, the CCO in effect pauses, with his C-suite peers and with his communication team to consider three pre-launch questions: *what?, so what?,* and *now what?* What is the subject (what's happened, what's about to happen)? So what does that mean to our company (how does this impact, or provide the chance to manage the impact on followers, stakeholders, and advocates)? So, at the present time, right now, what's the current action (the management plan, the mission, related to the vision) enabling us to communicate persuasively?

Foster counseled toward courage. This today can mean slowing down in a do-it-now atmosphere, to take charge of this pause before strategies and action, to assure there is smooth collegial and collaborative action. The CCO function today (engaging in the demanding, hyperactive arenas of social communication) may well include the Foster-level courage in two ways: first, leading the productive pause that prepares for maximum success, and then assisting and counseling those who will be outfront, personally leading and communicating. Again, the CEO and the CCO are the C-suite stalwarts, vision hawks who project and protect strategy and execution trustworthiness.

What are examples of ways to give the vision, and related missions, the power to influence? The CCO typically works with others in the C-suite (and beyond, into significant operational missions) to put together top-level remarks and speeches, both for in-company and public occasions, at times with the help of contract specialists (*e.g.,* speech writers). Content is then leveraged through the tone and skills of personal delivery. This requires personal attention to the leader's strengths and weaknesses, and his or her willingness to accept coaching or pre-delivery practice.

Reality—the scale of communication articulation—needs to be attuned to the hope of BAO: the company connects with, convinces, reassures, and inspires followers and stakeholders. This translates into making the communicator—especially the top of the organization—valued as influential on the company's behalf. An extraordinary example of corporate communicators collaborating with top executives is presented as a case study of corporate leaders "walking the talk," by Boris Groysberg and Michael Slind (2012) authors of *Talk, Inc.*

According to Groysberg and Slind, Cisco CEO John T. Chambers deals with the reality of dyslexia, which makes processing of written texts difficult. "(Chambers) can type only 15 words a minute," the *Talk, Inc.* authors said, "but he can talk 250 words per minute"; so, with help from his communication team, the CEO turned a presumably limiting condition to success. For his monthly video blogs, Chambers and his communications team went through talking points and, using a camera attached to his laptop, the CEO talked for two to five minutes in a conversational ("not 'corporate' speaking") tone. Employees received an e-mail link to the blog and were encouraged to submit text responses to appear alongside the CEO's post. Senior Vice President Blair Christie has emphasized that Cisco leadership communication is always about finding ways to assure meaningful links among senior leaders and everyone else in the company.

Dick Martin, who spent 32 years with AT&T, including five as executive vice president of public relations, employee communications, and brand management, has said that the CCO's role isn't to create more appealing corporate personalities. "The role is to lead a collaborative effort across the C-suite to build a common understanding of the company's enduring and differentiating purpose…and then help integrate that understanding into the company's core operations and, finally, into its external communications," Martin (2014) wrote in a Conference Board Review.

Thought leadership moves through stages toward executing within the context of the organization (Figure 4.2). Thought leaders may be

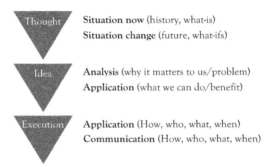

Figure 4.2 Leadership communication: thoughts lead to action

inside the organization, but more often they are outside—academics, social and business analysts, and others who take mega-views or sector views of situations, and communicate their perspectives. Organizations—business companies and other organizations—draw from these perspectives, analyze them within the organizational contexts, and arrive at ideas to solve problems and seek new benefits. Ideas become products, services, ways of executing, and they become leadership communication drivers. Execution to BAOs moves the company to competitive advantage.

The clarity or precision of mission statements tends to focus on immediate or near-term results. Although the overarching vision may be, in effect, "Visualize that far horizon, how great we will be one day," current mission statements may be motivated by a current BAO: "We plan to take that hill this quarter (year, five-year frame, and so forth)." Internal communication, as well as external guidance, effectively hews to missions, plans, and motivational communication. A second reason is that missions can be explained by executives and communicators in terms of value.[11] Leadership communication is tuned to stakeholder value. It describes the deal, conveys its win–win aspects, and constantly works to sustain it, all quite necessarily within the perception of the specific group of stakeholders. Let us review the elements of this process.

To reach her most effective service in the C-suite, the CCO is a thought leader. She serves along with the CEO as a *generalist*, seeing the big picture, coming up with coordinated strategies to connect with stakeholders in good times and bad; and she serves as a *specialist*, connecting with others at the top of the enterprise to apply communication expertise to vision-related missions, and executing toward results.

Stakeholder perception management is the CCO's responsibility. At its best, stakeholder communication answers the perceived stakeholder question: *"What's In It For Me?"* The CCO thinks this through. She

---

[11] Vision is converted to mission at least once a year in the first several pages of many companies' annual reports. In evaluating a company's leadership communication, its content and tone, its explanation of the win–win value deal with stakeholders, its language of leadership, an analysis should include study of the CEO or "chairman's letter" in the annual report.

plugs into the stakeholder ecosystem to sense the level of belief in the win–win, shared-value deal. She understands current thinking among employees about the deal of working for the company; among investors and analysts about the deal of buying its stock; and among customers about the value of obtaining, owning, and consuming its products and services. And the CCO engages in communication accordingly, attuning delivery to an understanding of need, strengthening deals or attempting to repair broken connections through communication. Every effort is made to strengthen stakeholder confidence, by providing information or evidence by which to judge or measure the potential yields of their individual deals.

Thought leadership, translated by viewing the big picture and converting it to ideas and action achievable in the current mission is where leaders at the top of the company—including communicators—shine. Prime Minister Churchill, himself a thought leader during the troubled times of war and recovery in Europe, read Peter Drucker's first major work, *The End of Economic Man*, which was published in 1939 and republished in 1995 (Drucker 1995). According to Drucker's website (www.druckersociety.at), Churchill described Drucker as "one of those writers to whom almost anything can be forgiven because he not only has a mind of his own, but has the gift of starting other minds along a stimulating line of thought."[12]

Perception in the marketplace—a strong grasp of stakeholder opinion—is the basis for building and refining strategic enterprise communication. The CCO needs to know what stakeholders think and how what they think helps or hurts your company's offerings and reputation. When the CCO tunes into stakeholder opinion—by monitoring and engaging directly in direct, old-line, and online social conversation—she is in the role of thought leader, valued as professional *counselor and collaborator* in the C-suite.

---

[12] www.druckersociety.at/index.php/peterdruckerhome/commentaries

CCO "New Model" Leadership:
Data Analytics—Work with CIO

Build expertise and capabilities in data analytics into communications planning and programs. How can you as CCO work with a chief technology or information officer to put into place the necessary tools and infrastructure to capture and accurately interpret enterprise and social data? Partner with appropriate leaders in the C-suite to use data to detect trends and systematically address gaps and deepen strengths. Use data collection and analysis to understand stakeholders as unique individuals. Leverage data to personalize and tailor communications and engagement to enhance the relevance of your company's mission, products, and services—and the two-way communication involving this.

CHAPTER 5

Influence: Replacing and Reasserting "Control"

What one word would you like people to use when they describe you? When Adam Bryant (2011, B2), of *The New York Times Corner Office* asked Bing Gordon, a partner with venture capital firm Kleiner Perkins Caufield and Byers this question, he replied: influence. In fact, Bryant used this response to title the column: "Power? No Thanks, but I'd Rather Have Influence."

As Gordon said:

Early on, I learned that I'm better with influence than power. And, in fact, I'm not power-hungry ... And there's a cost to having power, which is that people you have sway over actually own you, especially if you're in a business where there are more jobs than there are good people. *I like having influence.* I like being with interesting people and helping them become better and being part of the flow of ideas. And that's a little bit uncomfortable, as a boss. It doesn't make sense to people that the boss, who is kind of a figurehead and maybe a confidence-giving parent figure, just wants to be an experienced helper. As a person of authority, I'm kind of teacher–consultant more than a wielder of power" (Bryant 2011, B2)

One word: *influence*. Not *control*. We agree. Leaders, and importantly our enterprise principals—chief executive officers—who focus on the absolute ability to control situations are relying on the Achilles' heel of leadership communication. Jim Collins (Collins and Hansen 2011) was almost brutal in spelling it out, following his deep studies into corporate leadership. "Financial markets are out of your control," Collins (2011) told *Fortune* readers, referencing his book, *Great by Choice*, "Customers are out of your control. Earthquakes are out of your control. Global competition is out of your control. Technological change is out of your control. Most everything is ultimately out of your control."

Even the successful crisis counselor Eric Dezenhall, who wrote the book on crisis response and called it *Damage Control*, took pains to underscore the limits or the futility of efforts to be in control. When an enterprise is in a crisis, he observed, "a marketplace assault must be navigated, not 'managed' (which is) an arrogant notion that falsely assumes that you, as the principal, are in total control of your destiny. You're not; you're only in control of your role in a series of collisions between dynamic variables—quantifiable hazards, agendas, personalities, politics, the mood of the culture" (Dezenhall and Weber 2011, 26).

Influence Begins In the Corporate Culture or Character

So what can you do as a leader if you accept the limits of control? First reliance must be on the means to influence the firm's leaders and achievers in their effort toward best achievable outcomes.

Following his entreaty against futile control management, Collins (2011) proposed a form of an effective means to influence followers that he termed a "20-mile march" strategy—the idea of traveling toward a vision, a mission, or a goal with a steady gait that proceeds despite the fact that leaders have uncertain or no control over many of the contexts that surround the intended destination. "When you 20-Mile March," said Collins, "you have a tangible point of focus that keeps you and your team moving forward, despite confusion, uncertainty, and even chaos…" Peter Drucker expressed a similar view, observing that "effective executives do not race…they set an easy pace but keep going steadily … (they) concentrate on doing one thing at a time, and on doing first things first" (Drucker 1996, 100–112).

Harvard's Rosabeth Moss Kanter (2009) in her book, *Supercorp*, charted the impact of globalization and technology in escalating intrusion on previous models of control in all organizations, where chains of command implied a form of controlled, even dictated, performance. The new reality in vanguard companies, Kanter said, is the emergence of *circles of influence*.

"To focus people on serving customers and society, horizontal relationships across the organization are the center of action that shapes daily tasks," said Kanter, "rather than vertical reporting up a chain of command." (Kanter 2009, 148).

Leaders in vanguard companies, she counsels, want people at all levels to feel more self-motivated, not controlled (an idea we discuss subsequently, drawing on Daniel Pink's study of current motivational influences). In his book *Principle-Centered Leadership*, Stephen R. Covey (1990) acknowledges that most of us, and certainly organization leaders, want to have influence—positive influence—with people in our personal and professional lives.

If we are in an enterprise leadership role in a free-enterprise economy, we understand that principled performance and activated belief in shared value propositions are reliable management basics. The process of influence begins in the company's *culture*: its established, active character. If, as enterprise executives, we want to win new business, keep customers, maintain stakeholders, we need to influence positive, high-intelligence, high-emotional value behaviors within corporate cultures. But the question that Covey raises is about ways to make our motives their motives, and thereby their mission; *it's about the process of influence*. "How do we powerfully and ethically influence the lives of other people?" asks Covey (1990, 18). He explores three *routes to influence*: to model by example (followers see what is effective and encouraged), to build relationships that are caring (the leader cares about the follower at an appropriate personal and professional level), and to mentor through instruction (guide followers in ways to use their capabilities to achieve best outcomes).

Influence is Rooted in Collaboration

Positive influence and the "I" from our VICTORY (page 42) leadership circle—*integrity*—are bound together. The influential leader consistently follows a code of fair and ethical decisions. She adheres to principles that are clear, sound, and respectful. Through her example, kept promises, and integrity, she wins influence *with* others—the word with being an important enabler. As early as the 1920s, before use of the buzz-word empowerment, Mary Parker Follett was advancing her concept of power-with rather than power-over management. She said the way to develop power-with is to organize and manage so "you can influence a co-manager while he is influencing you" (Graham 1995).

Modern studies of organizational influence find that virtually all major decisions are reached collaboratively. As leadership analyst Perry Buffett confirms, executives now commonly work in collegial groups—boards, councils, committees—arriving at decisions more or less infor-mally.[1] Although all the participants know and respect the titles of their fellow collaborators, that factor tends not to be a barrier in the influ-ence-sharing process. The before "ultimate authority" remains that of the leader who reports to the board—that is to say, the CEO—but he has helped transform followers into colleagues who will implement the deci-sion. This powerful application of transformational leadership—engaging followers as colleagues in framing and formulating strategic moves—displays a leadership mindset advocated by Covey (1990): seeking first to understand, in order to be understood.

The oracle of financial performance, Warren Buffett (2011) brought our point forward when he said in one of his famous annual letters to investors: "An executive's ability to influence peers and superiors as they undertake a broad range of crucial decisions involving such issues as strategy, budgets, brand positioning and pricing, and capital invest-ments is a valuable skill—a skill that could be called influential com-petence." The tide of support for motivating *influential competence* may well begin with hiring, Suzanne Sinclair, director of leadership talent

---

[1] Perry Buffett, senior associate with Booz & Company, Chicago, specializes in leadership alignment and organizational change. On the need for values that don't change, Sidney Taurel, chief executive, Eli Lilly, said: "The first thing I think any leader should be judged by is a very strong set of values. I think there's a difference between leading and managing. Leadership is really to do with getting people to follow you to a place you haven't been, which is the future. It has to do with change. People won't willingly follow someone into the unknown unless they can trust that person's instincts and values. ... In the middle of change, you have to have some things that don't change, which are strong values. I think that is essen-tial for any leader." Source: NWA WorldTraveler, August 2007, pp. 48–51, 74.

acquisition at Allstate Insurance, has noted. "You have to understand your colleagues' agendas," she has said, "and how their agendas fit into the issue you are raising" (Buffett 2011).

CCO Role in Influential Competence

Communication—two-way, consistent, open, and understandable—is the lifeblood of influential competence. The role of the CCO in internal positive influence is to enable the chief executive in his role in activating two vital aspects of motivation and performance: (1) a reliable, readily accessible exchange of information; and (2) a culture that is as autonomous and self-governing as can be achieved.

At IBM, the leadership works to achieve influential competence so as many individual employees as practicable can influence the company's success as a consultant and partner in the expanding world of big data and advanced technology.

Companies in every business category are opening up to—or being opened by—access to information that in previous generations were considered privileged, kept close to the chests of top executives, whether through fear of competitive prying or through lack of trust within their own organizations. Circles of privacy and protection had not evolved to circles of inclusion and influence.

New-reality writers—Daniel Pink, Dov Seidman, Guy Kawasaki, Tony Hsieh, Chip and Dan Heath, Dick Martin and others examining modern routes to enterprise success—have described the forward path of business with leadership that motivates workers and creates cultures toward sustainable success in an atmosphere of widely transparent, high-tech availability to information. Motivation means providing means of reaching enterprise goals through individual satisfaction. Employees and rising leaders find joy in their own achievement, and sharing the thrill of achievement with others of like mind. People in companies are able to access people in other companies online. Crowdsourcing competes with company sources of information and expectation. Blind-obedience cultures are gone forever. Informed cultures are growing. The common ground of the current employee (or, if you wish, "co-creator") culture is defined by levels of self-governing, information-rich, influence-sharing, teamwork. The requirements and satisfaction of external stakeholders—customers, investors—are recognized as the dominating control over what happens inside the company.[2] What is the good news for company leaders? They can take competitive advantage of the new conditions through strategic engagement, starting with open communication inside the organization.

A barrier to leadership influence may be the inability of a potential follower to comprehend. Language, education, and other variables need to be dealt with by the leader and, when it is valuable, with help from his communication expert.

At the personal, internal-company level, Covey (1992, 202) has suggested ways to communicate influentially when there is not a common level of understanding: "Give more time to the process, be patient, and express nonverbal *[sic]* communication—how one looks at the other person—in a way that is congruent with what you are saying. Seek harder to understand, to show you care."

Turn the "I" of Influence Into an Empowered "We"

Bill George, former CEO of Medtronic, has made a specialty of interviewing and writing about leadership in best-selling books, including *Authentic Leadership* George (1978) and *True North* George and Sims (2007). "Authentic leaders," he has said, "discard the notion that leadership means having "legions of supporters following our direction as we ascend to the pinnacles of power" and realize that it's all about empowering others. "It is great teams, not charismatic CEOs, that build great organizations."

Jaime Irick, a West Point graduate and executive at General Electric, told George (2007, 135) his story: "We spend our early years trying to be the best. To get into West Point or GE, you have to be the best. That is defined by what you can do on your own—your ability to be a phenomenal analyst or consultant or do well on a standardized test. When you

---

[2] The books—Seidman's (2007) *How: Why HOW We Do Anything Means Everything*, Pink's (2009) *Drive: The Surprising Truth About What Motivates Us*, the Heath brothers' (2008) *Made to Stick*, Martin's (2012) *Otherwise*, and Kawasaki's (2011) *Enchantment: The Art of Changing Hearts, Minds, and Actions*—typified a vast outflow of commentary in print and online attesting to the change of influence and the challenge of communication.

become a leader, your challenge is to inspire others, develop them, and create change through them."[3] Rising as a leader in an aggressive company, Irick realized an important fact: "If you want to be a leader, you've got to flip that switch and understand that it's about serving the folks on your team. The sooner people realize this," Irick told Bill George, "the faster they will become a leader."

George puts influence into that context: Leaders set aside personal ego needs and recognize the unlimited potential of empowering others.

Teamwork works; it grows shared values and motivates

The bottom line on influence within modern, successful companies can be described most simply as teamwork. CEOs in our experience are now more frequently engaged team leaders than they are isolated bosses. They encourage and conduct frequent team meetings. They of course brief their teams of leaders on what they are thinking, what they are committed to achieving, and what they fear or question that could jeopardize their best achievable outcomes. They listen to team players, they participate in, and they support the circles of influence.

Team Leadership and Motivation

In their classic book on teamwork, Jon Katzenbach and Douglas Smith (1993), conclude one of their chapters with an oriental message that sheds light on team leadership and shared influence.[4] It is from the Chinese philosopher, Lao-Tzu: As for the best leaders, the people do not notice their existence. The next best, the people honor and praise. The next, the people fear; and the next, the people hate. When the best leader's work is done, the people say "We did it ourselves."[5]

---

[3] In 2012, Irick was President & CEO of GE Lighting Solutions.

[4] The Wisdom of Teams was first published by Harvard Business School Press in 1993, and a copy was given that year to one of your authors (Harrison) by a leader in AT&T and in American public relations, Marilyn Laurie.

[5] For other Lao-Tzu quotes, go to: http://www.goodreads.com/author/quotes/2622245.Lao_Tzu?auto_login_attempted=true

Bill George and his associates interviewed dozens of leaders in preparation for his books on leadership and his teaching at Harvard. Nearly all of these leaders had one thing in common. Each had gone through a transformative passage that made them recognize that leadership was not about their success at all. They realized that leadership is not only about getting others to follow them. They came to believe that the essence of their leadership is aligning their teammates around a shared vision and values and empowering them to step up and lead.

Leaders create leaders. Influence becomes inclusion. Former CEO George calls authentic leadership the transformation from "I" to "We."

Reasserting the Role of Control

In 2006, among her many perceptive *Wall Street Journal* columns during the latter years of the George W. Bush presidency, Peggy Noonan (2006) described the White House as a place where sensitive information was carefully contained. After the incident of the accidental shooting of a fellow hunter by Vice President Cheney, Noonan said that chief executive communications were assumed to be within "a never permeable dome of silence."

There was, of course, no such thing. The shooting story leaked and cascaded across media channels in the way that all information does when it is newsworthy—that is to say, interesting and of value, to public and stakeholders.

In an open and democratic society, information within government, as within publicly owned companies, is not as containable as perhaps it

CCO "New Model" Leadership: Focus on Influence

Virtually everybody is able to access or express all kinds of information and views about companies. For the CCO, successful accountability for information flow is essential; reliance on or expectation of information control are potentially counterproductive. The CCO's focus is on

influence, to increase the impact of two-way, value-sharing information flow. It involves making your company both participant and the
reliable resource in the constant conversation that will proceed, essentially without your control, about your company. The website strategy
can influence the level of understanding in the ongoing conversation,
leveraging support and trust.

arguably once was, when the media channels were fewer and iconoclasts
rarer. Noonan learned one never says "never." Presumptive, controllable
domes of silence have been long and irreparably shattered.

In another case of assumed secrets becoming public knowledge,
detailed aspects of the 2012 Penn State University coaching scandal were
displayed in an investigative report by former FBI Director Louis Freeh
and his law firm. A *Washington Post* columnist observed, "Among the
most shocking revelations in the 162-page Freeh report is that there isn't
a shocking revelation to be found" (Hamilton 2012). The rumors, the
facts, the shadings, the things the university thought were concealed were
in fact beyond its control.

The obvious lesson is the reality of leadership communication: *There
is essentially no privacy in public life.* Some sage has said if more than
one person knows it, you have to assume everybody will know it. We
have counseled that a C-suite leader would benefit from a cautionary
reminder note to self: *EKE. Everybody Knows Everything.* Anyone who
cares to know anything about your enterprise can get some, and perhaps
a lot of, information, right or wrong, correct or incorrect, timely or not,
from some source at some time. The leadership communicator's hope
of influence is providing stakeholders with as much of the ongoing real
story—Arthur W. Page's "truth with proof"—as practicable, aware of the
waiting whirlwinds of EKE.

Gatekeepers Are Endangered

Only transparency can stanch the flow of damaging leaks, speculations,
and trust-shaking inferences among followers and stakeholders.

Amazon.com CEO Jeff Bezos, interviewed in 2012 by author and columnist Tom Friedman (2011–12), described the current landscape for business and information. "I see the elimination of gatekeepers everywhere." Bezos was actually referring to cloud computing where anyone anywhere can use Amazon's open portals to do many things—sell things, get jobs, start a company, self-publish—all without intermediaries.

The open-access principle holds for enterprise information. Internet portals, personal communication devices, endless chatter, and the ease of leaks have changed the lives of corporate gatekeepers, in no instance more profoundly than that of the CCOs. Companies—and their leadership communication chiefs—are just one of many voices reporting, tweeting, tweaking, and twisting business news and views.

The chief communicator is information *central*, but he is not information *control*. He collaborates with others in the C-suite to design strategies, shape messages, put comments together with appropriate sources in the enterprise, prepare the internal source executives for response, compose talking points, line up media outlets for special attention—overall, to assure strategic management of the vital communication process.

However, any assumption of CCO as gatekeeper, implying control, must be deemed as shaken, as the prominent Internet leader Bezos observes. Information is an open commodity. For better or for worse, correct or incorrect, from qualified and other sources, it wildly and widely abounds in the social media.

How Can We Source Reliable Information?

So how do CCOs adjust to the incredible shrinking control they once might have had over information flowing to stakeholders? We suggest two avenues for adjusting to open-portal realities. They are *reliability* and *relevance*. You go back to the deal—the values that bind leadership to desired followers: What do stakeholders want to sustain their interest in your company? They want reliable, trustworthy information. When do they want it? Now—or, more accurately, as soon as reliable information, from the source, is relevant to their particular interest.

Alan Greenspan, who led the Federal Reserve Bank for nearly 20 years, was a powerful communicator. He was exceptional at connecting with listeners. He used two strong devices. One was artful phrasing that provoked a listener to think. The other communication device was to state a simple fact, a point that required no thinking; it merely reinforced a truth. An example of the first device was when Greenspan described a bullish Wall Street view on a matter of national financial significance as "*irrational exuberance.*"[6] He stopped the presses, the media delighted in adding to the financial lexicon an offbeat, quirky, and memorable comment on a condition that may or may not prove to be realized or true.

As for an example of plain-talk Greenspanism, an editorial commentary in 2012 (Surowiecki 2012), recalled this 1999 comment from the Fed chairman: *"In virtually all transactions we rely on the word of those with whom we do business."*

"Irrational exuberance" is word-smithing that evokes listener rethinking. Relying on the other party's word in a business relationship, stated simply, requires little thought. It reminds the listener of an essential principle. It is accepted as truth as soon as it is heard. In effect, it is the reason for corporate communication. It underscores reliability. The company speaks to the stakeholder in a truthful, plain-talk manner, where source reliability is king.

Although we are chary about the relative persuasive power of specific words, because the influence requires both competence and emotional intelligence about the individual or group—for example, employees— the communicator is trying to persuade. We get into this in subsequent chapters; here, it is useful to consider some of the many approaches to the predictive response to words that one smiths.

Word-smithing requires thinking otherwise—realizing that the stakeholder may well be skeptical of information from corporate sources. Thinking as the other person thinks is explored in a book by Michael Maslansky, with Scott West, Gary DeMoss, and David Saylor (2010). *The Language of Trust: Selling Ideas in a World of Skeptics* focuses on the communicator's skill in using language to connect and persuade. Based on research into how people respond emotionally to communication,

---

[6] "Irrational exuberance" is a phrase used by the then-Federal Reserve Board chairman, Alan Greenspan, in a speech given at the American Enterprise Institute during the dot-com bubble of the 1990s. The phrase was interpreted as a warning that the market might be somewhat overvalued. Quoted in Wikipedia http://en.wikipedia.org/wiki/Irrational_exuberance

the authors suggest words, phrases, and techniques to address situations where there appears to be a failure to communicate.

Maslansky, who has lectured to our communication class students at Georgetown, emphasizes the need (1) to learn how your intended connection thinks; and (2) to use language that builds, or rebuilds trust, when the facts, actions, and record are on your side, but you just can't quite get over that last hurdle—acceptance.[7]

Context, Content, and Tone Need Adjusting to Connect With Company Critics

Maslansky makes the point that, with indicators consistently showing a decline in public trust, companies must communicate in ways that are more likely to connect, even with skeptics. Maslansky counsels that how you tell your corporate story is as important as the story you tell, and that information contexts, content, and tone need to be adjusted to a post-trust era mode. The book author pounds the point in his trade-marked missive: *It's not what you say, it's what they hear.*

Contexts provide reasons to accept a company's message. Maslansky uses the example of an airline end-of-flight announcement to passengers which, while essentially meant to expedite the plane's readiness for the next flight, provides assisting flight attendants as a reason for passengers to clean up their seat areas.

Content involves emphasis on areas immediately grasped by intended stakeholders. Maslansky's new approach examples include the following:

1. turn facts and data into stories, narratives that touch specific stake-holders;
2. put much more emphasis on now and the future than on past experience or evidence;
3. use fewer big and bold statements; more small and credible statements; and

---

[7] For more information, see http://www.amazon.com/Language-Trust-Selling -Ideas-Skeptics/dp/0735204756/ref=sr_1_1?ie=UTF8&s=books&qid =1271995056&sr=8-1

4. provide more focus on outcomes achievable by the recipient than on the enterprise's current, though it may be an honest, intention to deliver.

Tone needs shifting toward caring almost exclusively about *them*, and not about you, Maslansky counsels. This means anticipating their objections, embracing alternatives they respect, and relaxing about persuading—letting the act of *informing* become an acceptable influence.

Gregory Ciotti, whose well-written *Copyblogger* entries (and books) are worth the attention of corporate communicators, has stated, "Many companies are proud of the features that their product (or service) can offer, and that's fine, but you have to remember that when you are focusing on writing persuasive copy, it all comes down to answering your customer's #1 question: *What's in it for me?*"[8]

That, as you know by now, is the question that we feel is one that the CCO and the corporate team neglect at their peril as they engage with officers in the C-suite, with those in the internal culture, and with external stakeholders. The CCO's ability to "see ourselves as others see us"— that is to say, the stakeholders' perceptions—keeps this highly relevant focus as a sustainable principle. Bottom line here is you are an agent of relevancy to the scales of value among those with whom your enterprise needs fair engagement. Think otherwise; put yourself in the mindset of the stakeholder, and address the question "what's in it for me?" Observers, stakeholders, critics, and force multipliers are your potentially active circles of influence: favorable, unfavorable, undecided, or uninterested unless something happens to make your enterprise news- or comment-worthy. Your ability to have the most reasonable degree of control over information flow also means intimate knowledge of the channels and people that convey information. You will score best when your information is relevant to editors, content generators, and re-generators with an interest or stake in your enterprise's success or failure. This applies both to online interactive writers and to old-line traditional writers. Peers in the

---

[8] See Ciotti's blog of 2013 http://www.copyblogger.com/persuasive-copywriting-words/

C-suite will expect the CCO to know what is happening in this universe of judgment, and how to influence fair, if not favorable, consideration.

Employees: Our Most Reliable Sources

Harold Burson, founder of Burson Marsteller and acknowledged as the virtual dean of enterprise positioning, reminds us that every employee is the ultimate, presumed reliable source to somebody. The Trust Barometer findings, an annual survey by Edelman (2014) public relations, shows that an average employee is as much as three times more credible than a CEO as a source of information about the company. If you are the CCO, here is where some of your control has not entirely eroded. Your information flow strategy has to start and be sustained within the potentially truest circle of believers and authentic communicators.

However, this is not a shoo-in. Reliance on employees as a credible source of information—effective truth-tellers and advocates—must be earned by leadership. Executives and managers must vest genuine trust in them. Trust is a two-way street. If you want employees to act as public advocates for the company, helping you strengthen the stream of reliable and relevant information, you need to exercise openness in internal communication. As counselor and business executive Richard Edelman argues (Groysberg and Slind 2012), "When a leader communicates with employees, the goal should not be simply to talk at them. It's allowing them to 'talk out.' You talk to them and then you allow them to speak more broadly. And then you benefit as well."

When CEO Sam Palmisano took over as IBM's chief years ago, he let thousands of employees have a say in what the company ought to be doing to keep pace with, and drive, change. CCO Jon Iwata served as strategic communication counsel in IBM's business transformation, continuing with successor CEO Virginia M. Rometty in implementation and further development of the C-suite's employee engagement strategy. Asked by the *New York Times'* Corner Office writer (Bryant 2012) what leadership lessons he has learned, Chris Barbin, head of the IT cloud company, Appirio, said, "look first to company employees." "(Transparency) is a huge part of our culture," he said, "and what I think makes a company and team really thrive and work." The reference was specifically related to negative information, such as cutbacks, certainly the most relevant matter in any organizational culture. His point was broader: "You should never surprise an employee." In fact, the goal is to enable employees to get in on the best achievable outcome by becoming reliable communicators, inside and outside the enterprise.

Tom Salonek, CEO of Intertech described his leadership communication guidance in a 2012 blog:[9]

> From the very beginning, we have sought to instill a culture of openness at Intertech. Our employees are given a copy of communication guidelines the day they join our company. We so fervently believe in open, two-way communication that we have gone to the trouble of writing down such principles as: Engage in direct communication. Venting to a third party doesn't change any situation and can disrupt office harmony. Address concerns, criticisms, and wants to the appropriate members of the company. (Salonek 2012, September).

Groysberg and Slind (2012, 121) observe: "Leaders…now listen to employees in part because those employees have something to say—not just on their own behalf, but also on behalf of their organization."

Website: Plugging Stakeholders into Your Best Hope for Control

To this point we have talked about the *what*, the *when*, and a potent *who* component of information flow. Let us consider more carefully the *where*. If you as CCO are "information central" in the C-suite, where is your reliable, relevant switchboard? Where is the one place that your "gatekeeper control" has the potential for enduring clout? We believe the strategic resource has to be *the company website*. If you are the chief communicator, accountable for information flow, your job is to make your company's website the go-to place for reliable, relevant, and trust-building internal and external information.

---

[9] INC 500 firm is a seven-time "Best Places To Work" winner. See: doi: http://www.intertech.com/Winning-Business/Articles/Tom-Salonek-Big-Biz-Show.aspx.

Content, form, and the speed of posting information deliverables (which may at times become *virtually immediate*) are factors for victory in this often-vital test of corporate leadership communication.

When your stakeholders are pounded by less-reliable sources or sources that compete with you for reliability, you need to get them to your website. Communication strategies begin with content. The corporate site must answer the question of stakeholders: *"What are they (or if you are an employee of the company, 'we') saying?"* In addition to building the best possible base for information you control, the question for you as information source is, *"if I build it, will they come?"*

You know you are not communicating in a vacuum. As CCO, you are fully aware that stakeholders (including the company's employees) and those that influence the perception of those stakeholders are regularly, sometimes intently, accessing the interactive media for news and views that have the potential to impact your company.

Your communication strategy will assure the easiest, quickest access to headline, short-form, and finally, long-form (company website-housed) information related to the company. Connection strategies will include popular interactive links (*e.g.*, Twitter, Facebook, LinkedIn, Tumblr), news engagement sources (*e.g.*, *The New York Times*, *Huffpost*, *The Wall Street Journal*), and search engines—which continue to be major drivers of online traffic.[10]

Corporate Communicator New-Reality Principles

The new reality, and it is not all bad, is that leadership communicators can now play a more significant role in the flow of information between the organization and its stakeholders, relying on these principles:

- Assume everybody knows, or soon will know, everything. (Our reminder is *EKE!*)
- Understand that everyone (including you) constantly seeks answers to the question, "What's in it for me?"
- Know that trust is easier when the value is clear.

---

[10] Pew (2013) found a search engine (e.g., Google), the second-largest source of website traffic coming from the population as a whole, far ahead of social media.

- Know that stakeholders, when surprised, look for explanation and reassurance.
- Expect, if you surprise, to receive a lot of hits and no free pass.
- Understand that we are in a period of hunger for drama that stimulates the open process of identifying villains and heroes.
- Expect analyses—good, bad, and irrelevant—from experts and common folk.
- In leadership communication, there are two keys: describe things constantly and tell the whole story.
- Expect that half-truths, fuzzy near-facts, and outright inaccuracies will make their way into public discussion, analysis, and judgment, good, bad, and irrelevant.
- To sustain followers, who create as well as abandon leaders, provide a plan they will understand and say, "I see what's in it for me."

The CCO helps keep the conversation honest, within the context of changing realities. Control, modified into value-sharing influence, has become collaboration.

How does the CCO reinforce the strengths of leadership? Peter Drucker (1996, 93–95) gave this answer: "The effective executive asks: What can my boss do really well? What has he done really well? What does he need to know to use his strength? What does he need to get from me to perform?"

CCO "New Model" Leadership: Owned Media

Establish the capacity to create owned media—information, knowledge, apps, and so forth—and to distribute this content directly to targeted individuals through social networks and smart devices. Examine measurement and listening instruments and revise or augment as needed to provide ongoing feedback and sensing.

PART II

The Influential CCO: Skills and Competence

In Part I of our examination of the remarkable sway of communication in achieving enterprise objectives, we began to define the compelling collaboration of the expert communicator with other C-suite leaders. In Part II, we look more closely at the skills required and the influence brought to bear by the Chief Communication Officer (CCO) and his team. Chapter 6 lays a foundational core competence for the effective CCO: strong command of the facility of listening. We recognize this as the starting place for strategic communication influence, and in Chapter 7 show its application for the CCO as a strong factor in corporate culture (as well as in two other primary CCO accountabilities: his management of multichannel information flow and of critical stakeholder perception). Chapter 8 provides guidance, with specific company examples, on setting the tone for stakeholders that influences them to follow, support, and in the best case advocate for the values of the enterprise. We acknowledge in Chapter 9 that the messenger becomes the message when enterprise leaders present directly to stakeholders, as well as those—such as investment analysts—who advise and influence stakeholder decisions; and we suggest ways to assure desired connections. Influence continues as the theme in the concluding chapter in this part of the book; we explain the shared deal of corporate governance (Chapter 10) and we provide guidelines for the CCO in public company communication.

In summary, the five chapters in Part II cover much territory toward our goal to prepare you to learn and to lead toward the highest levels of enterprise achievement. In Part III, we will provide guidance on protecting corporate reputation and dealing with disruption; concluding with our view of leadership communication's future opportunity.

CHAPTER 6

Listening: Where Communication Begins

"Growth starts here!" proclaimed General Electric CEO Jeffrey R. Immelt (2010), in his annual letter to shareowners as the company emerged from the worst economy since the Great Depression.

It was 2010. The chief laid it out for his team and for those who follow and believe in his leadership: It is time to reset the vision, refocus the business model, and transform for competitive success. Ways that worked well in the past need to be reviewed and reworked. If hard times exposed weakness, it was time for leadership to discard and re-deal. Matching the urgency of the moment, Immelt adjusted GE's leadership strengths. Defining the new growth path, he underscored the strategic art of listening.

While "*inclusiveness*" had long been one of GE's highly regarded leadership attributes, often influencing other companies, Immelt (2010) now specifically cited "*listening*" as vital to leadership development and execution of corporate missions. "Leaders must be humble listeners," he explained to shareowners (and of course to everyone in the company who reads and respects this yearly message from the boss). "We will stay open to inputs from all sources. We are here to work on teams and serve our customers."[1]

To read Immelt's annual report message as his followers might have read it, the chief was telling them: *Create stakeholders in our success by*

---

[1] GE was voted #1 in Developing Leaders in the 2010 Hay Group/*Business Week* poll. Visit http://www.haygroup.com/ww/press/details.aspx?id=24434 to see how companies are rated. See http://www.ge.com/ar2010/ with CEO Immelt's "Growth Starts Here" letter. It is worth reviewing as a leadership communication guide and annual report model.

understanding what our stakeholders want and what we need to do to deliver.
Let go of any ego notion that we know it all. Get out there and listen and
learn.[2]

Business-side Listening Is a Management Mainstay

Corporate leaders, and especially those charged with communication
leadership, must bring the art of listening into both personal and strategic business corridors. At the personal level, listening is the communication ability to become absorbed in what another person is saying. In
his book on mentoring, Gordon F. Shea described the value both to the
speaker and the listener of respectful listening, which is different from
listening during a meeting or discussion. At the one-to-one level, Shea
(2002) said,

> Respectful listening means allowing (the person you are men-
> toring, or coaching) to talk without interruption and accepting
> what is being said is genuine, at least to the speaker. Listening
> to another person for that person's sake is not a discussion… [it
> is to give] the other person an opportunity to gain insight into a
> problem by articulating it, to sort things out, perhaps to develop
> a solution, and almost always to gain emotional release and relief.[3]

At the business management level, GE's repositioned principle—*business*
success begins when management respectfully turns its ear to stakeholders, seek-
ing mutual-benefit connections —is as true in this over-communicating era,
as it was 50 or more years ago when the dean of management studies, Peter
Drucker, boiled it down in his books on the manager's job.[4] Ask yourself

---

[2] We can assume that "humble" is used by Immelt in the same sense that Jim Collins
(author of *Good to Great* and *Built to Last*) used it in describing leaders that build companies that last. Such "Level 5" leaders, Collins said, combine humility with a fierce
passion to achieve missions and sustain a vision of success.

[3] Gordon F. Shea is a counselor and the author of books and articles on organizational
development, leadership/management, communications, team building, and workforce development.

three questions, Drucker told managers: *What do my customers need and expect? What will it take to assure that they get it? What's my job today?*

Following Drucker's admonishment, business-related listening strategies took hold in corporate management. *"Listen, understand, deliver"* was for many years the slogan by which Navistar, the truck, engine, and school bus manufacturer (successor to International Harvester) inspired employees and built stakeholder trust.

Tom Peters, as a McKinsey consultant, advanced Drucker's management guides in the 1980s. Interviewing business executives, he began asking, *"What's your listening strategy?"* With that question, delivered in his books, blogs, and direct counsel with executives, Peters pushed that First Business Commandment—"listen to the customer"—into an element that business leaders (and, we would argue, communicators) commonly consider as an origin of the plan (Peters and Waterman 1982).[5]

Listening to customers and other sources of stakeholder influence is recognized as a strategy for optimum performance in every aspect of business. In his management articles and books on company success principles, Harvard's Michael E. Porter (1980),[6] includes "the bargaining power of its customers" in the five forces he has identified as facing or being available to any company selling a product or service.[7] Porter's emphasis is on competitive strategy. In Porter's construct, it is impossible to consider

---

[4] Drucker wrote several books on management between 1939 and the early 2000s (he died in 2005). One of your authors (Harrison) favored Drucker's 1973 classic, *Management: Tasks, Responsibilities, Practices* to learn how to apply Drucker guidelines to business communication. doi: http://www.druckerinstitute.com/link/about-peter-drucker/. Tom Peters (see next footnote) called Drucker "the dean of this country's business and management philosophers."

[5] http://www.tompeters.com/ *In Search of Excellence: Lessons from America's Best-Run Companies* (1982) by Peters and Robert Waterman, McKinsey consultants, advocated management ideas gleaned from winning companies, including the value of aggressive learning from people served by the business.

[6] http://www.hbs.edu/faculty/Pages/profile.aspx?facId=6532 Porter's 1980 book, *Competitive Strategy: Techniques for Analyzing Industries and Competitors* quickly became the bestselling business book up to that time.

[7] The four additional forces identified by Porter in *Competitive Strategy* are the competitors the company currently faces, the threat of new competitors, the threat of substitutes for the company's products or services, and the bargaining power of its suppliers.

any strategic move toward competitive victory that does not involve the power of stakeholder advocacy stimulated through communication input and feedback—in short, strategic listening. Consider the following outcomes of "incoming":

- Listening to the competition discloses ways to defend against or defeat their competitive moves.
- *Listening sparks marketing, sales, and customer relations.*

Digital listening strategies are at the forefront of corporate social media marketing campaigns, yielding measurement of return on effort and investment (ROE and ROI). This is a change from the cautious Internet entry in the first decade of the century.

In the early years of online access, company marketers moved cautiously. Surveys of company experience (such as those conducted with *PR Week* magazine in 2008 and 2010 by the MS&L consultant firm) revealed a limited ability (or effort) to link social media marketing activity to sales and revenue, or to isolate for efficiency the impact of social media from other outreach activities (*PR Week* 2010).[8] Product safety company Underwriters Laboratories, for example, launched its first social media campaign only toward the end of 2008, when the company used Facebook, Flickr, Twitter, and blogs to reach mothers who were concerned about creating a safe home environment. In a 2010 survey, MS&L reported that a quarter of respondents did not then have working systems to measure social media relevance. The primary way for companies at that time to guage the impact of social media was through broad and, by today's standards, rudimentary measurement of website traffic, sales or revenue, brand awareness, and favorability.

The digital force of measurement today helps companies sharply zero in on competitive customer dynamics. Social media "listening" is at least equally essential in marketing as in stakeholder relations, with efficient feedback and data analytics evaluating brand awareness and identifying market targets. As MS&L Group's Jim Tsokanos noted, "You can now

---

[8] http://www.prweekus.com/social-media-survey-2010-the-social-connection/article/177511/2/

measure share of voice, share of mind, and... understand [the] impact on product sales" (MS& L Group 2010).

Listening is a reliable basis for C-suite financial considerations. Decisions require awareness of the constant input from markets, government tendencies or actions, financial institutions, and many other influential sources. Physical, actual listening to investors—with the sometimes-dramatic quarterly conversation with analysts—keeps C-suite leaders informed and provides the basis for communication. The chief financial officer of Trulia Inc., who took the company public, learned how to focus on the points most likely to stir investors by sitting in on quarterly earnings calls with Wall Street analysts who he had known in his previous role on eBay's executive team. CFO Sean Aggarwal made a habit of digging into management-analysts earnings calls (readily available on the Internet); he told *The Wall Street Journal* that listening to analysts' questions served him well, preparing for Trulia's road shows promoting its initial public offering (Chasan 2013).

Listening Informs and Inspires Design and Technology

Strategic listening can transform visions not only for the GEs and other major, long-term hitters. It can be the spark for startups. Venture capitalist Tony Hsieh credits comments from friends for the idea that made him a successful modern entrepreneur. After listening to friends say that they would not buy a pair of shoes without trying them on first. Hsieh decided to try something like marketing jiu-jitsu. If you understand what customers do not think they can get, he reasoned, why not find a way to *give them the desired unexpected.* He identified shoe supply sources and spread his concept online: *Order the shoes you want to see, examine them, try them on and, if you don't want them, send them back and I'll pay the postage both ways.* Hsieh's listening, understanding, and delivery strategy led to profitable business in his online shoe and clothing shop, Zappos.com.[9]

---

[9] After a few years of rocketing success, Hsieh sold Zappos to Amazon for $1.2 billion and continued to lead the company. For a useful context of Hsieh's success in achieving market trustworthiness, read Chapter 3 of Guy Kawasaki's (2011) *Enchantment* (e.g., customer experience as unexpected pleasure): *The Art of Changing Hearts, Minds, and Actions.*

Chief Communicator's Core Competencies Start with Listening

Although "listen to the customer" and get "public permission to operate" remain the bedrock business public relations principles that Arthur W. Page advised in his speeches from the earliest years of the professional function in the 1930s and 1940s, the expert communicator in the swirling technology and change impacting today's C-suite, has to be a listening virtuoso.

Mastery of listening may now be called a core corporate communication competence, vital in raising the CCO's odds for high performance in her three essential accountabilities: stakeholder perception management, culture influence, and information flow. We look at these with the following examples:

Perception: CCO and communication team listening strategies designed and executed bring timely, accurate, and actionable gauges of stakeholder perceptions to the C-suite table.

Corporate culture: Through feedback and other listening means (relying strongly on respectful, high EQ listening[10]), CCOs improve management's ability to detect contexts, tones, and reasons for cultural acceptance of leadership, and to overcome resistance to mission change.

Information flow: Since leadership communication is essentially a strategic conversation, CCO listening is definitive in the two-way flow of information that adds inestimable value to management's efforts to create and sustain stakeholder engagement.

Managing Stakeholder Perception Requires Listening

Stakeholder perception management, a primary responsibility of CCOs, begins by engaging stakeholders with well-reasoned information on the mission. Stakeholders are given a way to judge or measure the potential yields of their individualized deals—as employees, investors, customers, and such—if the mission is achieved.

---

[10] Emotional quotient, personal-attention considerations that partner with IQ

"OtherWise" is the watchword, as Dick Martin (2012), a former CCO at AT&T, says in his book by that name. Relevancy draws on the CCO's specialized effort to know, for each stakeholder group, the answer to the question "what's in it for me?", and on the CCO's ongoing collaboration inside the enterprise, especially within the C-suite.

As CCO, your generalized expertise in stakeholder perception enables you to aim company information toward *current scales of value* among specific groups of stakeholders. Other executives in the C-suite do not have the overview you do, because you and your team monitor and, when useful, engage in, all the channels of incoming and outgoing communication. However, each of the C-suite specialists usually has a specific set of stakeholders in mind where there is news to be made, or news to which the company needs to respond. People in finance, led by the CFO, visualize investors—how they will react when they get this information. Operational or business section leaders think, *how will this be received by my customers, outlets, suppliers, and business partners?*

The CEO ideally would want all stakeholders to at least understand the practical rationale and value of any particular origination—and in almost every case, she will have a discreet stakeholder in mind, such as those who watch the stock price and are sensitive to governance issues. You will quickly comprehend that board members are prime stakeholders in information impact on company leadership.

Former Bayer CCO Elliot S. Schreiber[11] is among the leadership communication experts who assert that sustainable corporate reputations come from producing value that meets expectations. He expresses this as the best achievable outcome: if leadership performance produces expected value, the company has reputational respect.[12] But where does this long tail begin?

---

[11] Elliot S. Schreiber, Ph.D., Clinical Professor & Executive Director, Center for Corporate Reputation Management, Drexel University, LeBow College of Business. He has served as counselor to corporate leadership, including his role as Senior Vice President and Chief Communications Officer, Bayer Corporation. See his blogs, including "Not Building Reputation Squanders Shareholder Value" in the Arthur W. Page Society blog, Page Turner; he argues for effort to leverage "reputation capital."

[12] More on this when we study the highly salutary impact of financial performance on corporate reputation in Chapter 14, drawing on the book by Rosenzweig (2007), *The Halo Effect.*

As communicators, we must reel the leadership communication process back to the points at which stakeholders—and those who influence stakeholder opinion (analysts, commentators, the media: online and otherwise)—are given information. When C-suite missions and strategies are communicated, they will inevitably become translated into promises and propositions that are the basis of the specific "deals" or value expectations among stakeholders.

CCOs must understand how content, contexts, and tone of presenting mission-related information—for example, financial target estimates, announcement of product, management, or operational change—affect stakeholder perception.

The perceived value proposition is prime territory for the corporate communication team. When the CCO understands stakeholder views through *strategic listening*—monitoring and engaging directly in stakeholder conversation through oldline and online media—he or she is enabled to provide professional counsel, as a strategic collaborator in the C-suite. Surveys of company experience (such as those conducted with *PR Week* (2010) magazine in 2008 and 2010 by the MS&L consultant firm) revealed a limited ability or effort to link social media marketing activity to sales and revenue, as well as to isolate the impact of social media from many other outreach activities.

Listening Strategies Can Perceive Seeds of Risk, Even Crises

Norman R. Augustine (2000, 31), a former CEO of Lockheed Martin who later chaired the American Red Cross, once said about crisis management: "The bottom line of my experience with crises can be summarized in just seven words: Tell the truth and tell it fast."

That remains valid counsel for CCOs and others in corporate leadership who are in the throes of a crisis. However, as Georgetown University graduate students are demonstrating, a cybersphere-conscious, crisis-avoidance update might more usefully advice: *Find ways to systematically listen to the truth as it is perceived by stakeholders and deal with it fast and continually.*

By strategic, well-aimed monitoring of blogs, tweets, and other online mentions of the enterprise, its products, its competition, and its leadership, CCOs receive a substantial inflow of perspectives. In general, this kind of managed effort to gather reactions, opinions, which can be sorted for relevancy and value, is considerably useful in the enterprise necessity of producing a constantly relevant information outflow. On occasion this monitoring will reveal a problem that can be addressed and influenced by C-suite or operational attention. Our testing of systematic stakeholder-monitoring in our student classes has indicated its value as a "pre-crisis intelligence" device, assigning each student a company to follow online, using a common format of questions and topics related to the company. This online traffic monitoring over the course of 90 days enables the would-be CCOs to sense the kinds of positive, generally company-supportive stakeholder perception as well as views that show confusion, concern, bias, and even crisis-potential activity.

The point is that CCOs need to know as much as an analytically-aided human can know about what's going on that has an impact on the business. Competence in information flow and stakeholder perception determines the level of respect and effectiveness of the CCO in modern American corporate leadership. In any C-suite, the CCO arms herself and her team with information and data in specific fields of stakeholder interest that can be compared with, or added to, the company's ongoing intelligence gathering in marketing, production, and risk management. In Part III, we provide considerably more information—as well as guidance for the CCO—on risk analysis and crisis communication.

Listening Out, In, and Up

The best achievable outcome for leadership strategies and performance, which we have positioned as the "north star" on our VICTORY compass, is to listen and to hear a "Yes" from the stakeholders.

We draw on attributes recognized as influential in creating believers, followers, advocates[13]—stakeholders who can achieve and support company missions. Each trait is an opportunity for trust-building and collaboration at some level in the stakeholder ecosystem. The organization's CCO understands that listening is the ongoing, timely, direct, and powerful

---

[13] Recognized by corporate leaders (*e.g.*, Immelt, GE; George, Medtronic; Palmisano, IBM; *et al*) as well as leadership teachers and researchers (*e.g.*, Collins, *Good to Great*; Kanter, *Supercorp*; Peters, *In Search of Excellence;* et al.)

connector to stakeholders. It is also, as we examine in Chapter 7, an essential factor in the condition of listening up to top management.

Leadership and followership get to "yes" through organized, collaborative, and strategic *listenership*. No corporate individual is more responsible for this to work than the CCO. The CCO at the top of the organization is positioned to be the "connector," as Rosabeth Moss Kanter describes the effective C-suite player.[14] A "partnership for high performance" is the influential position for those at the top of the enterprise. That is the central message of *Authentic Leadership*, the influential book by Bill George, who took Medtronic to a strong leadership culture, and went on to teach leadership at Harvard.[15]

This means listening out, in, and up. The CCO has accountability for *listening out*; she's plugging into the universe of stakeholders expressing themselves. She also has to *listen in*—to keep up with what others in management are saying, need, or want to say (or *should consistently convey* to sustain mission support, stakeholder engagement, and culture commitment). And then there is the rare, job-critical opportunity to *listen up*.

The CCO has to be all ears in her relationship with the CEO. She needs to know constantly what, when, where, and how the chief executive—the ultimate voice of the company—needs, wants, and is able to communicate. How does the chief communicator become the listening virtuoso at this level?

The Ultimate "No Spin" Zone

Successful professionals in the public relations business generally abhor "spin" as a description of preferred communication strategy. We shudder when a boss or colleague or client, challenged by a condition that requires response, turns to us and asks, "Okay, how do we spin this?"

---

[14] "Connectors are those people who serve as bridges...assembling resources and mobilizing action," Kanter (2009) says in *Supercorp*. Kanter expresses the reality that personal contact and relationships are often as important as technical talent, adding "she who has the best network wins." Your authors and other CCOs can attest that this is as true in the C-suite as in any slice of collaborative life.

[15] In addition to *Authentic Leadership*, Bill George, former Medtronic CEO, is the author of *True North: Discover Your Authentic Leadership* (with Peter Sims). Learn more at www.truenorthleaders.com.

Despite some defense of the word as a common method of impacting opinion, "spin" to most communication professionals smacks of manipulation, hype, and other eroders of trust. It was refreshing therefore when a boss was quoted, in a 2012 *New York Times* interview, as declaring his office as the place where spin stops.[16] "I always tell my staff," said Shawn H. Wilson, president of Usher's New Look Foundation, "when you come in my office, you're in a 'no-spin zone.' Just be respectful."[17]

In his conversation with Adam Bryant (whose interviews with bosses have frequently exposed the good and the bad of leadership communication), Wilson came down hard on the danger of manipulating a message to achieve momentary advantage.

> I've seen the habit in other organizations, the CEO said, and I saw it creeping into our organization, where people tend to make excuses or spin the truth: "Well, this did happen, but it's because of this...I felt it was important as a leader to say: "Listen, I don't know why this happened, but we need to get to the core root of why it happened, and it has to be factual. It can't be all these other things (Harrison 2011).

Be respectful; be honest. That mantra means the most when it comes from the boss, because—if the chief communicator and his or her team take it and apply it—it takes root in the rest of the organization, helping to fulfill a CCO accountability: influence the ongoing transformation of the culture toward shared values and mission achievement.

As this chief executive told the *New York Times* reporter, "When we started that, I definitely saw a difference in the culture" (Harrison 2011).

One CEO's Guide for C-Suite Collaborators

What communication initiative can a corporate executive take to make sure he and the executive (or production) teams are on the same wavelength?

---

[16] See the interview at http://www.nytimes.com/2012/06/17/business/shawn-wilson-of-ushers-new-look-foundation-on-leadership.html

[17] Usher's New Look Foundation is a 501(c)(3) group established in 1999 to certify young people in four leadership pillars: talent, education, career, and service. More at http://www.ushersnewlook.org/

Typically, the executive or manager knows more about the people working with him than they know about him. He has access to background and interview information (if indeed he has not conducted the interview or recruited the employee).

The obverse—upstream insight—is not so easily available. One executive, the lead strategist for a firm specializing in feedback management, suggested a means of achieving more open, two-way communication: give followers a "user guide" to working with the leader. In a *New York Times* interview (Bryant 2013, B2), Ivar Kroghrud, cofounder and for 13 years CEO at QuestBack, said he provided this kind of information to those he worked with at the company:

- *I am patient, even-tempered, and easygoing. I appreciate straight, direct communication. Say what you are thinking, and say it without wrapping your message.*
- *I am goal oriented but have a high tolerance for diversity and openness to different viewpoints. So, again, say what you are thinking and don't be afraid to challenge the status quo.*
- *I welcome ideas at any time, but I appreciate that you have real ownership of your idea and that you have thought it through in terms of total business impact.*

At the end of this information provided to employees, Kroghrud added this: "The points are not an exhaustive list, but should save you some time figuring out how I work and behave. Please make me aware of additional points you think I should put on a revised version of this 'user's manual'." The reaction to his list, Kroghrud said, was "100 percent positive"— with the benefit of helping employees open up and avoid ingrained conflict based on lack of understanding.

CCO–CEO Research Underscores Productive Listening

Fortunately for the context of this book, the mystery of productive listening has been examined, *specifically related to corporate leadership communication*. Two communication researchers at an Arthur W. Page Society conference presented their findings on a survey, probing the theory that public relations success requires *mastery of listening*.[18] Listening occupies more time than any other communication activity in all of business. That was readily accepted. After all, in everybody's life, we listen as individuals more than we talk or make hand gestures or otherwise communicate. Professors Donald K. Wright and Don W. Stacks dug into the theoretical background of business communication to examine the process of *corporate listening at the top of the enterprise.*

With access to CCO opinion of success in the C-suite, Wright and Stacks in 2000 confirmed that public relations people fit the common frame of *listening* as the dominant communication activity of CCOs. They found that, on average, CCOs were spending approximately 50 percent of their time listening, about 15 percent of their time writing, and the remaining 35 percent doing all the other things, including talking.

This is no surprise to communicators in the upper echelons of corporate management today. If you are a CCO in a modern corporation, whether you are by nature voluble or tend to taciturn, talking is a lesser part of your communication. It may seem that you spend most of your time listening, in meetings, in your office, on the phone, but we suspect that the actual listening time—and here we are not talking about actual face-to-face listening—is far less than the other "receivables" such as reading incoming email, documents (memos, proposals, in-house drafts, and so on), and the time you spend on writing about this or that.[19]

---

[18] Both professors in communication and public relations studies: Donald K. Wright, then at the University of South Alabama, and Don W. Stacks, University of Miami. Their paper on CEO–CCO listening was presented at the 2000 Arthur W. Page Society Annual Conference, and each of them has continued to research, report, and help students as well as communication professionals understand and improve in critical skill areas, such as listening.

[19] Listening here is entirely focused on two-way, person-to-person, vocalized communication. Online communication, though absolutely essential in corporate communication (and may in fact be dominating all communication, both transactional and transformational) does not endow a full, precise listening analysis. We may have "listening stations" and we may usefully eavesdrop or participate in online "conversation"—especially to perceive at least online perceptions of stakeholders—but we lack the vital ingredients in listening: tone, signals, facial expressions, common time and place, and so on.

But the mystery that had not then been explored, and in fact still hangs in the air, is what the professional communicators at that Page conference bore down on: the connecting rod between top authority and top communicator.

Here's the destination. We now know, both because of this research and through hundreds of practical examples, that there is a decided distinction between "what" and "to whom" the CEO is listening. "Whether" the CEO listens depends on a great number of prevailing factors that are beyond the control of the speaker. However, a sensing of the contexts surrounding one's ability to communicate is an important skill to be mastered by the CCO. These contexts include, as the cited research indicates, the time, place, and mindset currently impacting the intake ability of the potential listener. We will get more deeply into the art and science of connecting in Chapter 9.

To be successful communicators, or to engage with stakeholders, including bosses, on any matter of importance to achieving company missions, the CCO needs to think as he or she—your important, first-tier stakeholder, the boss—thinks. How do CEOs and other peers (or to use an outmoded term which apparently still had some resonance during the research in 2000, to "superiors") listen in the C-suite?

Wright and Stacks posed five statements on how the CEO or others in the C-suite listen when the CCO (or, an outside counselor, say from a public relations consultancy) attempts to talk to them. The research team asked more than 100 corporate communication pros to express agreement or disagreement with these five statements.

Here are the insightful results of this line of questioning, statements, and CCO levels of agreement:

- Statement one: "This person [which means CEO or any other "superior"] is more concerned with what I say than with how I say it." *51 percent of interviewed CCOs agreed.*
- Statement two: "When this person is listening to me, he or she often responds before I finish my thought." *CCOs: 50 percent agreed.*
- Statement three: "This person listens for facts, not for central themes or ideas." *CCOs: 40 percent agreed.*
- Statement four: "This person often indicates he or she is listening, but I find myself having to repeat myself." CCOs: *23 percent agreed.*

- And the final statement, proposed by the researchers: "This person takes lots of notes when I'm speaking." *CCOs: only 9 percent agreed with this.*

The research team refined this line of questioning. They asked the CCOs in the Arthur W. Page Society, to focus only on the CEO, not on other corporate executives with whom the CCO has dealings in the C-suite.

Now we get to our question, what have we learned? Can we see some clues as to how to communicate with CEOs, how to make this C-suite partnership for performance—and of most importance, your side of the deal, stronger? You be the judge:

Researchers Find Eye Contact as a Critical Factor

Impression number one, confirming the obvious for most enterprise leaders, is that when they are presenting, the CEO may take few if any notes on what you are presenting. This special research shows, in that ultimate authority figures are more interested in looking you in the eye, than taking notes on what you're saying. We will come back to the take-aways on this and the rest of the findings, but let us say here that this is important for the expert communicator to know. You are in front of the CEO to counsel. It is a conversation with authority, respectful of time, contexts surrounding the conversation, and relevance not only to "what" but especially to "so what?" If you can know and express your *purpose* in presenting (the pre-encounter self-preparation mantra is focused on why you are there and how you can help), if you *think with the end in mind,* you will more likely achieve eye contact, which effectively is expressing *I see what you mean* and *I see what we need to do or think about doing.* The valuable point from the Wright-Stacks interviews of 2000 seems even more relevant in current, electronic-centric communication. When there is actual face time with the CEO, *eye contact, not note-taking, is your best gauge of worthwhile engagement.*

Communicators Must be Prepared to "Say That Again"

The second research finding is that CEOs are more likely to need things *repeated.* The CCOs said that this was true, although the CEO may indicate—eye contact, nods of receipt, or some other signs of openness—that seems to you to indicate that they are listening. Expect them to ask questions, but if none comes, repeat what you have just said.

A third reaction from surveyed CCOs—*it is easy for the CCO to know when the boss has stopped listening.* Executives at Amazon told how they knew when they had reached the limit of CEO Jeff Bezos' attention: he would pull out his cell phone and scroll or start texting or—in extreme displays of disengagement, he would walk out of the room. Whatever the signals, you know when the other person—friend, family member, business associate, journalist—is ready to move on. The point of this survey among communication professionals in the business community is that *the CCO needs to make key points first and adjust to the executive's attention span.*

The good news from this research is that CEOs, according to the interviewed CCOs, are eager to listen for current facts, specific to what they (and you) are focused on in the current (let's say, quarterly) timeframe. When you provide that, converting themes to controllable actions, CCOs said, people at the top of the organizations are practiced, uniformly better listeners than "other corporate executives."

Take Aways: Connect. Deal In Facts. Resist 'WIIFM?'

As we listen to what CCOs tell about their experience, we learn the following:

1. If you are the expert communicator in the C-suite, you know you can expect the chief executive most likely, among all the chiefs in the C-suite, to pay attention, at least for a minute or two, to what you have to say. And you will know, also most quickly among players at the top level, the point at which you have lost that attention.
2. You know that the CEO is most ready to hear facts, not rumors, not big themes or ideas, but factual information that is relevant, and may present some opportunity to, him or her, as leader of the enterprise.
3. When you want the CEO to listen, your attitude, and especially your eye contact matter. *You have a purpose.* You have come into the meeting with top management to bring up a point, to put forward an idea, *to be of service* to the purpose of the organization and its leadership.

This requires turning down your own fear and dialing back on personal, self-centered focus. It means resisting as much as possible that constant, often useful interior voice that asks, *what's in it for me?*

Dick Martin, drawing on his experience as CCO at AT&T, got the context right in *OtherWise*. "Become wise," Martin counsels, about the "other" group or the "other" person if you want to achieve a sustainable relationship, where there is shared trust. You might say, turn "they" into "we" and get to a mutual "yes."[20] Before any structured engagement with the CEO, there is an important "otherwise" oriented question that has the power to increase your potential to spur the leadership communication partnership. That question is: *What is in it for the boss to listen to what I have to say?*

Three preconversation questions can help you prepare for any meeting or engagement. These vital, focusing questions are as follows:

1. Why am I here?
2. What do I need to learn?
3. *How do I add value to this engagement?*

In meetings with the CEO (or, in fact, with any of your peers at the executive level), be-of-service questions such as these will encourage useful dialogue and mutual respect:

1. What is it all about, in your opinion?
2. What are some of the contexts that others may not be aware of and you know are important?
3. What do you think can be done better?
4. What kind of resistance or problems should we look out for?
5. And, the action question: As I look into the leadership communication options we can pursue, what is the best achievable outcome we might focus on with you?

---

[20] *Getting to Yes*, the book by Fisher and Ury (and now, Patton), a product of the Harvard negotiation program, still popular after all these years, is a mainstay of this book's authors, one of whom (Harrison) took the Harvard course in its early days. As shown in this book's early chapter, the ultimate destination of our VICTORY wheel of leadership traits is a direct lesson from the Harvard instructors, updated somewhat by our experiences, so the "Y" in our success wheel is "Yes," a mutual, shared-value, win–win agreement.

Think through those questions, with the CEO's interests and the company's mission in mind. Research and your authors' professional experience tell us that the CCO's influence in shared-value, autonomy-enhancing, information-sharing culture begins with these kinds of listening, question-asking, and collaborative learning strategies at the top of the organization.

Coaching the Star Player

"Executive coach" is a common term for an outsider who comes in periodically for a one-to-one with chiefs of the enterprise. On a less formal basis, "coaching" others in the C-suite—usually a combination of the kind of listening and "talking truth to power" we have discussed in this book—is an opportunity for the CCO to add value at the top of the organization.

In our experience, counseling or coaching the executive leader—bringing to bear your competence in corporate leadership communication—works best if (1) the executive already trusts you, (2) you fully understand both the executive and the contexts currently surrounding the executive, and (3) you do the coaching at the right time. Some guidelines are outlined in the following sections.

Trust Trumps All

It always comes back to trust. If the executive is not sure you are 100 percent on his side, that you understand who he is and what he is trying to achieve, that you are advising him personally and confidentially—overall, that he likes you and trusts you as a friend and an enabler, you will not be in his head when he is on the field of play.

These are events, situations, and other realities that neither the other executive nor you can control. If you are briefing the executive as a football coach would prepare his star quarterback in the privacy of the locker room before the game, you review the basic contexts. *Here is where we are, here's the latest on what will probably confront us, here's our best game plan, here's what's changed, here's what we need to get done.* As counselor to the executive, you can prepare for your briefing by raising, discussing, and answering three questions:

1. What is the executive's purpose?
2. What have we learned that affects the content and tone of your information?
3. What is the main point that you can make in some relevant way, at the beginning, somewhere in the middle, and at the end of your consulting with the executive?

Timing Is Important

Executive and coach engage when the executive is willing. It is up to the coach to figure out when this is. Scheduling a one-to-one "briefing" session, in private, where trust is highest, is usually tried and is usually a good idea. The coach's job is to take it at the right pace, drawing on what you the coach know about the executive's needs, skills, temperament so you keep the conversation right for the executive. A second, shared-control, short conversation that bolsters the executive's confidence a day before the information delivery—the game—is useful if you keep it upbeat: as in "here is the reality, chief, and as we talked about and you told me, here is our strategic opportunity...."

One more thing: call it pre-game forearming, if you were the football coach, you would tape key words or names of plays to your star quarterback's non-throwing forearm before he runs onto the field of engagement. For your star executive, prepping to go into an important engagement with followers, a media interview, or otherwise, but especially if it is a stand-up, without a speech script, teleprompter, or podium, consider providing him a discreet cheat sheet, say a 3 × 5 note card (color of blue is preferable, less obvious than white or yellow cards). Write on the card (1) the name of the group (possibly, name of key people or person, such as the host or introducer; (2) our purpose of the session (begin with the end in mind), and (3) our two or three key points. Call it pregame forearming.

CCO "New Model" Leadership: Stakeholder Data Analytics

Partner with appropriate leaders in the C-suite to use data to detect trends and systematically address gaps and deepen strengths. Use data collection and analysis to understand stakeholders as unique individuals. Leverage data to personalize and tailor communications and engagement to enhance the relevance of your company's mission, products, and services—and the two-way communication involving this.

CHAPTER 7

Culture: Understanding and Influencing

"Culture." What is it? Tevye says it pretty well in "Fiddler on the Roof."

"It's what we do, it's how we do it, it's tradition!"

"They always come to my house for Thanksgiving," a mother in America might say. "It's how we've always done it in our family."

"Culture" is the name we give to a group's behavior over time.

It is what people in a group do and do not do, if they want to be accepted in the group. It's what they (or others who have gone before them, or those who now lead them) strengthen or adjust, observe or reject—in effect, the ideas and things they have in common, they value, and they express through their behavior.

The chief communication officer's accountability in culture influence in fact wraps around the other two accountabilities, *strategic information flow* and *strategic stakeholder perception management*. In the corporate context, culture is the key to almost all the best achievable outcomes (BAOs) of performance. In fact, Andrew A. Grove, who served as the early, successful CEO of Intel, described culture as his company's "strong immune system" heading off intrusions that disable company performance (Pandya et al. 2004).[1]

As communicating leaders in a business setting, we want to understand how planned communication, strategic communication, communication in

---

[1] Grove co-founded Intel (short for Integrated Electronics) with Gordon Moore and Robert Noyce in 1968, initially focused on making integrated computer chips (invented by Noyce in 1959). He became president in 1979 and CEO in 1987. For more on Grove, judged "best of the best" among business people profiled in Lasting Leadership (Wharton School Publishing, © 2006 by Pearson Education, Inc..), see http://knowledge.wharton.upenn.edu/article/lasting-leadership-lessons-from-the-25-most-influential-business-people-of-our-times/

the hands and under the direction of professional corporate communicators, impact and improve or, worst case, hamper or confuse the belief in, and the execution and advocacy of shared values within the company.

If a company tells the outside world and its employees that it is socially responsible, then that responsibility needs to be reflected in the company's business practices wherever it operates. Mette Morsing and Dennis Oswald's 2008 study of integrating sustainability into business practices underscores walking the talk of shared value.[2] Responding in 2001 to pleas from the Mandela government to import and produce inexpensive medication for patients with HIV and AIDS, the pharmaceutical company Novo Nordisk was unexpectedly drawn into a court case, pitting the company against the South African government. Novo Nordisk's legal team mounted a defense that was perceived publicly as aggressive. Protests and negative news coverage ensued, placing at risk the company's reputation and declared mission of working for public access to health measures. Novo Nordisk leadership made a decision to change course, and withdraw from the legal proceedings. Company leaders explained that Novo Nordisk's position, defending sales and use of the product in South Africa, was not inconsistent with its stated goal of sharing values. Going forward, researchers Morsing and Oswald observed, Novo Nordisk has taken care to evaluate sustainability initiatives in terms of a core set of *organizational values* that include personal health access, and local social capital, wherever the operations may be. Today, company sustainability management systems include inclusive reporting procedures, with reference specifically to the "triple bottom line" of social, environmental, economic accountability.[3]

Former CCO Elliot Schreiber (2013) emphasizes that most of C-suite attention needs to be directed toward executing strategies—as Lou Gerstner, former chair of IBM used to say: "success is five percent

---

[2] www.emeraldinsight.com/journals.htm?articleid=1771024. Also see the philosophical research reference to the *Journal of Business Ethics Education*, 193–222 (2008) at philpapers.org/rec/MORNNA-2

[3] A write-up on the paper was found at Conference Board Paper No. DN-V5N15, AUGUST 2013, www.conference-board.org/directornotes

strategy and 95 percent execution"—but this doesn't happen without cultural focus. "When I have taught MBA and Executive MBA classes," said Schreiber, "I have been amazed how little care and consideration is given to culture as the greatest facilitator or killer of strategy. Culture is the way things are done and permitted to be done inside the company on a daily basis (Figure 7.1). We can have the most brilliant strategy the world has ever known, but if there is lack of organizational alignment around the strategy, it will fail."

At Nokia, cultural embrace of executing leadership strategy was the focus of CCO Susan Sheehan when she joined the Finnish company in 2010. Her mission was to strengthen Nokia's role as a challenger in the smart-phone sector that the 150-year-old company had previously led. Working with Nokia CEO Stephen Elop (with whom she had served as communication counsel when Elop was a senior executive at Microsoft), Sheehan told the *Holmes* news reporter Arun Sudhaman (2013) how Nokia was changing its internal culture—adjusting to its loss as market leader.

"We started on a mission around our vision and values," Sheehan said. "Our CMO and I looked at what Nokia's values were over the last 150 years. We went through a pretty deep archaeological dig through our history and our values. At the same time we spoke to professors and futurists to see where the industry is going; what are the big themes? And we looked at what are we good at today, why are people coming to work? We started asking these questions—why does the world need Nokia? Nokia used to always look inside for the answers so we looked outside as well. To help people embrace the new vision and values, we started on a road-show to 15 of our key sites.

"We took some risks and showed employees our product port-folio for the next year so they could see how the vision and values were coming to life. We said, 'this is our general story, now let us help you put it into your own words.' The results are that people are able to talk about Nokia in a genuine way, and it's their own story."

Culture is in the Mission Statement (Southwest Airlines)

The mission of Southwest Airlines is "dedication to the highest quality of customer service delivered with a sense of warmth, friendliness, individual pride, and company spirit." Often benchmarked for its customer relations, the company's leaders, beginning with founder and CEO, Herb Kelleher, believe that its people—its employees, associates, the folks who deliver the customer experience—generate its reputation.

Accompanying this Mission Statement is this note: "To Our Employees: We are committed to provide our employees with a stable work environment with equal opportunity for learning and personal growth. Creativity and innovation are encouraged for improving the effectiveness of Southwest Airlines. Above all, employees will be provided the same concern, respect, and caring attitude within the organization that they are expected to share externally with every Southwest customer."

Writing in Southwest's 1991 annual report, Kelleher described the impact of its culture. He said the company had reached its level of success because "our people have the hearts of lions, the strength of elephants, and the determination of water buffaloes" (Reputation Management 1995, August).

Figure 7.1 *Southwest Airlines mission statement*

Influential Engagement in Motivation

Internal communication, which enables employees to be informed and aggressively part of the success of the enterprise, must evolve as prevailing contexts evolve. "The problem," says Daniel H. Pink (2009), an expert in cultural motivation, "is that most businesses haven't caught up to [the] new understanding of what motivates us. Too many organizations...still operate from assumptions about human potential and individual performance that are outdated, unexamined, and rooted more in folklore than in science." In his book *Drive: The surprising truth about what motivates us*, Pink (2009) produces the results of human behavior studies to show how counterproductive carrot-and-stick, reward-and-punish management has become. High performance cultures thrive only when companies tie into the individual needs and interests of people in the culture, Pink contends. He points to three elements with the greatest impact in motivating performance and shaping the culture of the enterprise: *purpose, mastery, and autonomy*.[4] We like this leadership insight, and we see linkages in three corporate communication leadership questions:

1. *What is corporate communication's purpose?* The paramount purpose of leadership communication is to identify values that will benefit both the company and its stakeholders. In any situation, it is first to understand clearly the BAOs for the company if certain performance targets are reached. It is then the role of connecting employees to the value of their effort toward this high-performance objective.

2. *What is our mastery?* We have held that corporate communicators are experts in the interactive flow of information (listening, engaging with both leaders, and stakeholders); the implications inherent in stakeholder views (why they enter into and sustain their value deals and belief in the enterprise—and why some become advocates for it); and the way in which the corporate culture is influenced toward shared-value collaborative performance.

3. *What is our autonomy?* The evidence of corporate communication progress in leadership is the way in which the function connects with C-suite peer functions. CCOs in leading, high-performance enterprises are thought leaders and self-governing collaborators (independent thinkers adding strength to top-level strategies).

Jack Welch, whose success in management at General Electric was carried over into the Welch Management Institute at Strayer University,

---

[4] This discussion centers on in-company cultures, physical, oriented to the various workplaces. On another level—not one studied or perhaps contemplated by analysts like Francis Fukuyama years ago—are the online communities. Are they cultures? Are engagements through email or Facebook and other Internet communities a form of culture relevant to the company? These, of course are manipulated cultures or subcultures, as outsiders—folks in other cultures trying to sell products and services by plugging into the values of your employees' interest–community–culture.

made the point that "money is [just] a way of keeping score" in the motivation of successful employees. Pride in the job is a big factor. "Very few good people will stay in a job just for the paycheck," Welch said in a *Businessweek* column. Welch also said, "They also need to feel that they matter and that what they do for eight hours a day or more means something. You can fulfill those needs with open appreciation, a sense of fun, an exciting shared goal, and individual attention to the challenge of each job. It's a tall order for any boss, but the returns are incalculable."

Leadership communication, enabled by the CCO and the communication team in the C-suite, has an ongoing impact on the nature of the enterprise culture. BAOs are execution of strategies, group and individual productivity, and the degree to which individuals exhibit and sustain pride in the enterprise.

Culture Is an "Inherited Ethical Habit" (Francis Fukuyama)

Communication professionals have for some years found Francis Fukuyama's (1966) examination of national cultures useful in understanding differences in group or societal motivations and traditions that are relevant and useful to apply in influencing corporate culture behavior, especially because Fukuyama emphasizes trust as the central bonding element. In his book *Trust: The social virtues and the creation of prosperity*, Fukuyama makes the case that a nation's economic wellbeing is conditioned by the pervasive factor of the level of trust inherent in the society.

Trust, says Fukuyama, is what it is all about. From their shared values (identified as specific social capital), people form "communities of trust." Fukuyama holds that culture is a trusted, inherited habit (a view differing with economists who hold that culture is a group's rational choice), absorbed, passed on within the community, and immune to opinions outside the community that they view as odd or irrational. A trust-based culture, says Fukuyama, is a collection of shared values. He expresses this in terms of countries, religious, or other traditional beliefs. People in a particular culture, for example, may come to the view that pork is unclean, or that cows are sacred or that the eldest son inherits the entire estate.

Critical social questions having to do with trust become passwords to any particular culture: *What do we value? Whom do we trust? What authority do we honor?* The questions need not be stated. They are understood. They *are* "tradition!" They also describe the ethical manifestation of groups. Unwritten moral rules become the ethical codes by which communities—societies, nations, or parts of nations—regulate behavior.

For the corporate communicator, Fukuyama's concept of culture can be a key in the process of understanding critical stakeholders. Any gap between the culture of the company and the culture of various stakeholders will diminish the creation of mutual trust. Fukuyama's examination also underscores critical research questions for leadership communication: *What are the shared values within the company's various stakeholder communities? Whom do they trust? What authorities—what authority figures, for example—do they respect? And, therefore, understanding all of this, how do we communicate?*[5]

Much is discussed in leadership guides about "management" connecting with "workers." That is true enough, but an effective, efficient, and *happy* culture requires that the employees—while there are followers engaged by leaders—have to engage *with each other* in order to produce

---

[5] Fukuyama, a former George Mason University and Johns Hopkins University professor, who was earlier (1992) the author of *The End of History and the Last Man*, advanced the idea that when the culture of a nation permits a high level of trust, high economic results occur. The absence of trust leads to poor economic performance and its attendant social implications. "Challenging orthodoxies of both the left and right, Fukuyama examines a wide range of national cultures in order to divine the underlying principles that foster social and economic prosperity... (H)e contends that in an era when social capital may be as important as physical capital, only those societies with a high degree of social trust will be able to create the flexible, large-scale business organizations that are needed to compete in the new global economy." —Amitai Etzioni, *Washington Post Book World*. Fukuyama argued that the progression of human history as a struggle between ideologies is largely at an end, with the world settling on liberal democracy after the end of the Cold War and the fall of the Berlin Wall in 1989. Fukuyama predicted the eventual global triumph of political and economic liberalism: "What we may be witnessing," he wrote, " is not just the end of the Cold War, or the passing of a particular period of postwar history, but the end of history as such.... That is, the end point of mankind's ideological evolution and the universalization of Western liberal democracy as the final form of human government."

results.[6] In companies organized with labor unions, engagement may be to a greater or lesser degree formalized. In every set of work conditions, however, leadership communication can encourage individual and team interaction, that produces the personal sense of autonomy and mastery advocated by Pink, and trustworthy or goal-directed "tradition" cultures of the sort that Fukuyama identifies on much larger scales as essential to human advancement.

The "How" Perspective (Dov Seidman)

Visualize three workplaces, all making the same product and there is heavy machinery involved or there is a risk to life and limb to the workers as well as to others, as on an offshore drilling platform. The specific culture in each of the three workplaces is different. This view of workplace cultures is drawn by a social–ethical author and business counselor, Dov Seidman (2007), founder and CEO of LRN, in his book, *How: Why HOW we do anything means everything*[7] (Figure 7.2).

> **Workplace One.** Nobody questions the boss. You do what you are told or face the consequences. Somebody has required them to wear

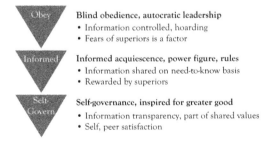

Figure 7.2 Three types of corporate cultures
Source: Adapted from HOW, Dov Seidman, 2007.

---

[6] We use the term "employees" because its meaning is clear. We do, however, clearly recognize the value of terms used by companies to encourage "employees" to be partners in achieving business missions. As management guru Gary Hamel said in a McKinsey interview in May 2013: "In most organizations, we don't call people employees anymore...we call them team members or associates... (They) are in fact "business partners" in a company's "co-creation with...customers."
[7] Since 1994, LRN has helped companies navigate complex legal and regulatory environments and foster ethical cultures. *Fortune* magazine called Seidman "the hottest advisor on the corporate virtue circuit."

hard hats and blue shirts and pants. Safety is an order. Employees vaguely understand what is behind the order, but they hardly ever ask any questions. They do their jobs, wear the blue outfits, and never take off their hard hats. Working is a matter of following orders. It is essentially an "obey and get paid" culture.

Workplace Two. Rules are as clear as the workplace is clean and well ordered. Top-down directives sift through the organization in predictable and controllable ways. Variations of individual behavior are minimized. Workers are informed about what is expected, they are told why it is needed, and they get rewarded when they do it. Workers accept this. Procedural, rational communication has reached them. Each individual wears the hard hat or the provided outfit because he or she knows it is expected. Workers acquiesce. They conform to what seems to be rational authority. "Nothing personal, it's just how we do things," they explain to others in the workplace. Theirs is an "informed, rational rule" culture.

Workplace Three. Conditions are clean, efficient, focused on output, but here there is a difference. Everybody here takes personal responsibility. Everybody has come to believe that safety is in everybody's best interests. It is a shared value. Values speak to their higher self. Each worker feels satisfaction in doing his or her job, wearing the hard hat, proud to be in the clean blue outfits, and encouraging others—in the other's best interest, safety and pride—to do likewise. This is a culture of some autonomy, or self-governing (Seidman 2007).

Seidman's analysis is useful in considering how leadership communication applies (or fails to apply) in various enterprises. There is limited or no application of Seidman's workplace one culture of *blind obedience* (which we shorthand as *OBEY* in our graphic) to modern Western capitalist enterprises.[8]

---

[8] Seidman actually talks about four "factory" cultures; however, the first—which he describes as a culture of "anarchy and lawlessness"—is so antithetical to anything you are likely to encounter in the United States and other advanced industrial nations that it is hardly worth our study of modern leadership communication. To read the results of a disturbing 1963 study conducted by Yale University psychologist Stanley Milgram (1974) on the ugly, even inhumane, result of obedience as a forced determinant of human behavior, see *Obedience to authority: An experimental view.*

If obey were a company mantra, leadership communication would be in a sad state. In Seidman's "workplace one" setting, information flow is managed to its downward detriment. Contrast our "everybody knows if more than one person knows" reality with an alternative reality where a boss hoards what he knows, communicating only when it suits the individual's interest, never mind the interest of the enterprise and its stakeholders. The rise and effectiveness of employee communication has eradicated such cultures. If there is still any unquestioned bossism in any company, it is safe to predict that social media will inexorably bring it to light.

Similarly, Seidman's workplace of *informed acquiescence* (*INFORMED, in our graphic*) is an outmoded, if not disappearing, cultural distinction. Here we can observe advancement in leadership communication, en route to the next level in the Seidman workplace hierarchy. In this reasonable rules culture, information flows, albeit in narrow channels, on a need-to-know basis. The culture is not yet free of subjective and arbitrary carrots (rewards) and sticks (punishment); these are still implicit in workplace two communication. (For an unusual example of a company at least appearing to have kept one foot in the past, with regard to worker sensitivity, see the Amazon warehouse story in the notes.[9])

We benefit from Seidman's characterization of the previous two workplace cultures to highlight the *values-based self-governance* of his workplace three (SELF-GOVERN in our graphic). Here we activate the engagement factor that has the potential to release individual mastery and

---

[9] The following is excerpted from a *New York Times* article from Sunday, August 18, 2013: "It was so hot in Allentown, Pennsylvania, in May 2011, that some workers at the Amazon warehouse there collapsed. Another company with different attitudes might have installed air-conditioning, or simply sent workers home during heat spells. If Amazon did that, however, East Coast customers might not get their Jay-Z CDs or diapers or jars of heather honey as quickly as they expected. So the company chose a different solution. It arranged to station ambulances and paramedics out front during five days of excessive heat, according to *The Morning Call*, the Pennsylvania newspaper that broke the story. Fifteen workers were taken to area hospitals after they fell, and as many as 30 more were treated by paramedics at the warehouse. Workers quoted by the paper said the heat index in the facility, a measure that includes humidity, was as high as 114 degrees. Amazon had little to say to the newspaper, even when it later installed air-conditioning."

team collaboration. Both Pink (2009), defining motivation, and Seidman (2007), defining management, give credence to what we consider both ideal and essential for enterprise competitiveness, corporate values-based PURPOSE.

"Best Workplace" Guidance

Research from the Hay Group (Goffee and Jones 2013,) found that highly engaged, productive employees are 50 percent more likely to exceed expectations than the least-engaged workers.[10] What does an engaged culture look like?

Best workplace guidance now seems to be: It is the culture where employees believe in the corporate purpose and know what is in it for them, information is not suppressed or spun (playing tricks with the truth), the company adds pride and worth to the individual, the work is rewarding, the employees trust the leadership and the leadership models the behavior that is expected; and, to summarize Seidman's "workplace two" feature, *there are no stupid rules.* The flow of communication is bilateral with purpose-centric encouragement from the C-suite to the farthest reaches of the enterprise, what public relations theorists James Grunig and Todd Hunt (1984) calls "symmetrical two-way communication."

Inclusion is the guiding word, believes leadership guru Warren Bennis. "Leaders make people feel that they're at the very heart of things, not at the periphery," Bennis has said. "Everyone feels that he or she makes a difference to the success of the organization. When that happens people feel centered and that gives their work meaning."[11]

A best practices white paper by the Institute for Public Relations (IPR) by Gary Grates, Keith Burton, and Coleen Learch (2013, 3) concluded that "it's all about the why." Cultures in successful companies are able to clearly and concisely articulate the purpose and value of change for future success, to begin with the end in mind—and remembering it.

---

[10] *Creating the Best Workplace on Earth,* by Rob Goffee, emeritus professor, London Business School, and Gareth Jones, visiting professor, IE Business School, Madrid; in *Harvard Business Review,* May 2013.

[11] (doi: http://www.successories.com/iquote/author/1895/warren-g-bennis-quotes/1)

IPR suggested an in-house communication mantra that succinctly captures the shared-value purpose can be helpful, citing as example a purpose-focusing mantra that FedEx employees have understood throughout the firm's four-decade history: three words, continually communicated: "People, Service, Profit."

The CEO's Role in Shaping Culture

The chief executive of NIC, Inc., a provider of online services for federal, state, and local governments, told a journalist (Bryant 2013, May 18, B2), "I firmly believe that the No. 1 job I have is to set the culture of the company." Harry Herington acknowledged that his behavior as chief executive drove the level of performance and success, its integrity, its trust of his leadership. His method of engagement was unusual, if not unique. He bought and learned to ride a motorcycle, a large Harley Ultra Classic painted law-enforcement blue, which he would ride to various venues where his employees were gathered and conduct the program he called Ask the CEO. Employees enjoyed the CEO's courage and candor. "They see me in a different light," Herington said. "That is where most managers and leaders struggle. How do you get to the point where (employees) perceive you as human? It goes back to the trust thing. They want to understand my thought process, and they want to understand basically the core of who I am" (Bryant 2013, B2).

In an intensive, multiday workshop for new CEOs, involving more than 50 corporations in 2004, the facilitators, led by consultant and author Michael Porter and associates (Porter et al 2004), summed up lessons the CEOs said they encountered in their rise to the top. Among these lessons were

1. The CEO actually do not run the company.
2. Giving orders is often a costly exercise.
3. It is hard to know what is really going on.
4. You are always, intentionally or not, sending a message.
5. You are not actually the boss.
6. Pleasing shareholders is not actually the goal of corporate performance.
7. You are, after all, still only human.

One of the CEOs in the workshop told his story associated with Lesson 2 about giving orders. In a previous company, the CEO—call him, Perry—was a success as a hands-on executive. His habit was to get directly involved in major programs, apply his energy and personality, and drive to completion.

In his new leadership post, Perry got an early opportunity to show his stuff when a pending advertising campaign to launch a new product reached his desk. He had a better idea for the campaign. He called a halt. He would get involved. The team members, who thought they were through after weeks of work, thought they were just coming in to apprise the new chief of the plan, were sent back to the drawing board.

The impact? A signal to managers: this CEO likes to be hands on, likes to take charge. Perry was changing the process, and the culture had to adjust. Here was the lesson of the cost of giving orders, as described in an article by Porter in the *Harvard Business Review*: the culture shifted from independence to dependence, from best effort by each individual to tentative effort in hope of approval. Perry soon had managers standing in line to bring him their ideas in the early stages. He had plans to approve or work on. He had problems to solve.

A CEO once told us that when one of his fellow C-suite officers showed up at his office, the CEO would look at them first to determine— *is this person bringing me a problem or is she bringing me the answer to a problem?* Our CEO friend said the ones who helped to lead the company were in the latter category. She, or he, would always arrive with at least two possible strategies to solve the issue under discussion.

In the case of the 50-CEO study reported by Porter, the can-do, got-to-do CEO did change the immediate culture in the C-suite. He found himself in charge. People slowed down the performance. The individual who had led the team that came in to show the boss their work was so discouraged that he took another job at another company. The CEO was puzzled, shocked into realizing, he told fellow CEOs at the workshop, the cost of giving orders. He had become not the leader and the facilitator of leaders. He had become the boss and the bottleneck.

The bike-riding CEO of NIC correctly observed that followers want to understand the human and his thought process. Employees want to see what the boss values—and whether their respective values work together. Style is an important indicator of cultural value.

When Brent Saunders became CEO of Bausch & Lomb, brought in by the board to turn the company around, he was escorted to his Rochester, N.Y. office. The room was huge, with a magnificent skyline view. "This isn't going to work," he told associates, "If we want to create one company, one culture, one team mentality, then we should all sit together." He moved all the executives from the lofty quarters to the company's manufacturing plant building a few miles away. It was a symbol, he said, that everyone was in the turnaround together (Bryant 2013, B2).

The question is always, "does the culture enable the achievement of missions, moving toward the rewards of victory?" The point of the Harvard CEO study was that the CEO will impact the immediate C-suite culture, for better or for worse; and that giving orders rather than encouraging initiative, disables leadership communication and the rise of new leaders. Communication—its context, its content, its style—enables a more autonomous culture, one that produces shared values.

Starbucks CEO Howard Schultz has acknowledged that there may be legal or ethical reasons why some in-house information is not ripe for mass consumption, but he found this to be no excuse for people with power to ignore, or fail to act upon, the truth as they understand it.

> "Few leaders will be able to resolve issues in ways that please everyone," Schultz believes, "but without the right information up front they are ultimately powerless. That is why I respect people who speak to me with candor and why I have always tried to foster an environment of transparency so others feel comfortable sharing even negative news." Schultz said he tries to be the role model: "I strive (to be) direct in my own communications admitting what I don't know and letting my natural curiosity drive me to understand the heart of a matter."[12]

In a memo to Starbucks leaders, after he had stepped down from, and before he resumed, the chief executive position in 2007, Shultz sent word

---

[12] Schultz, chairman, president, and chief executive officer of Starbucks, is the author of the best seller *Onward: How Starbucks Fought for its Life without Losing its Soul.*

to senior leaders that the company's very future was on the line, because certain standards of success were not being acknowledged.

> "I was emotional as well as pointed in my critiques of our busi-ness," he said in the 2012 newspaper interview, "because I wanted our senior leaders to understand that the company's future success was at stake if we did not acknowledge various faults and act to fix them." "I knew that some people would disagree with (the memo) and be upset with me," he went on, "But I felt that as leaders, we had a responsibility to face even unpleasant truths about our busi-ness. Only by acknowledging that we were straying from our core could we get back on track."

The chief executive's internal memo leaked, according to the com-pany, appeared online and in national business news articles. Schultz said he was not pleased with this but said he "found solace knowing that the memo had sparked open dialogue throughout our organization about things we needed to improve." He credited the leaked memo as a catalyst for honest conversations that made a successful course correction… "[It] jump-started the company's eventual turnaround," Schultz said (Bryant 2013, B2).

Suggestions for the CCO in the Purpose-Driven Culture

Rosabeth Moss Kanter (2009), in her influential book, *Supercorp: How vanguard companies create innovation, profits, growth, and social good*, examined the traits that drive vanguard (that implies clearly leading) companies and puts a lot of emphasis on making values and vision a daily part of the C-suite conversation. Linkage of cultural values to leadership vision needs to be vocalized constantly at the top of the organization, Kanter (2009, 148) holds, to focus employees on serving customers and society, with emphasis on connections. She is describing an obligation of CCOs when she cites the growing importance of connectors in organi-zations. "Connectors are those people who serve as bridges between and among groups," Kanter observes, "assembling resources and mobilizing action." As she states, "In essence, she who has the best network wins," we underscore your role as connector vital to best outcomes in the company cultures.

How do you, if you have accountability for information flow and stakeholder perceptions, get started and raise the impact of values and culture engagement?

Borrowing from engagement theorists Kanter, Dov Seidman (2007), Daniel Pink (2009), from other counselors and—most importantly— drawing on direct experience as C-suite communication leaders, we have prepared a go-to-it values and culture nine-point *engagement* kit for new and rising CCOs.

1. **Gut check.** Start with what you know about the culture, what goes here, "how we do things," what works, what does not...tradition! Use your conversation leadership skill to probe, gently, not challenging, views of C-suite peers. Affirm or adjust your gut view of what can be done.

2. **Describe reality.** What is the cultural condition? Based on informal review, place your company on the Seidman scale—informed acquiescence or self-governance. What values and vision guides are in place that you can work with? If there is a vision or mission statement, evaluate its relevance. What are the contexts surrounding the company (competitors, world or local news, whatever else affects the stakeholder listening climate)? Are current contexts and tone right for what is? What can be shaped, what can be kept, how do we build on the base? If there is no employee-culture-relevant standard—no creed carved in stone or posted online—what can you infer from sources, preferably published? For example, in the most recent annual report to stakeholders, what was the outlook (vision or mission) in the chairman or CEO letter?

3. **Shape authentic themes.** Huddle with your communication team. Address tough questions about engagement and the paths to autonomy and self-governance. Begin to shape themes that will authentically recognize purpose, vision, and shared values in the company's stakeholder relationships (we call them *win–win* deals). Consider the theme of moving toward greater good outcomes. Draft plans to work

these themes into the managed information flow, and to test them in the stakeholder ecosystem.

4. **Think networking.** Build some belief and advocacy within the leadership. As Kanter counseled corporate executives on *vanguard*-ism, be a connector who opens new possibilities by socializing, assisting, and guiding values-based commitments among others who have goals to achieve. Think how stakeholder (starting with employee) engagement can join with and help leaders achieve various goals.

5. **Adjust the big portal.** What is your best chance to amplify and to some extent control authentic engagement? This has to point to your company's owned website content. This is the always-open, 24/7, most frequently used check-in point for outsiders (and employees and their families and connections) to see what the company thinks is important. Make the website your big portal for engagement. Evaluate and tune the access, the content, and the tone of this conversation center to convey, prove, and advance authentic vision and shared values.

6. **Simplify, then oversimplify.** In their classic book on market positioning, Al Ries and his co-author Jack Trout (1981) said communication is a battle for people's minds. Frequent cultural value messages have to be sharpened to cut into minds already cluttered with ideas, bias, and competing communication. Corporate communicators are operating in societies diagnosed by Ries and Trout as already infected with the *disease of over-communication*. They said the only antidote is *oversimplified messages*. Their counsel: "You have to jettison the ambiguities, simplify the message, and then simplify it some more" (Ries and Trout 1981, 8).

7. **Tune in to WIIFM.** In all levels of engagement communication— incoming and outgoing, remember that everybody listens to their *What's In It For Me* (WIIFM) station. From the top of the organization to its farthest reaches, from employees to investors, personal relevance is the key to believing, practicing, and advocating values shared with the company. This is why it is so important for company leaders to listen, to understand, and to relate to the constant conversation that is going on in the stakeholder universe. And that is why you, as expert examiner of stakeholder perceptions, are in the best

possible position to counsel executives and managers on authentic and effective engagement.

8. **Have a plan, work the plan.** It may be as open and intensive as the plan IBM's Sam Palmisano put in place when he became CEO. He forced the curve of employee engagement toward agreement on and participation in the driving purpose of the company. Shared values and autonomy, which we know as the motivators for high performance, become the culture with that sort of aggressive, democratized approach. The plan need not be that grand. IBM communicators were fortunate to have a leader who saw the need for a cultural adjustment and was willing to throw open the engagement door. The key is to have a plan that is rational, real, and achievable, even if it is just one small step at a time.

9. **Keep learning.** Besides learning what is needed and what you can do in communicating, keep up with the state of this growing art of culture leadership. Dov Seidman, Daniel Pink, John Baldoni, and other corporate observers are accessible online. The range of leadership or communication books continues at a pace of several hundreds a year. Academic studies—like those at Georgetown University—are available, along with management guides. We recommend commentaries and current developments on organization sites (such as awpagesociety.com; instituteforpr.org; PRSA.org) and communication professionals sites (such as the site that identifies closely with leadership communication as we teach it at, Maril MacDonald's *letgoandlead. com*, and the site for public relations job-seeking and career-development, Ron Culp's *culpwrit.com*). For a general search related to culture, Google corporate culture (reaching sites such as *mckinsey.com, bcg.com, wharton.upenn.edu, inc.com, forbes.com, hbs.edu, georgetown. edu,* and of course, *amazon.com*); and plug in to see what works for you in your organization.

Bottom line is that information management and stakeholder perception management—the first two accountabilities of the CCO—are in fact the company's strongest potential influence on the company's character and culture. The core competences of the CCO become an engagement force in the C-suite. The CCO is (to be somewhat glib, but to make a real point) also a CEO—that is to say, potentially the chief engagement officer.

CCO as Conscience of the C-Suite?

There is a potentially troubling aspect to the obey influence in organizations. That is when the lines of business ethics and morality are crossed. Following a case of business ethics in 2013, James B. Stewart (2013) of *The New York Times* interviewed experts in organizational psychology for, as he put it, "clues about why otherwise ethical, law-abiding, well-educated, and highly compensated people often do something they either know or should know is wrong." One expert—Edward Soule, associate professor at the McDonough School of Business at Georgetown—acknowledged the danger at the morality-management intersection. As human beings, Soule believes, "we are predisposed to be obedient to authority, no matter how malevolent it may be." He cited work done by Yale University psychologist Stanley Milgram on this. A professor of social enterprise at Columbia Business School told the *Times* columnist that workers may react to an assumed obey—overlook or abide untenable situations. Professor Soule pointed to a natural instinct to obey. "For evolutionary reasons, group membership is a central feature of the human condition," he told Stewart. "Neuroscientific research has shown that the mere thought of being rejected from a group is painful." The *Times* columnist concludes that in some corporate situations, people learn that "if you defy authority, you get into trouble."

The key to influencing company culture is communication that consistently encourages truthful, fair, and certainly lawful and moral behavior. Codes of ethics, guiding principles, and personal C-suite and supervisor modeling behavior are ways in which communication does not allow a vacuum for any degree of dishonesty. Professor Shannon A. Bowen (Bowen et al. 2010; Bowen and Stacks 2013) in several publications and in particular in her co-authored book, *An Overview of the Public Relations Function*, takes on corporate ethics as a necessary, not merely sufficient condition for profit in her chapter on public relations ethics.

How much accountability does the communicator in the C-suite have for influencing the company's culture? It varies, company to company, of course, but it is safe to observe that the opportunity is growing.

One analyst of corporate leadership, *London Evening Standard* columnist Anthony Hilton (2012), suggested that a competent company communication officer might be the right person to assume what is now the company lawyers' accountability for deciding how conscientiously the company regards laws and standards. His argument was that corporate attorneys too often take a legal compliance mentality that lets the company slip past the letter of the law, veering dangerously close to violating the spirit of the law. Lawyers are not built to be the conscience of the company, in other words, and Hilton advanced the case that CCOs, attuned to culture, values, and stakeholder perceptions, need to take on the role of conscientious culture advocate and enabler.

Arthur W. Page Society (AWPS) leaders come close to this view. Its 2012 research and direction report, *Building Belief: A New Model for Activating Corporate Character and Authentic Advocacy*, argues that the CCO has a responsibility to work across the enterprise to define and activate corporate character. AWPS President Roger Bolton, himself a veteran in employee engagement during his C-suite role in Aetna, has noted:

> From my perspective, everyone in senior management—or in the company at large, for that matter—has an obligation to build and protect brand and reputation by adhering to a strong set of values and an appropriate mission to create value for customers, employees, shareholders, and society. And in the companies where I was privileged to serve, the general counsel and corporate attorneys played a highly constructive role in that regard (Bolton 2012).

The question of who should weigh in on the level of legal compliance is a case-by-case matter. There seems to be a decisive factor: *Is the company content with a culture striving to simply comply with requirements, or is it trying to create, reassure, and sustain stakeholders, including employees who see how close the company gets to legal limits?* Corporate management believes that CCOs today are well situated to weigh in on C-suite decisions that affect sustainable business cultures. "When this is done well," as Bolton said, "companies are focused on doing the things that are consistent with their espoused character—in essence earning trust with everything they do every day. In this scenario, compliance remains important, but doing the right thing is never in doubt."

"Giver" versus "Taker" Cultures

What does it mean when we say that shared values are strengths that create and sustain a company culture? In a sense, it is a matter of give versus take. With a culture that encourages leaders and employees who are givers (they help other employees and their leaders to succeed), and screens out takers (they are overly self-centered, closed-system individuals), companies can achieve lasting benefits. Adam Grant (2013) at the University of Pennsylvania's Wharton School uses the story of "Ed and Alvy" to illustrate this idea.

Ed and Alvy were the leaders of a certain Hollywood film company's creative division when a new CEO was hired. Under financial pressure, the new chief ordered layoffs. Ed and Alvy disagreed. Their team was doing a good job, they argued, adding value that would be lost if jobs were cut. The new boss dug in. "You have to cut at least two people in your team," Ed and Alvy were told. He asked for the list of names to be on his desk by the following morning.

At nine the next day, the CEO found the list on his desk. He opened and read the list. It contained two names. You guessed it: the names were Ed and Alvy. The team was needed, they said; and the new boss heard from others in the C-suite that he could not afford to lose these two leaders.

The CEO relented. He was not ready to slash key personnel. Ed and Alvy kept their jobs and so did all the members of their team. Several months later (this was in 1985), an executive from another company came in. His name was Steve Jobs and he wanted to buy the creative division of Lucas Film. Jobs bought the unit, used it to start a new company, which he called Pixar. A quarter of a century later, under the leadership of Ed Catmull and Alvy Ray Smith, Pixar had become a strong and enduring force in the film business of Hollywood.

The spirit of dedication and success prevails in the culture set by leaders who communicated shared-value reality. They, the leaders, would put their own jobs on the line for the good of a values-adding team. Commenting on this story in his examination of taker cultures versus giver cultures, Professor and author Grant observes, "When it comes to giver cultures, the role-modeling lesson here is a powerful one: if you want it, go and give it."[13]

CCO "New Model" Leadership: Corporate Character

Initiate a cross-C-suite effort to define your company's corporate character. Try to answer this question: Does the company's internal culture and its external reputation reflect (and help move forward) the company's differentiating purpose, mission, and values?

---

[13] Grant's book, Give and Take, A Revolutionary Approach to Business, is a goo perspective related to culture.

CHAPTER 8

CEO Letter: Leadership's Cardinal Communication

What is the single most controllable, highest profile, and possibly most potent, thrust of leadership communication in a public company? This chapter presents the case for the chief executive officer's letter in the corporation's annual report. Published and freely distributed before the company holds its yearly stockholder meeting, the annual report is the *proactive narrative* on the company's current condition and outlook. Here is where every phase of the enterprise—the business, the products, its people, and financial performance—is laid out for shareholders (investors) and other stakeholders. The CEO provides the top-view perspective, summarizing achievements, challenges, and prospects for the year or years ahead, and asking for support in ongoing or future success.

In addition to responding to the concerns and interests of company shareholders, the annual report is commonly considered a means of supporting the company's marketing, of building employee understanding and pride, and in the best achievable outcome, of creating new followers and stakeholders. The report is typically professionally produced, published as a full-color booklet or brochure, and is posted in various forms for public access on the company's website.

This volunteered annual report differs distinctively, in content and format, from the rigid, formal (Form 10-K) report required each year by the Securities and Exchange Commission (SEC) (Figure 8.1), but the company takes care to assure that the data in both publications are consistent—and the SEC report is often included, as the thin pages at the back of the corporation's narrative report.

The most-widely read section of an annual report is the CEO letter, because it "sets the tone from the top" and provides an insight into the thinking of the leadership of the company. We have studied CEO letters

---

The Securities and Exchange Commission on the purpose of an Annual Report[1]

The annual report to shareholders is the principal document used by most public companies to disclose corporate information to their shareholders. It is usually a state-of-the-company report, including an opening letter from the Chief Executive Officer, financial data, and results of continuing operations, market segment information, new product plans, subsidiary activities, and research and development activities on future programs. The Form 10-K, which must be filed with the SEC, typically contains more detailed information about the company's financial condition than the annual report.

"Reporting companies must send annual reports to their shareholders when they hold annual meetings to elect directors. Under the proxy rules, reporting companies are required to post their proxy materials, including their annual reports, on their company websites. Companies sometimes elect to send their Form 10-K to their shareholders in lieu of providing shareholders with an annual report. Some companies may submit their annual reports electronically in the SEC's EDGAR database."

Figure 8.1 SEC Guidance, Form 10-K

from numerous companies to evaluate and appreciate the important leadership communication factors at play. The CEO letter is the most personal and direct opportunity for the leadership to level set with stakeholders, while providing the annual appraisal of the corporate performance against the goals promised and then setting the framework for the next targets to conquer. In other words, the purpose of the CEO letter is to relate the current reality of the company's performance and then provide the path to hope, both when the current performance is beating expectations… and, especially when it is not.

The CEO letter typically:

- Affirms the corporate vision;
- Advances the strategy and mission;

---

[1] http://www.sec.gov/answers/annrep.htm

- Reports on the previous year's progress and projects the near-term outlook;
- Reiterates how the company's strengths uniquely position it to win in the competitive marketplace, and
- Seeks to influence continued support for the company and its management. (This call for sustained engagement is almost always the closing paragraph of every CEO letter.)

Sample CEO Letters

Here are some examples of how CEOs used their letters to communicate the leadership factors listed above to their stakeholders in their company annual reports issued in 2012.

General Electric[2]

In CEO Jeffrey Immelt's 2012 annual report letter, he affirmed the corporate vision:

> GE works on things that matter. The best people and the best technologies taking on the toughest challenges. Finding solutions in energy, health and home, transportation and finance. Building, powering, moving, and curing the world. Not just imagining. Doing. GE works.

He then advanced the strategy by describing a conference the company held in Silicon Valley the previous year to launch what General Electric called the Industrial Internet, which drove home key messages for attendees:

> It was a reminder of two things. First, few companies can do what GE does: the scale we operate on and our decades of investment are a competitive advantage. Second, in an uncertain economy, long-term growth and competitiveness require the endless pursuit of innovative productivity.

And he reported on the future outlook for GE:

---

[2] http://www.ge.com/ar2012/#!report=letter-to-shareowners

We like the way GE is positioned in this environment: a great portfolio of world-class, technology-leading businesses; a strong position in fast-growth global markets; leading-edge service technologies that achieve customer productivity; high visibility with a backlog of $210 billion; and a strong financial position. We want investors to see GE as a safe, long-term investment. One with a great dividend that is delivering long-term growth.

With that assessment, Immelt outlined the five "choices that drive the future":

- First, we have remade GE as an "Infrastructure Leader" with a smaller financial services division;
- Second, we are committed to allocating capital in a balanced and disciplined way;
- Third, we have significantly increased investment in organic growth, focusing on R&D and global expansion;
- Fourth, we have built deep customer relationships based on an outcomes-oriented model;
- Fifth, we have positioned GE to lead in the big productivity drivers of this era.

He also outlined the competitive advantages of GE going forward:

- Leading in the shale gas revolution;
- Extending GE's lead in advanced manufacturing;
- The power of the industrial Internet through a major investment in software and analytics;
- Fueling airline productivity;
- Localizing for underserved healthcare markets.

Finally, he affirmed the culture of GE: *We are mission-based. We search for a better way. We drive solutions for our customers and society. We are a "We Company." It is driving accountability for outcomes. It is fostering smart risk-taking and business judgment.*

Johnson & Johnson[3]

Alex Gorsky used his first shareholder letter as CEO of Johnson & Johnson to position the company in its responsibility for providing high-quality healthcare solutions:

> Johnson & Johnson works at the very center of this challenge, across the broadest base of any company in global healthcare. Every day we are working to help people everywhere live longer, healthier, and happier lives. We recognize that with our global leadership comes a responsibility; one we consider a privilege. I'm pleased with how we are meeting that responsibility, but I'm far from satisfied.

He used the opportunity to affirm his commitment to the legendary J&J *Credo* (Figure 4.1, page 63):[4] "My overarching goal as CEO is to ensure that our nearly 128,000 employees in more than 275 operating companies around the world will always be united by Our Credo and our single purpose: Caring for the world, one person at a time."

And he tied the company's legacy of caring to its actions in responding to the 2012 Hurricane Sandy that affected J&J's New Jersey headquarters community (20,000 first aid kits, blankets to shelters, and more than $5 million in Red Cross funding) and the efforts of J&J people to assist in the relief efforts:

> It is this example of caring by individuals that inspires caring in the whole community, and reminds me of how firmly and fundamentally compassion is woven into the fabric of our culture.

Finally, Gorsky had solid 2012 business results to report, led by an impressive long-term record:

> We generated significant cash flow and maintained our AAA credit rating. Importantly, we continued our track record of consistent

---

[3] http://2012annualreport.jnj.com/chairmans-letter
[4] http://www.jnj.com/sites/default/files/pdf/jnj_ourcredo_english_us_8.5x11_cmyk.pdf

performance, with 29 straight years of adjusted earnings' increases and 50 consecutive years of dividend increases. Johnson & Johnson is one of only six companies in the Standard & Poor's 100 Index to achieve that record.

ExxonMobil[5]

Rex Tillerson opens his 2012 letter to shareholders by reminding them of the company's vision:

> …Our unique competitive advantages and steadfast commitment to ethical behavior, safe operations, and good corporate citizenship enable us to deliver long-term value to our shareholders while helping to supply the world's growing demand for energy.

Tillerson points to strong 2012 results and the benefits for shareholders:

> Over the last five years, we distributed $145 billion to our shareholders, and dividends per share have increased by 59 percent, including a 21-percent per share increase in the second quarter of 2012.

The competitive advantages, mentioned in Tillerson's letter and given extensive treatment in the annual report, include a balanced portfolio, disciplined investing, high-impact technologies, operational excellence, and global integration.

Berkshire Hathaway Inc.[6]

In un-characteristic CEO style, Warren Buffet opens his 2012 CEO letter by addressing the bad news for the year—first, subpar performance in book value versus the S&P (in spite of a total gain for shareholders of

---

[5] http://cdn.exxonmobil.com/~/media/Reports/Summary%20Annual%20Report/2012/news_pub_sar-2012.pdf

[6] http://www.berkshirehathaway.com/2012ar/2012ar.pdf

$24.1 billion), and second, the failure to make a major acquisition ("I pursued a couple of elephants, but came up empty-handed.")[7] He hastens to add that the lack of a major acquisition in 2012 was made up for in February 2013 with the agreement to buy 50 percent of the holding company that will own H.J. Heinz. And he pledged that he and Charlie Munger "have donned our safari outfits and resumed our search for elephants."[8]

With the bad news out of the way, Buffet reports on the positive results in 2012:

- $10.1 billion aggregate pretax earnings by their five most profitable noninsurance companies (BNSF, Iscar, Lubrizol, Marmon Group, and MidAmerican Energy);
- 26 bolt-on acquisitions by Berkshire subsidiaries;
- Insurance operations, with GEICO leading, that "shot the lights out last year;"
- Two new investment managers that outperformed the S&P 500 by double-digit margins;
- Record Berkshire employment of 288,462;
- Increased ownership positions in Berkshire's "Big Four" investments (American Express, Coca-Cola, IBM, and Wells Fargo);
- Record $9.8 billion investment in plant and equipment projects.

---

[7] Warren Buffet, 82, is the world's 3rd richest man according to Forbes, with a net worth of $54.9 billion (as of 3/24/13). His lifetime philanthropy has resulted in $17.3 billion in gifts. In 1962, Buffet began buying shares of a struggling textile company, Berkshire Hathaway. The firm, which Buffet famously said was "the dumbest stock" he ever bought, has long since shed its textile assets to become Buffet's famed investment vehicle. Buffet is often called "The Oracle of Omaha" for the city where he has lived most of his life, demonstrating the value of his investment advice, which he shares—often in memorable, folksy quotes—in his annual shareholder letter. www.forbes.com/profile/warren-buffet.

[8] Charlie Munger, 89, is at the time of this writing the Vice Chairman of Berkshire Hathaway, often described by Warren Buffet as "my partner." A native of Omaha, Munger met Buffet at a dinner party in 1959. Prior to joining Berkshire, he was Chairman of Wesco Financial Corporation (now a wholly owned subsidiary of Berkshire Hathaway). His net worth stood at $1.1 billion (3/2013), which, he announced in 2013, will decline as he makes charitable gifts ("I don't need it where I'm going.")

He summarized the company's investment strategy:

> In summary, Charlie and I hope to build per-share intrinsic value by
> (1) improving the earning power of our many subsidiaries; (2) further
> increasing their earnings through bolt-on acquisitions; (3) participat-
> ing in the growth of our investees; (4) repurchasing Berkshire shares
> when they are available at a meaningful discount from intrinsic value;
> and (5) making an occasional large acquisition. We will also try to
> maximize results for you by rarely, if ever, issuing Berkshire shares.

Ford Motor Company[9]

Ford CEO Allan Mulally opened his 2012 letter by reminding stakeholders of the company's commitment to its mission of delivering profitable
growth, called One Ford plan.

"We remain laser focused on the key aspects of our plan, which remain
unchanged":

- Aggressively restructure to operate profitably at the current
  demand and changing model mix;
- Accelerate development of new products our customers want
  and value;
- Finance our plan and improve our balance sheet;
- Work together effectively as one team, leveraging our global
  assets.

"By following this plan, we will continue to build great products, a strong
business, and a better world."

He listed the achievement of several important milestones:

- Restoring Ford's investment grade status;
- Reclaiming the Ford Blue Oval;
- Resuming regular dividend payments; and
- Achieving 14 straight quarters of operating profit.

---

[9] http://corporate.ford.com/doc/ar2012-2012%20Annual%20Report.pdf

Mulally then reported on the 2012 progress and competitive strengths in the product and business arenas as well as the environmental and social milestones.

"Great Products"

Among the 2012 product achievements, Mulally pointed to the following:

- Launching 25 vehicles and 31 power-trains globally;
- Announcing plans to revitalize the Lincoln brand as the Lincoln Motor Company;
- Sales of 2.3 million vehicles in the United States (second straight year above 2 million). Ford is the only brand to top the 2 million mark in the United States since 2007;
- Sales of 1 million for the first time in Asia-Pacific, including a record in China;
- Focus as the best-selling nameplate worldwide and Fiesta as best-selling B-Car; and
- Ford was the only brand to have three vehicles in the top 10 best sellers worldwide.

"Strong Business"

2012 business results included the following:

- Full year pretax operating profit, excluding special items, of $8 billion, or $1.41 per share;
- Strengthening the balance sheet with $24.3 billion in automotive gross cash (exceeding debt by $10 billion);
- Strong liquidity position of $34.5 billion, an increase of $2.1 billion over 2011;
- $3.4 billion in cash contributions to worldwide funded pension plans;
- Largest manufacturing expansion in more than 50 years;
- Adding 8,100 jobs in the United States;

- Transforming the European business for future profitable growth; and
- Strengthening the leadership team globally.

"Better World"

Environmental and social achievements in 2012 were as follows:

- Going further than competitors by offering an industry-best seven vehicles in the United States that deliver 40 or more miles per gallon, by:
- Producing the 500,000th fuel-saving EcoBoost engine in three years after launch;
- Introducing six new electrified vehicles (hybrids, plug-in hybrids, and a pure battery electric vehicle); and
- Serving communities with 25,000 employees and retirees volunteering more than 115,000 hours at 1,350 projects.

Mulally ended with projections for the near-term future as he provided the path to hope, and concluded:

> Overall, we expect 2013 will be another strong year for the Ford Motor Company with pre-tax operating profit about equal to 2012, Automotive operating-related cash flow to be higher than 2012, and pre-tax profit for Ford Credit to be about the same as 2012.

IBM[10]

Reporting "…record operating earnings per share, record free cash flow and record profit margins, with revenues that were flat at constant currency," IBM CEO Virginia Rometty started her 2012 CEO letter with the

---

[10] http://www.ibm.com/annualreport/2012/letter-from-the-chairman.html

aim of putting the results in context with IBM's model of "Continuous Transformation" through the following strategic proof points:

- "We remix to higher value" in R&D, acquiring new capabilities and divesting nonstrategic assets;
- "We make markets" by category, geography, and client;
- "We reinvent core franchises" (e.g., System Z as the latest reinvention of the mainframe and Information Technology Services shift to high-value service of data center energy efficiency, security, and business continuity and recovery);
- "We remix our skills and expertise" (e.g., increased analytics with more than 8,100 experts);
- "We reinvent the enterprise itself" to "achieve our goal of $8 billion in productivity savings over the course of our 2015 Road Map;
- "We use our strong cash flow strategically" to reinvest in the business and deliver consistently strong shareholder returns.

To reiterate IBM's competitive strengths and industry leadership, Rometty describes a *new era of computing:*

Today, another new wave is sweeping in—powered by Big Data, analytics, mobile, social and cloud. We anticipated this several years ago with our point of view on building a Smarter Planet—a world that was becoming instrumental, interconnected, and intelligent...

Arguing that IBM is well-positioned for this new era—which IBM calls "Smarter Computing"—Rometty defines three characteristics of the new era:

1. Smarter Computing is designed for Big Data.

   Every two days, as much data is now generated as in all of human history up to 2003. This is "Big Data," and it constitutes a vast new natural resource that can revolutionize industries and societies—with the right technology, capable of analyzing and extracting value and insight from it.

Rometty advances two direct benefits for IBM:

- Strong growth in IBM's analytics business led them to raise "our 2015 Road Map target for Business Analytics from $16 billion to $20 billion of revenue."

We are also rapidly advancing the marketplace applications for our breakthrough "cognitive" computing system, Watson, which is already demonstrating its potential to transform healthcare and finance. We will introduce our first commercial Watson offerings this year.

2. Smarter Computing is built on software-defined environments. Here again, Rometty argues that IBM is strategically well-positioned:

Hardware build for these new environments will be of significant business value—exemplified by IBM's systems today. From System z, to Power Systems, to storage, to our new PureSystems family, IBM systems are software defined.

3. Smarter Computing is open.
Rometty points to IBM's success with Linux, Eclipse, and Apache in developing IBM businesses to work in the ecosystems.

Today, we are repeating this strategy through a number of collaborations such as OpenStack, a new open source cloud platform; Hadoop, an open source platform for Big Data; and several promising open source hardware projects.

Opportunities presented by this new technology era, according to Rometty, are allowing IBM to engage with *new clients and new markets:*

- Chief marketing officers (200 percent growth, or $2 billion, in 2012);
- Chief procurement officers (expected increase in investment by 30 percent through 2015);

- Human resources leaders (*"One analyst has ranked IBM as number one in enterprise social business for the past three years."*); and
- City mayors and urban transportation managers.

Rometty also forecasts that "Front-office" transformation *"has the potential to fuel the biggest wave of business technology investment since the era of enterprise resource planning (ERP)."*

Finally, Rometty closes her letter by affirming how the IBM model supports the IBM value of *being essential.*

It speaks to IBMers' aspiration to be essential to each of our vital constituencies—our clients, our communities, our partners, our investors, and one another. We see this as our purpose as an enterprise—to serve their plans for success, their need to transform, and their own unique sense of purpose.

Hewlett Packard[11]

Taking head-on the turnaround efforts under way at HP, CEO Meg Whitman positioned 2012 this way in her letter to stockholders:

Fiscal 2012 was the first year in a multi-year journey to turn HP around. We diagnosed the problems facing the company, laid the foundation to fix them, and put in place a plan to restore HP to growth. We know where we need to go, and we are starting to make progress.

In her report on the financial performance for 2012, she asserted that, "we are already seeing tangible proof that the step we have taken are working." By the numbers:

---

[11] http://h30261.www3.hp.com/phoenix.zhtml?c=71087&p=irol-irhome&jumpid=reg_r1002_usen_c-001_title_r0002

- $10.6 billion in cash flow from operations;
- Rebuilding the balance sheet by reducing net debt by $5.6 billion; and
- Returned $2.6 billion to stockholders through share repurchases and dividends.

The multiyear restructuring program, announced in May 2012, according to Whitman, had initiated efforts to:

- Optimize our supply chain;
- Reduce the number of stock-keeping units and platforms;
- Refine our real estate strategy;
- Improve our business processes;
- Implement consistent pricing and promotions;
- Refocus R&D;
- Better understand customer needs;
- Align our portfolio;
- Speed our time to market.

She also indicated that they had modified their incentive compensation structure for senior executives to increase shareholder value focus. In addition, 2012 "was a landmark year for product announcements:"

- The first new line of multifunction printers in seven years;
- A new line of Windows 8 PCs;
- HP ElitePad.

Whitman characterized 2013 as "a fix-and-rebuild year" with anticipated disruptions from 2012 organization changes, cost reductions, investments in tools, systems, processes and instrumentation, and disciplined capitol allocation. She also said that 2013 would bring product innovation, an improved commercialization strategy focused on cloud computing, security and information optimization, and rebuilding their go-to-market capability.

Looking to the future, Whitman reiterated HP's competitive strengths in terms of:

unparalleled scale and distribution…to reach customers and partners in any corner of the globe at the best possible price. Our brand is trusted by customers around the world. We have talented and resilient employees that are committed to our customers, and a culture of great engineering and innovation.

She also referenced today's "new style of IT," which will "demand much greater agility, lower cost, and a higher degree of accessibility." This environment, Whitman claimed, made HP an ideal partner:

> Our diverse portfolio sets us apart, and we are the only company that can deliver hardware, software, and services that meet the needs of all of our customers, from the enterprise to the consumer.

She marked her first full year as CEO with statements of confidence that HP's position as a world-class technology leader, delivering unrivaled solutions for our customers...will increasingly equate to improved financial performance and increased stockholder value.

CEO Letters: CCO Guide to Best Practices

As evidenced by the examples of the CEO letters summarized in this chapter, it is fairly easy to highlight the best practices employed among top Fortune 500 companies:

- Describe the current reality and influence continued support for the company and its management.
- Share and reinforce the company's vision and how it is differentiated or uniquely positioned to win in the competitive marketplace.
- Tally up the achievements of the past year and use them to demonstrate the company's strengths and management expertise.
- Explain the company's challenges and put in perspective the impacts of any extraordinary events, such as a one-time write-off.
- Establish the priorities and target milestones for the coming year.
- Give credit to the performance of specific teams of employees who are living the corporate values and demonstrating positive cultural behaviors.

- Outline the strategic goals for the longer-term and position them in terms of corporate values and culture.
- Humanize the company by putting the vision and mission in perspective to achieving goals that contribute to a greater societal good.
- Leave a lasting impression of a CEO and aligned leadership team that are accountable and transparent, engaging and informative, and confident and authentic.

The best CEO letters will leave readers feeling as if they have just had a meeting in person with the CEO and come away with answers for every question, encouraging strong support for the company's leadership and strategic direction, and, in the best case from the perspective of the enterprise and its leadership communicators, a compelling desire to invest in more of the stock.

Set the "Tone from the Top;" Make the Letter Receiver Centric

Based on the preceding discussion and samples from top Fortune-500 companies' Annual Report CEO letters, we suggest six points to remember when working with the CEO on maybe his most important letter.

1. **Investors want to feel they are "insiders" to the corporate thinking.**

   Jack Welch (GE) and Warren Buffet (Berkshire Hathaway) consistently acknowledged their personal attention to writing their CEO letters—and their letters have been cited, over time, as being among the most engaging, transparent, and investor-focused annual communication devices. (see Jeff Immelt's [GE] letter above.) Personalized efforts by CEOs in writing their letters are a boon to the CCO's leadership communication program. As the letters put the corporate vision into relevant, current perspective, they serve also to achieve that most difficult positioning of conveying to investors and other stakeholders the personal interest—and in best cases, the charisma—of the leader, the ultimate authority and voice of the enterprise.

2. **The goal is to inspire confidence in management and a belief in the corporate strategy.**

It requires serious engagement by the CEO and senior leaders. Too many CEOs simply do not invest enough personal effort in the letter and regard it as "just another 'check the box' task"—preferring their annual colonoscopy over this ritual letter. See comment above on the personalized efforts of CEOs.

3. **The CEO letter should speak directly to the shareholders, and it should not duplicate the narrative in the Annual Report.**

An obvious indicator that the CEO did not write his or her letter is when it parrots the Annual Report. Shareholders ask: "Didn't the CEO have something of value to add?" In addition, the CEO letter should honestly and straightforwardly summarize how the results were achieved, even if the marketing-influenced narrative of the Annual Report mainly highlights the positives. If underperformance is a fact, the CEO should unambiguously state the reasons and outline the steps the company is taking to course-correct the strategy and change the results. Meg Whitman's letter (HP) is a demonstration of stating the unambiguous: "Fiscal 2012 was the first year in a multiyear journey to turn HP around. We diagnosed the problems facing the company, laid the foundation to fix them, and put in place a plan to restore HP to growth. We know where we need to go, and we are starting to make progress."

4. **Shareholders are interested in understanding the contribution of the intangibles to corporate results as well as the tangibles.**

Many companies forego highlighting the impact of intangibles, because the accounting is fuzzy, but many intangibles are the real secret sauce of the company's true success (e.g., brands, trademarks, reputation, customer loyalty, quality of management, strategy execution, product innovation, human capital, market share, quality of corporate governance, independence of the Board of Directors). CEOs should acknowledge the intangibles and provide metrics when or where they are viable to demonstrate the corporate value and complete the corporate success story (i.e., if Starbucks did not talk about its intangibles in terms of brand, reputation, customer loyalty, product innovation, and quality of associates, the tangibles would not come close to telling the full story of their success).

5. **Shareholders want to be reassured that the company has alignment from top to bottom about the mission.**

Companies often discount the importance of a richly vibrant culture to achieving the shareholder's objectives of increasing value. Talking about the culture and the employees' commitment to the mission can provide a powerful message to align shareholders with the company's mission. (Jeff Immelt of GE declared in his CEO letter: "We are mission-based. We search for a better way. We drive solutions for our customers and society. We are a 'We' Company." It is driving accountability for outcomes. It is fostering smart risk-taking and business judgment.)

6. **Shareholders are increasingly interested in corporate governance and how the Board of Directors is exercising its fiduciary responsibility on behalf of all shareholders.**

Most CEO letters do not report on the role of Boards of Directors currently, but this issue will become more important as activist shareholders bring proxy proposals that increasingly focus on the role of the Board and its members. CEOs should include a focus on the Board governance role in future CEO letters to demonstrate the importance of the Board's responsibility and activity in support of *all* shareholders.

CCO "New Model" Leadership: Build Stakeholder Relations via CEO Letter

The CCO's position is such that she stands to put the company's achievements—and failures—in perspective, related to its mission, vision, and values. While serving as values advocate, she is also fostering relationships with those who invest in the company and those who govern. *The new model CCO helps set the stakeholder relations tone for the year when shaping the CEO letter's strategy and content.*

CHAPTER 9

Language and Presentation

Influential communication involves the skillful expression of ideas and motivation. The first obligation for the leader of an enterprise is to influence thinking and behavior that impact the organization's success. In competitive business environments, this means going public with information with the hope of building credibility and support for the company. Communication from the top is aimed ultimately at achieving victory in competitive business environments.

Two communication factors shape the influence toward that goal. One is *language*, the words that flow in leadership communication. The other is the result of the leader's *personality* when the individual delivering the message becomes the message.

Deborah J. Barrett (2010), author and Rice University professor in professional communication, has described "a master of leadership communication" as one able to analyze a group of stakeholders in every situation and develop a strategy that facilitates accomplishing an objective with that group, at that time, in that place. "Leaders need to be able to structure and write effective, simple and complex correspondence...from text messages and emails to proposals and reports," Barrett said. Within each context, she said the leaders "need to be able to write and speak in the language expected of leaders, language that is clear, correct, and concise. In addition, they need to be able to create and deliver oral presentations *confidently* and *persuasively*."[1]

At his or her most influential level, the chief executive will routinely excel in the use of words to establish connectivity and stir action. For the

---

[1] At Rice University, Dr. Barrett was a lecturer of MBA communication at the Jones Graduate School of Management from 1988 to 1991, and from 1998 to 2006. Her book, more formally presented than our text/reference, is recommended for both theoretical and practical applications of communication and leadership.

communication counselor to C-suite executives, the language of leadership and guidance in personal delivery must be areas of competence.

In their books on communicating at work, Tony Alessandra and Phil Hunsaker (1993) support our sense that leadership communication engages information content, context, and tone or style. They cite three "V elements" in message influence: verbal, vocal, and visual. *Verbal* means words—the language of leadership. *Vocal* means tone—how the message builds rapport with the receiver. *Visual* incorporates everything that the reader senses and the viewer or listener sees or hears.[2]

The Language of Leadership

We begin with the end in mind. The purpose of leadership communication—thoughts turned into language—is to influence stakeholders to accept, believe, and advocate the values of sharing in the success of the enterprise. Following are guidelines for the chief communication officer (CCO) and those in the C-suite and beyond who shape and convey communication that leads to best achievable outcomes.

Belief is Not Automatic

Information flow is impacted by a lot of filters, some enabling, some disabling the intention of the sender. Communicators for any enterprise must understand that the *content* of what they initiate will be affected by prevailing *contexts*. Acceptance of the enterprise message is conditioned by external and internal business contexts, the communicator's reputation and skills (in our VICTORY circle of leader traits, Chapter 3, we tag the reality that nothing good happens if the leader is not trusted), and the record of the company (forever green on the Internet) in the guideline taken from Arthur W. Page is about telling the truth, and proving it.

The *context challenge* for business communication is very high, as author and counselor Michael Maslansky (2013) pointed out to students in a lecture on leadership communication at Georgetown University:

Living through the horror of the 9/11 era, the 2008 financial collapse, and a lifetime of accumulated consumer experiences, Americans are more skeptical now than at any other time in our history…. They think financial services companies will take their money. Pharmaceutical companies put profits over patients. Politicians are all liars. And corporations will do anything for a dollar. Communicating in this difficult environment requires more than selling products or telling stories. The only way to reach consumers who are more sophisticated and skeptical than ever is to re-establish credibility.

Maslansky's book, *The Language of Trust: Selling Ideas in a World of Skeptics* recommends tools to use language that builds, or rebuilds trust, "when the facts, actions, and record are on your side, but you just can't quite get over that last hurdle—acceptance" (Maslansky et al. 2010).[3]

President Ronald Reagan is credited with a slogan for skeptics on the receiving side of communication: "trust but verify." Corporate speakers, on the delivery side, might gain credibility through a twist on that. In a speech constructed by one of your authors for a corporate chief executive officer (CEO) facing a skeptical audience on the topic of pollution reduction in the 1990s, the theme was "don't trust us, track us." The CEO acknowledged the need for clean-up proof. His company provided a way for stakeholders and critics to receive current, credentialed information on an open, ongoing basis about the progress of the company's greening program.[4]

How does the CCO activate *followership belief* in Barrett's "mastering leadership communication?" In her book, *Leadership Communication*,

---

[2] Tony Alessandra taught marketing and sales at University level for eight years before becoming a full-time professional speaker. His clients in speaking/presentation skills include Fortune 500 companies and professional associations. He has been a speaker at conferences of the Arthur W. Page Society.

[3] "Based on pioneering consumer research, The Language of Trust shows you how to regain the confidence of your clients and customers and communicate with them on their terms. You'll learn what words to use, what words to lose, and how to structure your message to overcome skepticism and build and keep the trust of your audience." (Marketing review).

[4] Speech by E. Bruce Harrison for the chief executive of Union Carbide Company at the 1992 United Nations "Earth Summit" on sustainable development, in Rio de Janeiro, Brazil. The "track us" offer was substantiated through public disclosure of tests of pollution levels, conducted by a leading research firm.

Deborah J. Barrett (2010, 407) writes: "Mastering leadership communication becomes a priority for all individuals who want to lead others and want their groups, their organizations, or the broader community to follow them, trust them, and consider them leaders."[5] This book is about that purpose, underscored in the guidelines that follow; however, one basic move for any enterprise has to be to make the company website a constant source of relevant current and historical proof of the company's performance and values. The site will contain statements, speeches, questions and answers, access to records, and evidence. And, this enterprise front door needs to be lively, reliable and, we recommend, able to swing both ways: conveying information and inviting questions and feedback.

Make Truth-Telling a Language Habit

Leadership language is *situational*, in that it needs to be right for the occasion. However, there is a constant imperative for messages in any and all situations; that is, *to tell the truth.* The Arthur W. Page Society, made up of CCOs whose jobs involve conveying language at the highest levels of corporate endeavor, cites truth-telling as its very first corporate communications principle. "Taken at face value you wouldn't think this axiom requires explanation," said one of the founders of the CCO society, Edward R. Block (2004), who headed communications at the top of AT&T.[6] "But…at the highest levels of policy-making, the truth can be elusive. Inevitably, there are endless, sometimes bewildering, consider-

---

[5] The index of Barrett's (2010) book also provides a useful "Self-Assessment of Leadership Communication Capabilities."

[6] Ed Block was a founding director of the Arthur W. Page Society. Prior to his retirement at AT&T in 1986, he was senior vice president, responsible for public relations, employee information, and advertising. His mentors at AT&T were two senior executives who had reported to Arthur Page when he headed the corporation's communications and served on the AT&T board of directors. The excerpt here is from Building Trust: Leading CEOs Speak Out: How They Create It, Strengthen It, and Sustain It, a 2004 publication of the Arthur W. Page Society, edited by John A. Koten, a founding director and the first president of the Page Society, who during the course of corporate experience at Illinois Bell, AT&T, New Jersey Bell, and Ameritech, reported to seven different CEOs. Koten said in the book, "Their personalities varied, but their expectations for ethical behavior were uniformly high." See awpagesociety.com

ations to take into account when top management seeks consensus on the right policy, the right course of action or even a response to unanticipated events." Even in circumstances when all the facts, in every detail, may not be available, he counseled, "you always know intuitively what the truth is." Block counseled CEOs and CCOs to avoid obscuring reality. "Employees, customers, shareowners, and the news media easily recognize dissembling or spinning half-truths," this thought leader in corporate communications warned; "when management's actions or statements don't pass the 'smell test,' credibility is the immediate casualty."

Block called truth-telling the first line of defense in protecting a company's reputation and the leadership's trustworthiness.

Think "Otherwise"

George Nelson, the American designer, summed up what's needed in a lively book on communicating (*How to see*): "A cat may look at a king, as the old saying goes, but the visual message is more interesting if the (cat) also knows what a king is." The sender "must use a code of language that is intelligible to the receiver."[7] In another approach the radical activist, Saul Alinsky (1969), noted that you cannot use the "Queen's English" when speaking in a ghetto. The choice of language, of vocabulary, of intensity is the essence of clearly communicating.

If you, as CCO, are the collaborator in the C-suite and the facilitator of connections beyond the C-suite, the strategy for connecting is to know where you are aiming, to correctly assess surrounding contexts, and to understand as fully as possible what the primary intended recipients are prepared to absorb and understand. We will address this in discussing leadership presence—the potential power of direct, personal communication—later in this chapter. Here, we repeat our "think otherwise" guideline: tune in on the mental channel your stakeholders are constantly listening to: WIIFM, *What's In It For Me?* How do your words resonate with their needs and their ability to decode and grasp with your meaning?

---

[7] Quoted in Writing to Learn by William Zinsser (1998), writer, editor, and teacher (Yale, New School in New York), one of a series of highly readable books on writing, recommended by your authors. Writing to Learn is a Harper Collins book, New York, 1998.

Make the Encoded Message Decodable

The authors of *Communicating at Work* (Alessandra and Hunsaker 1993, 14) envy the communication process of the *Star Trek* drama, where Mr. Spock could mind-meld information perfectly to another Vulcan. "However, since we haven't figured out how to use Mr. Spock's mind-meld method of direct transfer," say the authors, "we are stuck with…an imperfect system that contains considerable opportunity for misunderstandings." Alessandra and Hunsaker (1993, 15) simplify the process this way:

Speaker > *encoding* > MESSAGE > *decoding* > Listener.

Corporate speakers and writers (leaders and their communication counselors) select words that they hope will convey to receivers (stakeholders as well as neutral and critical publics) the intended meanings and (to stakeholders) connecting values. The "imperfect system," described by Alessandra and Hunsaker (1993, 15), involves the fact that even the best-quality, aimed-at listener or reader receives the message through a series of filters: his past experiences, perception of the sender, emotional involvement with the message, understanding the verbal content, level of attention,…on and on. "In a sense, he (the intended receiver) translates the message into his own words, creating his own version of what he thinks the speaker was saying," Alessandra and Hunsaker state.

Get Feedback

To activate improvement in leadership communication (to "sharpen the saw" as Stephen Covey recommends),[8] you need feedback. This is the most readily done inside the enterprise, through internal surveys, ques-

---

[8] Covey (1989, 2004), in *The 7 Habits of Highly Effective People*, gave "sharpen the saw" as habit #7, following be "proactive, begin with the end in mind, put first things first, think win/win, seek first to understand, and synergize." Covey said that "sharpen the saw" means having a balanced program for self-renewal in the four areas of a person's life: physical, social/emotional, mental, and spiritual. In Covey's (2004) subsequent book (to which we refer here), *The 8th Habit: From Effectiveness to Greatness*, he provides advice relevant to communicators and other leaders, dedicating the book "To the humble, courageous, 'great' ones among us who exemplify how leadership is a choice, not a position." We take this as a proper incentive for CCOs, as to how they lead in the successful corporation.

tions asked of audiences after an in-house presentation, and through informal (but planned and strategic) conversations with leaders, managers, and employees. CCOs, whose team members are most frequently involved in preparing internal communication, are generally in charge of feedback follow-up, working with human resources when it is mutually useful. External feedback strategies include engaging in social media research, monitoring stakeholder conversations, blogs, and other online flow related to the company's information outflow.

Connect With Internal Stakeholders Where They Are Connected

Ben Adler (2013) started each day by going outside and getting the home-delivered *New York Times*. "I read the *Times*," Adler wrote in an issue of the *Columbia Journalism Review*, "for the same reason that I eat Hebrew National hot dogs, tie my necktie in a schoolboy knot, and aspire to buy a brownstone: because it's what my parents did." Adler's parents became adults in the early 1980s. "I'm 31, a dinosaur," Adler commented, as he compared his own conditioning to those whose parents entered adulthood in the age of the Internet. In a well-researched article, useful to read in full, Adler examined the way in which Generation Y, the rising, effectively dominant class of information *consumers* (individuals born between 1978 and 2000) are dealing with information. Adler's conclusion is that millennials expect a steady diet of quick-hit, social media-mediated bits and bytes. And they expect to get in on the action.

What does that mean for corporate communications? The substantial change in journalism (newspapers are adjusting or disappearing) is reflected in substantial change in business information flow, and especially in employee communication, driven by the forces of technology and transparency. CCO Jonathan Atwood of the global firm Unilever paraphrased the information expectation of employees in his company: "Employees are telling us 'talk to me now, when I want to be talked to, how I want to be talked to: send me an email, send a text message, weigh in with Twitter and Vimeo' (https://vimeo.com). What they don't want is a long, well-constructed letter from the CEO."[9]

---

[9] The Unilever communications executive made his point at a colloquium sponsored by the World Environment Center, at the National Press Club, Washington, DC, on May 10, 2013. Your author (Harrison) participated in this event.

Digital Devices Dominate

A formal letter from the CEO may well be necessary; it is good for establishing the record, which the CCO, the board, and many others may need, and it can be considered for posting on the company website. What it can lack, if it is not in sync with the employees' and other stakeholders' needs, is *immediacy*, particularly reaching employees how and *where* they are connected. Employees get information and opinion through their mobile devices and Internet-connected desktop computers. And again, our reminder: leading companies turn their websites into belief builders and value enhancers. This is where CCOs can lead in C-suite influence, through the control of content, relevance to context, selection of tone, access to *and speed of* information flow, up-to-the-minute, two-way, 24/7.

Strengthen The Company's "Language of Trust" Online

The Internet has made the conversation with stakeholders—information flow and feedback—an endless proposition. The trust challenge is never closed. In online engagement, the corporate communicator can understand online language and wink–wink terms (from one of the earliest, LOL, has flowed a stream of such shortcut terms), but we like Maslansky's take on forms of delivery to overcome skepticism and build credibility. Maslansky offers online language-of-trust guidelines such as these:

1. Use online style and content limits to express the same main points (headlines, attention grabber) that you use in news releases, speeches and blogs.
2. Respond to online critics with rational, proof-supported comments rather than suffer the "silence that cedes the floor."
3. Use online facilities—such as links to messages of others—to broaden the conversation in ways that help you tell your story. And,
4. Use the company website to capitalize on the broadened online conversation.

Rosanna Fiske, an associate professor of public relations at Florida International University, has noted that students need PR studies with a clear understanding of social, economic, and lifestyle preferences and how these affect communication, consumer behavior, culture, and technology usage. It is not just about 140-character messages. It is about having the right words at the right time, said to the right people through the right medium, in the right tone and sentiment—all the while keeping in mind the importance of the public interest.[10]

Communicating relatively long distance with stakeholders, CCOs can benefit from a review of basics: knowing the best way to reach those stakeholders, confidence in understanding current stakeholder values, and competence in reaching them so you and your company touch those values.

The Presence Factor

Woody Allen said in an interview with Frosty (2008) that "eighty percent of life is showing up...so that was what I would say was my biggest life lesson..."[11] We hold that to be true in business leadership. Personal presence is at the highest level of the communication scale. The business communicator's trust-building leadership words meet their test when the leader delivers them in a speech, an interview, a phone conference with investors, or unscheduled interactions, such as a response to a pop-up media question. If the active sender of information is seen and heard by the active receiver, the connection is obviously at its highest potential strength. The strongest element of the Alessandra-Hunsaker analysis— visual communication—is activated. Positive leadership "presence" skills can move, convince, inspire, and entertain—in short, connect the speaker to the listener in a planned manner.

---

[10] See Alessandra and Hunsaker (1993, 15).

[11] Allen said: "I made the statement years ago, which is often quoted that 80 percent of life is showing up. People used to always say to me that they wanted to write a play, they wanted to write a movie, they wanted to write a novel, and the couple of people that did it were 80 percent of the way to having something happen. All the other people struck out without ever getting that pick. They couldn't do it, that's why they don't accomplish a thing, they don't do the thing, so once you do it, if you actually write your film script, or write your novel, you are more than half way toward something good happening. So that I was I say my biggest life lesson that has worked. All others have failed me" (Frosty 2008, 2). http://col-lider.com/entertainment/interviews/article.asp/aid/8878/tcid/1/pg/2

Everything changes when the messenger becomes the message, because personalities engage. As pollster and "words that work" expert Frank Luntz (2007, 72) has said, "Personality goes a long way. Those character attributes that together make up personality—that tell us something about one's affiliations and sympathies—are a critical component of communication. When they clash with your listener's expectations, the most precise and on-target language in the world won't save you."[12]

Make Presence a Work Habit

Company leaders were exhorted by management experts years ago to "manage by walking around" instead of spending most of their time in their offices (Peters and Waterman 1982).[13] Accessibility—easy engagement of executives and managers with employees—is increasingly the management habit (as underscored in Chapter 7 by observers such as Dov Seidman and Daniel Pink). The management habit of presence means focus on people on whom the leader depends to achieve missions (which ultimately add up to the leader's vision). "[This] means, when you're with people, giving them your full attention, so that they will feel recognized and motivated," say two "presence" counselors, Kathy Luban and Belle Halpern. "When you're not present to the people you lead, it weakens their willingness to commit."[14]

Preparing To Present

Notre Dame Professor James O'Rourke (2008) teaches business communication at the University and, frequently working with CCOs, coaches corporate officers in public speaking. His excellent resource book, *The*

---

[12] Dr. Frank Luntz has counseled Fortune 500 companies on using words, language, and presentation skills to achieve corporate goals, has analyzed speaking skills and audience impact of political candidates and office holders, and was called America's "hottest pollster" by the Boston Globe. Our reference here is from a book well worth studying for business messaging: *Words that Work: It's Not What You Say, It's What People Hear*, Hyperion Books, January 2007.

[13] See *In Search of Excellence* (his 1982 book which touted "management by walking around") and additional views of Tom Peters, his presentations and blog at tompeters.com

[14] See Chapter 1, "Presence: What Actors Have That Leaders Need," page 10.

Truth About Confident Presenting, asserts that all communication is context-driven. Presenters can best prepare by understanding the contexts of audience, purpose, and occasion.

In corporate leadership settings, questions such as these need to be resolved by the CCO team before drafting or prepping company spokespersons. Who is your audience? What are their needs and interests? Why are you speaking to this group, on this occasion, about this topic? Does the occasion call for a serious, challenging talk or a polite, informative presentation?

CCOs who help others in the C-suite present information must first analyze internal contexts (what is going on in our company) and surrounding external contexts (what's happening in the world around us in the community, the industry sector, the national scene) right now. What is in the news or social media streams, either about your company or about circumstances that will confirm or challenge what you plan to present?

We remind CCOs who draft presentations of the value of thinking *otherwise* (visualizing stakeholder values, desires, and fears) in advance of communicating your needs. Get into *their mindsets* as you aim for your shared-value, best achievable outcomes. Barrett (2010, 9) says, "The more we can relate our presentation to what is in the minds of the (intended) audience, the more easily we will be able to garner their attention." O'Rourke's (2008, 30) truth—"All that really matters is what the audience wants"—is a workable reminder for connecting, informing and, always to some extent, influencing desired outcomes.

The 'What, So What, Now What' Formula for Preparing

If you are writing a news release, you get into the journalism mode. You ask yourself five questions: who, what, when, where, how?[15] The corporate communication team works out the answers before drafting the

---

[15] To these basic questions, our journalism teacher way back when would add: "and sometimes why"—the implication being that the answers to the five questions would likely be factual, which is the reporter's meat; but the "why" might lead the reporter into the fuzzy area of speculation; and that, interpreting the news, was—at least in the old days of newspapers without the Internet—an area to be left to the editorial page and columnists. Now, news delivery 9–5, 24/7 is much more an admixture of facts and opinion.

release. Who is the source of this, what do we want or need to say or disclose, when must we (or what is the deadline to) get this ready for internal review (with external release date in mind), where is this going, and how do we get it out there (modes of delivery).

Something similar happens in preparing to present. We suggest simplifying the questions to three to organize the remarks or speech: *What, so what, now what?* This boils down to a presentation process approached in this order:

- **Step One**—A simple, clear statement based on your knowledge of what is the occasion, what are the contexts, what are the stakeholders exposed to and probably thinking, and what do we need them to "get" right away and take with them.
- **Step Two**—so what?—gets into the relevance of that initial statement: what it means to the audience, the community, the country, the shareowners, the nation, and the workers... whatever it is. The point is to connect immediately with the audience and give them something to think about. The "so what" is effectively "so what does this mean to you" or "why you should care about this" or...whatever engages the receiver in terms he or she can understand and care about.
- **Step Three**—now what?—brings it home. It describes the road ahead, the likely outcome, or the desired outcome that "we" or "the company and...you" can achieve. We have said that leadership communication is about expressing reality and hope. The influential speaker will describe the situation as it is, pulling no punches. That is openness that engenders belief. The influential speaker then points to the road ahead. He or she is the leader who sees the trail to best achievable outcomes, to some form of victory.

If you follow this three-step process in your thinking, you are likely to give your speaker or leader the logic that supports persuasion, the belief that accompanies credibility and the value prospects that create followership, and even advocacy.

Presentation is Akin to Theatre

Luban and Halpern, with backgrounds in the theatre, have made the point that the perceived strength of actors to connect with audiences is the same kind of strength that political, social-cause, religious, education, and, yes, business leaders require to make their connection to their particular followers. They define the burden (and of course the opportunity) in their book, *Leadership Presence*: "Great leaders, like great actors, must be confident, energetic, empathetic, inspirational, credible, and authentic."[16] They draw on theatre for four elements in developing presence (*PRES* is their acronym):

P: Being *present*, in the moment, able to handle the unexpected.

R: *Reaching out*, through listening, empathy, making an authentic connection.

E: *Expressiveness*, able to use facts, words, voice, and body to express (deliver) a congruent message.

S: *Self-knowing* (not the same as self-absorbed!), able to reflect your values in your decisions and actions, again consistent, authentic.

Show Authenticity

Presenting as an authentic, believable person is the aim of a business leader even more, in our view, than it is of an actor on stage. Earlier in this book, we recounted the surprising but apparently favorable impression of the CEO who arrived at a company event in goggles and helmet on his Harley. The CEO evoked attention and respect as a leader who was about to tell his followers to trust the company's vision and work with him to achieve it. The bravado arrival fit the occasion. The messenger became the message. He showed daring, energy, and confidence. Authenticity was perceivable.

Luntz says, "Whether your arena is business or politics, you simply must be yourself."[17] Being "yourself" may well mean surprising others, but that surprise needs to be strategic and authentic. Luntz uses the

---

[16] Halpern and Lubar (2004) have applied the lessons they have learned as performing artists to the work of their company, The Ariel Group, which has counseled executives at major companies, including General Electric, Mobil Oil, Capital One, and Deloitte. In *Leadership Presence* (2004), they make their strategies available to everyone, from CEOs to young professionals seeking promotion.

[17] See Chapter 3, "People-Centeredness: Humanizing your approach."

example of candidate Bill Clinton appearing on the *Arsenio Hall Show* during the 1992 presidential campaign, wearing sunglasses, and playing the saxophone. Within the contexts of timeframe, politics, diversity, and Clinton's established display of intelligence and leadership, this decidedly public display of coolness worked *because it fit,* adding to the candidate's authenticity. Observes Luntz (2011, 31–32): "Clinton had a certain genuine cool. He could get away with being a bad boy saxophone player because, audiences could sense, he really did have that naughty side."

Luntz notes that the power of "show" is infinitely stronger than the power of "tell." We are not recommending gimmickry. We are underscoring the added value of showing in an authentic way one's humanity and leadership ability.

A story told to us by Senior Vice President Greg Elliott (2013) of the truck and engine manufacturer, Navistar, makes the point that the ultimate stakeholder question of the leader is always "do you care about me?" Elliott recalls his initial discomfort when his boss arrived at a hastily arranged, emergency news conference dressed not in a suit and tie but in a sport shirt and sweater. "I remember thinking, the sweater is not right," said Elliott; "I was afraid that the chief would not get or show the respect that we needed to convey." The occasion was extraordinary—confusing, painful, and sad. Early that day, an armed gunman had come into the company's manufacturing plant. He had shot and killed several people before turning the gun on, and killing himself. Now, late in the day, in the aftermath of tragedy, ambulances and police having left, CEO John Horne came into the plant to express his grief and to provide comfort. He said a few words to the group assembled, and then walked among the workers, shaking hands, comforting, wearing the sweater that had seemed wrong to his public relations counselor. "Then I saw that he was absolutely right," said Elliott. "It was not about him. It was about the employees and their family members. The chief was sincerely engaged." He was the personification of the needed message of personal, authentic caring, not as boss, but as consoling friend.

Putting It Together

If you are the speaker or if you are the CCO coaching a leadership speaker: remember the basics of connecting, the purpose of influencing, and the impact of context, content, and tone. Who is your audience? What are their needs and interests? Why are you speaking to this group, on this occasion, about this topic? Does the occasion call for a serious challenging talk or a polite, informative presentation?

Your Performance as a Presenter

How, when, and why do we humans perform at our best? What makes us fail or choke when we are trying very hard to succeed? Whether playing golf, acting on stage, solving a math problem, or giving a speech, personal panic can interrupt.

Sian Beilock (2010), a University of Chicago psychology professor, says concentration on real or imagined contexts seems to be the problem. It's not so much that the objective—the task, the challenge—is extraordinary. It is more about how we as humans think and feel when the challenge is at hand. We turn off the automatic parts of our brains (the parts that have already learned how to do a certain thing). And, we turn on at overwhelming strength the challenging *contexts* that surround our doing the intended thing. In *Choke: What the secrets of the brain reveal about getting it right when you have to*, Beilock gives the example of the golfer about to swing at the ball during a competitive event, but whose brain shifts into thinking more about the conditions that can limit her performance than she does about her practice routine of hitting the ball.[18]

It happens in sports so regularly that coaches use ways to gain psychological advantage, with moves to shake the rhythm and confidence of the opposition. The field-goal kicker focuses on the goal—but the opposing team, understanding the psychology of icing, calls time out, and the kicker has too much time to think about what could go wrong, what could break his routine of kicking straight and long; his brain goes into choke mode.

And it happens in personal, physical presence. The public speaker shifts from the confidence and pleasure of delivering a planned, rehearsed

---

[18] Sian L. Beilock is a professor in the Department of Psychology at The University of Chicago. Her research program sits at the intersection of cognitive science and education. She explores the cognitive and neural substrates of skill learning as well as the mechanisms by which performance breaks down in high-stress or high-pressure situations. Dr. Beilock's research is funded by the National Science Foundation and the U.S. Department of Education (Institute of Education Sciences).

message to the discomfiture of focusing on the people who are looking at him, wondering now more about what they are thinking than on what he thinks and has to say.

Be Present, Know Your Purpose

Professional athletes know how to stay with the presence of who they are, where they are, and what their purpose is. The batter knows the kind of hit he needs and plans to make: a long ball to a specific part of the outfield, a ground ball through a weak place in the infield, a bunt to advance a team player. He has done it all before. He is resolute in his purpose. An actor knows how and why she enters a scene, with whom she will be talking, and the purpose of the scene in advancing the plot.

The athlete and the actor do one more thing. They play the mental game. They release all of the contexts that surround to distract. They concentrate on the best achievable outcome. Athletes have preperformance routines. These routines are private and personal. Waiting his turn at the plate, the batter may swing two baseball bats a certain number of times—always the same two bats, always the same number of times. He may walk to the plate in exactly the same way each time, take his position in the same way, place his feet in the same way he always does, maybe grinding one foot or the other into the turf, hoisting his bat to his swing position exactly as he always does, moving it in a small circle or holding it rigidly straight—well, the options are endless, and the choices are highly personal. But the routine is reassuring. He creates inner calm with his preperformance routine.

Golfers have preshot routines. Before the professional walks to the tee, she does whatever she always does to prepare to perform perfectly. It may be to select the club, the exact club that feels right for the shot, to swing it once or twice in just the manner that she knows is right for the aim and distance of the drive. She brings calm to herself, perhaps by meta-talk: words in her head, silently hearing words that encourage, silently singing or hearing a song or tune—always the same words or song or tune, trustworthy, calming.

There are books out on the "mental game" of tennis and golf, and acting. Great actors are known for their silent, totally alone preparation offstage, before they enter the scene, becoming mentally in tune, letting their instinct gather strength, not worrying or caring, and certainly not choking by the context of theater or audience.

"I'm Glad I'm Here ..." Pre-presentation Routine

With regard to prespeech self-talk, we recommend the guidance of Dorothy Sarnoff (1989), and her book, *Never Be Nervous Again.* Sarnoff, an actress who became a speech coach, has found reassuring methods of focusing on best outcomes in speaking before a group.[19]

Inspired by Sarnoff, one of your authors has used and recommends the calming effect of saying to yourself, silently and confidently, before you start your presentation, the following sentences: *"I'm glad I'm here. I'm glad you're here. I know what I know."*

Reflect on these three sentences. Before you go on stage or to the podium or into the presentation, just think these thoughts, alone, calmly, happily, with a smile in your heart and on your face.

- ***I'm glad I'm here.*** The internal message to yourself goes like this: Here is exactly where I want to be. I'm here because I chose to be here. I have something to share. I am talking to friends. I am happy to be here with you. I'm glad I'm here.
- ***I'm glad you're here.*** Your meta-message is along this line: If you were not here, we couldn't have this time together. I

---

[19] Dorothy Sarnoff, Chairman of Speech Dynamics, Inc., has counseled CEOs of Fortune 500 companies, politicians such as Senator Robert Dole and Lloyd Bentsen, newscasters such as Lesley Stahl, and numerous media personalities. In her book, she shares her time-tested techniques to help you conquer your nerves and come across with authority, enthusiasm, and ease in any social situation or public forum. Whether you're talking to a dinner companion or to your boss, meeting with the PTA or with a room full of television reporters, you'll never have to be nervous again. She offers a step-by-step program that will help you: Prepare and rehearse like a pro for professional results, Nip your butterflies in the bud with on-the-spot relaxation technique; Tailor your personal appearance to achieve maximum effectiveness; Sharpen your delivery and get your audience's attention. The book has 250 quotes and anecdotes that can make any speech special, tips for using visual aids, facing the camera, and adding wit and spice throughout your presentation. Available at Amazon.com in paperback and hard cover.

couldn't get to know you. I'm thinking about you when I tell you my story. I care about you. I'm glad you are here.

- ***I know what I know.*** You are thinking to yourself: I will tell you what I know. I am interested in you and I want you to know what I know. I wouldn't be here if I weren't knowledgeable in my field. I know what I am talking about. If you ask me a question, I will tell you what I know. If I don't know something, I will not pretend that I do. I will say I don't know and I may ask you what you think. And I will try to find the answer for you later. For now, I know what I know and that's what I know.

Remember: you are saying this to yourself. This is your calming mental, "pre-shot routine," just as an athlete might do with his or her preperformance. Smile and relax. You will enjoy this outcome.

So, as soon as you face your audience, **BEFORE YOU SPEAK,** you look at them and say SILENTLY to yourself: ***I'm glad I'm here…***

You now have activated our three-step guidance, enabled by answering these questions before you engage with others, whether in a presentation, as part of a meeting, in coaching or counseling C-suite peers or those who work with you. Mentally—or on a note-to-self card, ask yourself:

1. What is my purpose here?
2. What can I, or what do I need to, learn in this engagement?
3. What value can I add at this time, to this person or group that he or they can take away and benefit from?

Purpose, shared learning, shared values=a good formula for leadership communication in conversation and presentation.

Presentation Skills and Style

Corporate communicators must be good presenters. "Show what you know" is a reasonable expectation of the CCO and her team.

The CCO and the communications team need to be competent in presentation, and may well go through professional training sessions. This competence requires the C-suite communicator's awareness, and personal application of basic presentation guides. We offer these reminders, based on our experience and advice from practitioners such as Don Rheem[20] and Marty Zwilling.[21]

Facial Expression, Especially the Eyes

The speaker's face needs to match the delivered message. A smile, for example, puts energy into the delivery, whereas a frown or "frozen" face takes energy away. And, most important, all counselors agree, the eyes are the most powerful part of a speaker's body language. They express everything from happiness to annoyance, from interest in the subject and in the audience, to lack of interest in being the speaker and in what he or she is saying. An engaging speaker makes eye contact with the audience—looking at different sections of the audience or at individuals in the audience—as frequently as possible. Frequent eye contact is interpreted as honesty, the desire to engage and connect, and the pleasure of being "here." (Remember the Sarnoff (1989) mantra, *I'm glad I'm here, I'm glad you're here*...say it in your mind and it shows on your face.)

Posture

An erect posture—with shoulders back and a chin level—expresses confidence, authority, and connection. A slumped posture, leaning on the

---

[20] Don Rheem is an award-winning former print and broadcast journalist, Washington Bureau Chief, Cabinet-level speechwriter, and White House correspondent, Don brings more than 20 years of experience to his marketing and communications initiatives for his clients. Mr. Rheem is a professional speaker, facilitator, and media consultant. See more at http://rheemmedia.com/about/don-rheem/#sthash.djCqaJYC.dpuf
[21] Marty Zwilling's passion is nurturing the development of entrepreneurs by providing first-hand mentoring, funding assistance, and business plan development. He is the Founder and CEO of Startup Professionals, a company that provides products and services to startup founders and small business owners. He writes a daily blog for entrepreneurs, and dispenses advice on the subject of startups to a large online audience of over 225,000 Twitter followers. Follow Marty Zwilling on Twitter at www.twitter.com/StartupPro

rostrum or furniture, can indicate lack of interest, insecurity, weakness, or untrustworthiness. Folded arms or crossed legs, perhaps turning away slightly, seems to mean detachment.

Space Occupied

Speakers need to be the center of attention, to dominate the space and to welcome, in fact, to invite attention to allow the audience's virtual participation in the presentation. This means: the effective speaker will stand up, with an open delivery, embracing the space with open arms when it is appropriate. If the room allows, it means moving away from any podium or table to focus on various parts of the room, to get more eye contact with individuals wherever they are seated. Speakers successful at this include CEOs such as Cisco's John Chambers, who moves regularly to gain eye contact with groups; and stand-up comedians such as Chris Rock, who has said he moves constantly while on stage to elicit undivided attention. If he stood still, Rock told an interviewer, some audience members would start texting on their smart phones, expecting the performer to be in the same place when they look up, but when he moves around, they have to pay attention.

Coaching

In our view, CCOs are often on thin ice when they assume the role of presentation coach to others, and especially to others in the C-suite. Coaching requires constant correction, dealing with egos that can be a delicate proposition, expressing doubt, and other uncomfortable conditions that can damage the collaborative, peer-level relationship between the CCO and his peers. For this, among other reasons, including respect for peers and respect for specialty experts, CCOs most often outsource the role of coaching key leaders and company people on presentation skills. Bring in a consultant. In confidential or private group sessions, specialized experts will work with company executives on whatever is needed: delivering a speech, handling questions and answers, responding to media questions and on-camera interviews, relying on scripts, notes, or teleprompter, the value of eye contact, posture or body language, and other aspects of effective presentation, suited to the individual's style and natural strengths. The CCO can get feedback afterward, both from the consultant and from the corporate speaker, and can stay in the corporate person's corner as available counsel.

CCO "New Model" Leadership: Content, Context, and Persuasion

Focus your team on the drivers of stakeholder belief and advocacy—content, surrounding contexts, and presentation. Discuss ways to work with C-suite leaders on information timed and tuned to connect with each stakeholder universe, external and within the culture. Discuss what causes someone to believe, to act, to have confidence, or to advocate. Develop a schedule for persuasive communication initiatives, and means to coach for presentation effectiveness.

CHAPTER 10

Limits: Corporate Governance

When she enters the C-suite, the chief communicator feels the influence of operational limits. There are, of course, internal limits set by management: the enterprise's approval processes, agreement on handling, and the release of information. And there are limiting influences—effectively, controls—from outside the organization.

Welcome to the world of corporate governance, where at least three forces will frame the CCO's responsibility to operate corporate communications to the firm's advantage. Two of these forces are close at hand, direct and constant. They are the company's board of directors and its shareholders. The third force is outside but always there, hanging over the process of free enterprise. We mean of course, the considerable ordinary and potential power of government itself. Later in the book, we get into the role of C-suite communicators in government relations. Here we will simply observe that government controls—rules, regulations, direct engagement, and, at the extreme, government take-over, even—through agreement—in a democracy, such as happened with General Motors following the U.S. financial disarray in the century's first decade.

Here is a sort of basic primer on corporate governance, essential for the CCO to understand before and while she is doing her job.

A Governance Guide for CCOs

The following best practices guide for the chief communicator to engage with C-suite colleagues on corporate governance underscores the vital skills of listening, learning, and contributing to best achievable outcomes for the enterprise.

- Understand the company board of directors' oversight role and its fiduciary responsibility to operate in the best interests of all shareholders—and focus on areas where *communication may add value.*
- Understand the specific *shareholder value* propositions for the largest 10–15 shareholders and how ownership in your company may activate support for management positions.
- Understand how activist stakeholders may give rise to various shareholder resolutions and proxy positions.
- Review and embrace the *corporate governance principles* of the company.
- Research, understand, and be an expert in the *best practices* of leading companies in the governance arena.
- Follow the "hot button" issues at other companies and the trends emerging in the energetic debate about corporate governance. *Listen with a Google alert on corporate governance.*
- Engage in the company's *risk management process*, especially involving any issue that may have reputation and stakeholder risks (including what management reports in the SEC-required annual *risk factors* report in the SEC 10-K section).
- Become a *chief collaboration officer* within the C-suite on emerging issues that may require escalation to the board's attention. Bring the outside perspective to other C-suite members.
- Find ways, working with others in the C-suite, to be of service to, and interact with, board members on an ongoing basis through relevant committee work or focus (i.e., corporate governance, risk management, audit, legal affairs, and public policy).
- Bring *early warning intelligence* to the CEO and CFO related to the board's deliberations—not waiting for a potentially disruptive situation to develop.

Consider ways to connect to performance. Companies that set tangible sustainability goals are four to five times more likely to improve their environmental and financial performance than companies without such goals, according to a 2013 white paper by the engineering and consulting firm CH2M Hill. The study drew on source material from 23 companies, including SEC 10-K forms.[1]

A Governance Primer

Here is a simplified, quick reference primer on corporate governance, essential for the CCO to understand before and while she is doing her job.

Board Influence

The board provides oversight on management's performance. Elected by shareholders, board members are charged with a fiduciary responsibility to act in the best interests of company's shareholders. Board committees (such as audit, compensation, nominating and governance, and risk management) look in on management decisions, strategies, operations, and plans.

Shareholder Influence

Shareholders elect the board, which may include a company executive (*e.g.,* CEO) and in some cases, an employee representation (*e.g.,* union member). Shareholders are influential because they provide money through the purchase of an equity interest (*e.g.,* shares of common stock). Controls are in the form of votes approving not only directors but also items that are proposed by management and the directors—or, another channel of limits or allowance on corporate behavior and management, resolutions (*e.g.,* on environmental, economic, or social matters) proposed by stockholders.[2]

---

[1] In addition to SEC 10-K filings, the study, *Sustainability Goals that Make an Impact,* conducted in 2012 and 2013, drew on corporate sustainability reports, green rankings and analysis, and interviews with senior sustainability executives. Point is to tie positive information to the 10-K required information.

[2] To be clear, there is a distinction between the power and influence of investors and shareholders. Investors include both shareholders, who have an equity stake in the company, typically through share ownership, and bondholders. Holders of bonds do not have the authority to vote at general meetings, nor to vote or nominate members of the board of directors.

Government Influence

Corporate communication in the United States took on new importance in the 1930s, when public company performance came under federal government scrutiny through creation of the U.S. Securities and Exchange Commission (SEC). Set up to protect investors, maintain orderly markets, and spur capital formation, the SEC influences—in fact requires—information flow on plans, risks, performance, and other aspects of the company that investors and other stakeholders now have the right to know.

Muscle was added over the years to SEC overview or control power, and in 2002 when Congress—reacting to multiple corporate failures and scandals (e.g., Enron, WorldCom, Adelphia, Tyco, Global Crossing, and the accounting firm Arthur Anderson)—approved the Sarbanes-Oxley Act. Known in public corporate suites as SOX, the law established the Public Company Accounting Oversight Board to look in on and regulate the auditing profession in its role of reviewing corporate financial statements and issuing opinions on the reliability of the company's books. Control burdens on company leadership are substantial as the result of SOX. CEOs and chief financial officers (CFOs) must now attest to the accuracy of the company's financial statements. Board audit committees must now have members that are independent and they must say whether some member of the committee is, in fact, a financial expert. The company's external auditors must rotate their lead partners every five years and cannot do certain consulting work for companies where they are an auditor.

Can the make-up of the C-suite be questioned under SOX? No, but the 2002 law does say that a specific audit firm cannot audit a company if anyone in a senior management position at the company worked for the audit firm in the past year.

In 2010, the SEC increased its interaction with companies under authority of the Dodd–Frank Wall Street Reform and Consumer Protection Act. Enacted by Congress in response to the late-2000s financial crisis and recession, it brought more changes to U.S. financial regulation, affecting almost every part of the nation's financial services industry. Among requirements: public companies now must disclose their leadership structure (getting into the matter of whether the company's CEO is also the board chairman), whether there is a lead independent director on the board—among other influences on C-suite decisions and information.

Big Board Influence: Governance Standards

Companies listed on the New York Stock Exchange (NYSE) and other stock exchanges must meet specific governance standards required by NYSE (known as the Big Board). These influence company decisions on the independence of directors, regularly scheduled meetings of non-management directors, and the establishment and authority by the company of a nominating or corporate governance committee composed entirely of independent directors.[3] Beginning in 2010, and updated in 2012, the Business Roundtable has published guidelines for best practices in corporate governance.[4]

Other Factors Related to Communication

Among changes under discussion in the governance arena are so-called say-on-pay rules, which would empower shareholders to express their views on their approval or level of satisfaction with the public company CEO's pay and overall executive compensation program.

Guidelines for Company Communication

Public companies communicate frequently with investors and other key constituencies. Those who have a stake in the company are informed through proxy statements, annual and other (*e.g.*, corporate social responsibility, sustainability, and philanthropy) reports, and shareholder meetings. Corporations report financial performance through annual and quarterly reports, earnings news releases, concurrent investor and media conference calls, and in annual stockholder meetings. Although much of this is to follow required government rules—especially to make clear the company's financial performance and results—companies are steadily increasing information flow to communicate positions on issues of importance to their investor-owners and to the analysts who follow them. Public companies typically construct and keep up-to-date website sections devoted to investor relations information. Posts feature company news

---

[3] (http://nysemanual.nyse.com/LCL/Search/default.asp).

[4] (http://businessroundtable.org/uploads/studies reports/downloads/BRT_Principles_of_Corporate_Governance_-2012_Formatted_Final.pdf).

and video presentations, information on industry conferences, leadership statements and speeches, as well as relevant financial indicators tracked by investors and analysts.

Corporate governance guidelines are issued by public companies annually, normally as part of the proxy statement sent to stockholders. Adopted by the board of directors, the guidelines outline the directors' responsibilities to provide effective governance over the company's affairs for the benefit of the stockholders. It is worth the CCO's reviewing, if in fact he does not join with legal and other C-suite officers in drafting, the proxy statement governance guidelines. Areas in the proxy that are directly related to corporate communication include the CEO's performance and company ethics. Leadership, vision, integrity, and other aspects of desired—essentially required—management behavior, and accomplishment of strategic objectives are among typical topics within the proxy purview. Codes of business conduct or ethics, which apply to directors, executives, and all employees, are another area for CCO engagement. These codes, found in corporate proxy statements, are also posted on public company websites; which is effectively the chief communicator's front line of controllable communication.

Social Media

Companies use social media outlets such as Facebook and Twitter to disclose key information (e.g., the current quarterly earnings) in compliance with the SEC's Regulation Fair Disclosure (Reg FD). But the company needs to announce in advance the selection of a social platform to investors. Investors must be alerted as to which social media channel the company will regularly use to send out this kind of information. Reg FD applies to social media the same way that it applies to corporate websites, where companies can disclose possibly market-moving information.

The general guideline is that this type of communication can be on a company's open access platform, *only if they tell investors to look for it there*. If a company does not alert investors to its use of the social media channels, its communication could constitute "selective disclosure" and thereby violate Reg FD rules requiring companies to distribute material information broadly and not exclusively. The SEC did not specify which social media channels would be acceptable platforms for communication.

Now more than ever, companies need to be sure they follow social media and communication policies. An Internet privacy attorney, Jeremy Mishkin of Montgomery McCracken, gave some advice to CFOs in April 2013 that was a heads-up for CCOs also:

> If I'm a CFO, I need to know not just what's on my company's Facebook page or Twitter feeds, but also what my executives' pages look like, so I don't have a situation in which a person associated with the company issues a statement that the SEC might view as a material announcement. (Provost 2013)

For example, General Electric includes the following notification on its investor relations website to inform investors of the social media sources it employs: *In addition to our Investor Relations website, GE's corporate blog, Facebook, and Twitter accounts contain a significant amount of information about GE, including financial and other information for investors. GE encourages investors to visit these websites from time to time, as information is updated and new information is posted.*[5]

Technology, as well as financial services, companies are sensitive to Dodd–Frank regulations along with changing rules at the federal, state, and local levels. In 2013, the fifth year of a survey of Risk Factors for Technology Businesses, conducted by BDO USA, regulatory pressures were for the first time cited as the major concern (Provost 2013).

CCO 'New Model':
Governance Leadership

Initiate a process (together with investor relations) for shareholder outreach involving the board (*e.g.*, voicemail, email, and corporate address). Monitor the feedback and be ready to advise board members on the frequently asked questions and proposed responses to shareholders. Determine which of the company's owned media channels (starting with the website) can best be activated to reach stakeholders on a 1:1 or a 1:many bases.

---

[5] www.ge.com/investor-relations

PART III

The Working CCO: Leadership in Context

In Part I we discussed how the corporate chief communication officer (CCO) becomes a valued participant in the senior management team, working with C-suite peers in constructing and communicating leadership vision, stimulating mission execution, and promoting the enterprise's shared value proposition. We drew on more than a century of public relations thought leadership to suggest corporate communication strategies that prove effective in companies competing with other companies for victory on behalf of stakeholders.

Throughout the book, we emphasize the dominance of contexts (circumstances that surround the exchange of information between the enterprise and its stakeholders) as they affect the content and tone of leadership communication.

In Part II we advanced your knowledge of the CCO's role with a special eye toward the skills she takes to the C-suite and her ability to influence, guide, and render effective communication.

In Part III we zero in on the prospect of unplanned disruptions in a company's execution of strategies toward best achievable outcomes. The context is crisis, periods in which CCOs become an exceptionally vital participant in corporate leadership. We chart the course of crisis conditions and the best practices for response from the C-suite communicator and her team. Our anatomy of a crisis, developed within our more than five years of classroom discussion and role-playing, prompts the CCO to prepare to be a C-suite activist: expert in current stakeholder perceptions, armed with pre-crisis intelligence (red flags or prodromes), and ready to engage with other C-suite and operational leaders in the appropriate message and spokesperson activity. The CCO, we suggest, becomes the agent for executing calmly managed communication strategies that align with the firm's overall crisis management plan. We show how the BAO of crisis is to achieve the earliest practicable point at which the disrupted company can gain a positive communication foothold, to begin repairing reputation damage and restoring stakeholder trust. We conclude with an overall look at corporate communication, our view of the road ahead, when the value of the function will continue to escalate, and CCOs will advance in enterprise leadership.

CHAPTER 11

Crisis Basics: "Topic A Bad News" and the CCO

How do you know when your enterprise is in a crisis? We put that question to a veteran corporate communicator who lectured in our Georgetown University class on crisis communication. Steve Harris (2010), who had served as CCO of General Motors, cut to the chase. His answer was, "When one negative situation is topic 'A' bad news at the top of the organization."

In the first class of the Georgetown crisis course, we engage our students in developing a working definition of corporate crisis that can be tested and applied to the case studies we examine during the semester. In the spring 2013 semester, the students arrived at this definition: "A corporate crisis is an event or condition that could pose a threat to stakeholder perceptions, disrupt normal business operations and affect the future sustainability and integrity of the company."

Crisis always shakes the wheelhouse of the CCO. As the disruptive impact of a crisis overwhelms the routine, the context, content, and tone of leadership communication must shift. The elevated need for C-suite counsel, and the execution of steadying communication, put the CCO in a significantly higher position in the drive to influence best achievable outcomes for the enterprise. This chapter and the next are aimed at preparing you, as the enterprise's chief communicator, to deal with change in business plans, mission focus, stakeholder, and media contexts.

Crisis as "Strategic Inflection Point"

Factors contributing to crisis fall within two categories: those beyond the reasonable control of the enterprise or anyone in it, and those that could—and in retrospect, probably should—have been controlled, perhaps averting crisis impact. The factors beyond reasonable power to control are wide ranging—from context in market conditions, to the content and tone of a negative (perhaps totally inaccurate or rigged) YouTube video that has gone viral (Capozzi and Ricci 2013).

Similarly, controllable (perhaps neglected) factors can range widely—from consumer discontent that was expressed but was not picked up or engaged, to corporate values or communication (related, *e.g.*, to safety in manufacturing) that were misdirected, poorly executed, or otherwise failed to influence employees' behavior.

A crisis can develop suddenly—death, disaster, public exposure of highly sensitive enterprise news events, to name a few exemplary causes—or it might be the irresistible cresting of a slow development. Andrew S. Grove, the long-time leader of Intel, whose computer technology company survived a slow-moving business phenomenon that became a crisis. Grove draws from mathematical studies to identify the *strategic inflection point* when the path of a routine condition shifts directions. At this point in a business, the enterprise can continue to succeed at a higher level, or it can be cast into a failing crisis. Grove (1999) explained,

> "An inflection point, occurs when the old strategic picture dissolves and gives way to the new, allowing the business to ascend to new heights. However, if you don't navigate your way through an inflection point, you go through a peak and after the peak the business declines. It is a point where the curve has subtly but profoundly changed, never to change back again."[1]

---

[1] Intel, under the leadership of Grove (named by *Time* magazine as its Man of the Year), survived the strategic inflection point challenge, to become the world's largest chip maker and one of the world's most admired companies. Grove's books are useful in understanding business and communication, especially in navigating in the Internet revolutionary age of business. Our quote is from Grove's 1996 book, *Only the Paranoid Survive: How to Exploit the Crisis Points That Challenge Every Company*, which has been widely read by corporate executives and CCOs. The 1999 paperback includes a new chapter on "the impact of strategic inflection points on your career."

Grove's company and competitors in the computer industry went through such a point, and some (but certainly not Intel) succumbed to a crushing crisis.

No matter the cause, the timing, or the corporate segment in which the company is situated, two points are clear: (1) the firm cannot ignore the crisis. And (2) corporate communication is at the center, if not at the front lines, leading the communication response, aiming toward regained control, trust, shared values, and competitive victory.

Anatomy of a Crisis

"Tornadoes are caused by trailer parks." That was one of the tongue-in-cheek laws coined by a master of leadership communication, Norman R. Augustine (1994), for a treatise on crisis management. Look at the empirical evidence, the former CEO of Lockheed Martin, told his followers. The first places hit and totally destroyed by a tornado's rampage are trailer parks and mobile homes. Therefore, he told readers of *Managing the Crisis You Tried to Prevent*, the place to start to reduce crises is to go look at the trailer parks in the company that are ready to attract the first winds of crisis.[2]

The advice to find potential vulnerabilities is certainly sound in the corporate sense, but as all enterprise chiefs (including Norm Augustine) have fully understood, tornadoes can come seemingly from out of nowhere and neither their paths nor their power is predictable. With the caveat in that story, we here offer a neat charting of the stages of corporate crisis (just as Augustine does in his piece). We know fully well that the course of crises rarely runs neatly. Our purpose is to provide some sense of the heat that rises in the course of crisis, and very importantly to point you to the place where

---

[2] *Managing the Crisis You Tried to Prevent*, by Norman R. Augustine, is the first entry in the collection in the Harvard Business Review on Crisis Management, Harvard Business School Press, Boston. Augustine served on boards of several major companies, including Procter & Gamble, had a career in the Pentagon, including undersecretary of the Army, was president of the Boy Scouts of America, and chairman of the American Red Cross. Another delightful book written with Kenneth Adelman (Augustine and Adelman 1999) is all about leadership, based on leaders in the plays of William Shakespeare.

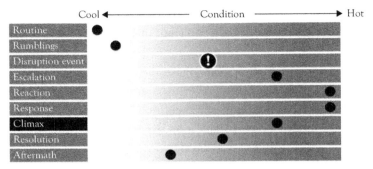

Figure 11.1 Anatomy of a crisis

cooling may begin. The stage that we call *climax*—the turning point—is that place. When this stage arrives (or is achieved through strategic effort), corporate communicators can turn the internal and external focus toward control. We provide, for general education and guidance, a simplified explanation as to the nature of these moving stages of discovery and response, beginning just before Augustine's tornado is caused by your company's "trailer park." In doing so, we walk through the crisis as depicted in Figure 11.1.

Routine

Business is proceeding as usual. Company operations—production, providing services—are proceeding in a normal, planned, and expected manner. Executives are performing to plan. Sales, customer relations, and employee engagement are on track.

Rumblings

Signals of problems are detected. Potential negatives could become obvious inside the company (*e.g.*, a production or supply interruption, a delay, a safety issue arises). There could be rumblings in the external stakeholder ecosystem (product or customer dissatisfaction, threat of a lawsuit that could become serious, unpredicted competition move). Some are controllable, some are not. In the extreme, the problem—controllable or not— could disrupt positive outcomes and perceptions.

Disruptive Events

Something happens. It may or may not be a total surprise. It may or may not have been predictable. The circumstance could arise or peak from within or outside the organization. An ongoing, acknowledged problem—similar to situations that have in the past been addressed and controlled—rises to an uncontrollable level. For example, a production problem becomes unsolvable. A deadline is missed. Expected income fails to materialize; a financial matter escalates to a critical state. Or an external event, outside the control of the organization, abruptly changes the rules. For example, new government regulations impose stringent new requirements that affect the company's standard operating model, threaten its margins or very existence, or both disadvantage the company in the competitive arena. Foreign competitors gain competitive advantage by cheating or abusing trade rule norms.

Or, an "out of nowhere" event occurs. There is an explosion, a fire, a natural disaster. A neglected, internal danger erupts. Competition changes a vital success option. There is a very serious episode of management or board mishandling. There is sudden death or disablement of one or more key executives. This is, as former congressman Joe Scarborough (2012) once described it on his Morning Joe television show, "the freight train out of the mist" that you did not see coming.[3] In the C-suite, and at all the points in the company where this turn of events has an impact, normal and routine process and execution are slowed, skewed, or stopped. Corporate leaders assess the situation. Is this a problem that can be handled? Has the company entered crisis conditions? Corporate communicators prepare for the first phases of crisis communication.

Escalation

The event disruption grows. The crisis has begun. Stakeholder and media reaction put the company in a defensive, stressful mode, cast in one or

---

[3] Scarborough's comment was directed toward political leaders who are blindsided by disruptive events during an election campaign. We find this an applicable warning in corporate leadership.

more negative perceptions, ranging from incompetence to villainy. While production or sales continue, executing strategies and plans, these are shadowed by concern about the ability of the management to fix or deal with the condition. C-suite attention focuses on crisis management, with corporate communicators at the forefront.

Reaction

The company becomes a target. This is the hot top half of the crisis, where stakeholder reaction challenges the company. External stakeholders—investors, customers, stores, dealers, distributors, service centers and others—are stirred. Bonds of trust are shaken. They worry about the impact on them. They think about (or actually engage in) withholding purchases, stopping or shifting investments, switching to competitors. A barrage of stories, blogs, tweets, and social media agitate concern. Politicians, office-holders, government regulators may get into the blame game and seek protection or restitution among their constituents. Corporate communicators are on defense. As Eric Dezenhall (2008, 103) observes in *Damage Control*, it is less a case now of making them like you and more of making them "stop attacking you."[4]

Response

The company acts to control the damage. Energy is directed to explaining, defending, and determining ways to regain traction on the slope of the crisis. Senior management and the board scramble to determine moves to correct, contain, and fix the negative situation. Corporate communicators activate internal and external communication programs, responding to questions, focusing on stakeholders directly or through public and social media, making executives available as spokespersons. This may be the period for earnest, transactional apology, remembering (as Eric Dezenhall

---

[4] Dezenhall (2008, 104) goes on to say: "Rather than going through the futile exercise of trying to get people to like your company, it is more feasible to get them to stop attacking your company."

[2008, ch 7] explained in his book) that "damage control means more than having to say you're sorry."

The communicator's purpose now is to generate accurate, honest two-way communication from the company side and from those affected by the crisis. The values of transparency are now a mixture of defense and offense, doing the media's job with (and at times, *for*) them, and using collaborative processes such as linking to principles understood by stakeholders (Dezenhall 2008, ch 5).[5]

Climax

The company is positioned for offense. Dramatic theater places characters in conflict until the point of no return, where the conflict is fixed, a situation is frozen to develop no further, and a character achieves purpose or will not ever do so. This is the play's *climax*. In the real-world drama of a crisis, with the company in conflict with other forces, *the climax is the turning point at which the company can begin to regain lost ground, lost trust, and lost stature.* Whatever the root problem, however intense and costly the crisis, the company now has the opportunity for greater control. Andy Grove, who was part of Intel's leadership team for half a century, calls this "the strategic inflection point" (Pandya and Shell 2006, ch 1). Senior management is able to commit to demonstrable, measurable correction, restitution (if needed), and repositioning with stakeholders. For example: faulty, damaging, or unprofitable operations may have been shut down; damage may have been curtailed or entirely stopped; critical financial conditions may have been turned around, enhanced, or settled. Corporate communication has the chance to get *ahead* of negativity, and provide open, honest, positive, caring information while collaborating with authorities and stakeholders on resolutions and recovery.

---

[5] Dezenhall (2008) counsels effective communicators to know how to associate issues, positions, or calls to action with a timeless value: "…something most people cherish or hold sacrosanct." Examples are security, justice, privacy, choice, safety. We agree with this counsel not as a gimmick, but as a path toward aligning company management and stakeholders' concerns and goals, as a covenant of honest, trustworthy effort, and two-way communication.

Resolution

The company re-enters the trust agreement. The crisis having crested, effectively ended with the climax, the company and those affected enter into the phase of resolution that can extend over an unknowable period of time. During this period, company leaders must reassert values than can be usefully shared by stakeholders. The shared-values promise will require a sustained level of commitments, delivery on expectations, possible financial commitments, possibly legal cases, and settlements. Sustainable communication at a level of openness and honesty is required, based on management's serious engagement in mutually beneficial, long-term relationships and benefits to stakeholders. Communication will say, in effect, "don't trust us, track us"—evaluate us from this point forward, determine what is in it for you to believe, follow and affirm us.

Aftermath

The company reconciles itself and enters a process of learning. As company leaders strive to reassert normal conditions—seeking the return to productive routine, affirmative relationships with all who have a stake in the company's success, and execution of profitable strategies—they face a hard reality: "there is no over" when a company has wrestled with a serious, highly challenging, well-publicized crisis. The story may never completely die. Impact can linger both inside and outside the company. A new perspective of the company may have taken root among employees—changes reflected in the company's culture, for good or bad—and among external stakeholders, as well as observers, commentators, bloggers, enabled by an Internet where content, the "history of the crisis" and views live forever. The external aftermath—with, for example, lawsuits, government action, and market moves by competitors—can recall the upside and downside of the crisis. Corporate communicators will need plans to deal with these bubbles of memory. The best lesson may be that which is captured in the title of the book by Intel's Andy Grove (1999): *Only the paranoid survive.*

Repositioning

The company, from "lessons learned," attempts to regain authenticity with stakeholders. Corporate leadership will need the strength of strategic communication to achieve the new normal of successful operations. Chief communication officers will usefully drive a factual, caring, collaborative, shared-values flow among stakeholders. Repositioning will move toward one sustainable goal: *earned trustworthiness.*

Crisis: Applying Communications

"Thank goodness, we were lucky that somebody knew what to do."

That—a veteran chief communication officer (CCO) of a company who had been through its share of crises told us—was without doubt the best compliment he ever got from a C-suite colleague. The certain crisis situation was cooling, moving from damage control to resolution and luck—an achieved outcome—was once again in the air.

Luck does happen, of course. But, as the saying goes, luck has the curious habit of happening at the intersection of preparation and opportunity. We now turn to ways of raising the odds for lucky outcomes through methodical, persistent preparation within the function of corporate crisis communication. We focus on the CCO's essential role through the typical stages of a corporate crisis: from rumblings and red flags of trouble to the turning point of climax, toward the winning prospect of resolution and a successful aftermath (Figure 11.1).

Preparation starts with the end in mind, the purpose of the CCO's work with his team, with others in the C-suite and beyond, extending throughout the enterprise.

CCO Purpose: Enable Effective Corporate Crisis Management

What specifically is the CCO's values-driven objective? We believe it is to apply the three strengths of corporate communication—mastery of information flow, intimacy and influence within the company's culture, and active interaction with stakeholders and media—to enable effective corporate crisis management.

We differentiate corporate crisis management and corporate crisis communication to underscore that comprehensive crisis management typically involves a lot of people, up to and including the chief executive and other senior people. In Chapter 12, we look at what we have learned from these experiences in a tactical framework. First, however, we need to look at crisis management from the strategic perspective of the C-suite.

Corporate Crisis Management: Benefit From Corporate Risk Management

The theoretical origin of crisis management is in *risk management*. Risk management is a company-wide function commonly conducted through a top-level risk management committee (typically involving the CEO, a chief risk officer, the chief financial officer, the company's general counsel, and other C-suite leaders) that may well engage on this area with the board of directors. In fact, a board-level *risk management committee* is becoming an increasingly important governance tool—involving board members in the corporate process.

Guiding principles for improving board oversight of risk were defined by the National Association of Corporate Directors in the October 2009 Blue Ribbon Commission report, *Risk Governance: Balancing Risk and Rewards* (New York State University 2009, October 1). According to the NACD report, every board should find ways to implement risk oversight principles such as these (our emphasis added):

- There is recognition that *management of risk is essential* to the successful execution of the company's strategy. The *risk appetite* implicit in the company's business model, strategy, and execution *is appropriate to the business.*
- Management implements *a system to manage, monitor, and mitigate risk* in the company's business model and strategy.
- The risk management system *informs the board of the major risks* facing the company.
- Expected *risks are generally commensurate with expected rewards.*
- An appropriate *culture of risk-awareness* exists throughout the organization.

Our observation: corporate communication has a collaborative opportunity in working with others in the C-suite (and possibly, directly with board members) on objectives such as these; and, the CCO may be directly accountable for influencing a "culture of risk awareness." This will require clear understanding of board and management commitment— what can and should constitute internal communication—and a strategy to achieve leadership and employee engagement.

Public companies registered on U.S. stock exchanges are required by government rules to warn investors about circumstances or events that could forestall or make irrelevant the company's plans for financial and operational performance. Company annual reports to the Securities and Exchange Commission (known as 10-K reports) list the presumed risks: statements about developments that could negatively affect the company's strategies or plans to succeed.[6] Risk factor identification is a benefit not only to investors who can see what management conceives as possible problems. It also encourages management toward a *proactive*, continuous pre-crisis focus.

If a crisis develops (which may or may not have been anticipated in the risk factors identified in the annual report), company management leaders have accountability to determine the cause of the event or culmination of circumstances. They must assess the physical, financial, legal, and operational effects of the disruption. And they must decide—with operational or production or sales interaction—when, how, and what actions (e.g., at plant or sales levels) to control the damage and move toward climax and resolution.

When a financial crisis disrupts a company's reputation and business strategy, corporate crisis management conducts the internal inquiry to get to the root of the problem, takes whatever action is needed to ameliorate or stop it, and deals directly with board and other external parties who have an immediate connection to the outcome of the crisis. When an accident, a contamination, or another disruptive condition threatens not only the company but the lives and interests—perhaps the physical wellbeing—of others, corporate crisis management attacks the problem, tries to stop further damage, assigns people away from other tasks to focus on the situation.

---

[6] Risk factors for a SEC-regulated company can be found at http://www.edgr.com

This is a general and simplified summary of leadership accountability for *corporate crisis management*.

CCO Engagement: Crisis Communication

Chief communication officers are part of the management team, applying their special competencies. Through *continuous* engagement with stakeholders to assess *current* attitudes or perceptions in the stakeholder ecosystem, CCOs can be among the first leaders in the C-suite to detect potential risks and disruptions. Through their influence on corporate culture, CCOs can boost employee and leadership commitment to intended outcomes as well as potential readiness to deal with imposed disruptions. And, through virtuoso performance in information flow, CCOs are hugely influential in the ability of the company to create accurate, open, and trustworthy engagement with media and stakeholders.

The expert communication team—comprising the CCO, staffs, and external public relations consultants (often from the major public relations agencies and firms who have specialized practices in crisis communication and management—puts into play the *crisis communication plan*, with full attention both to in-house communication up to and including those in the C-suite and those who may be in the field at the site of the disruption. The CCO moves into a position of high responsibility as counsel to management and as the director of dialogue with stakeholders, media, and others with a stake in the situation.

In sum, CCOs are engaged with other company leaders in the overall effort of *corporate crisis management* by planning and driving a *crisis communication process* that supports or enables high-level assessments, action, and best achievable outcome. That process begins with pre-crisis preparation and is implemented throughout the stages (the anatomy as presented in Figure 11.1) of a typical crisis.

Crisis Communication Checklist

Consider this bad—if not worst-case—scenario. You are the chief communicator at the headquarters of a fast-food retail company. A YouTube video appears. It shows—or even seems to show—an employee of your fast-food service engaged in some unsanitary—imagine the worst—food handling. By the time you find out about it, thousands of viewers have seen it; Twitter and blogs have made it viral; TV and radio have picked up on…and company headquarters, your wheelhouse, is at least astir. Social media's potential to turn an incident into a raging crisis requires the urgency and effectiveness of fire-fighting.[7]

As we have tried to establish in this book, the best effort to avoid crisis, as in avoiding or effectively dealing with fires, is in preparation and, if possible, prevention.

Looking for fire risks involves practice drills, equipment, skills, inspection of sites to remove hazards. Effective CCOs in the business sector readily grasp this analogy and understand the value of looking ahead and, as a pre-crisis intelligence method, listening, and engaging in social conversations affecting the company. *Asking questions, listening, and learning* are solid bases for pre-crisis detection and true crisis management.

Following the terrorist attack on the World Trade Center in New York in 2001, Howard Paster, then CEO of Hill and Knowlton public relations, is said to have noted that "Preparedness is a business imperative." While much has changed since 9/11 impacting communication (it is not the satellite-TV truck pulling into the corporate parking lot that you first fear; it is the YouTube video that has landed in a million emails), Paster's counsel prevails: Be prepared is the primary conditioner of crisis management. *Preparation starts with self-examination.*

Crisis Questions: A CCO's Checklist

Pre-crisis and in-crisis-related questions that the communication team can consider are provided here—questions that are scanned to see what is relevant and what needed to understand, know, and do. Remember that crisis is chaos only if it gets an irresistible advantage. *A Caveat: These are thought starters to guide the CCO in crisis communication response and management. While we have tried to put these in some logical order, it is unlikely that they would be used in this exact order. We do urge that the first question to always ask, in any engagement:* **what's it all about?** *Further, to listen,*

---

[7] Several cases of "viral" crises are developed in Capozzi and Rucci (2013).

learn, and adjust to the reality of each situation, including the reality of the other individual's perception of it.)

What's It All About?

- What is the source of what we hear or know?
- Is there any harm to any person?
- When can we, when do we have to, be ready to go public with a statement?
- What is our level of risk in this situation?
- Who is manning our listening station?
- What is out there—who knows what, when, where, why?
- What is on the Internet?
- Who do we need to call?
- Where do we meet, is our situation room fully equipped?
- How will we want to engage the CEO in communication with employees, with the board of directors, with media and with others who need to know or will weigh in with questions?

What are The Contexts?

What other news about us, industry competitor news, events in which we are participating, upcoming analyst call, board meeting, product or news announcements (positive or negative)—that surround and influence what we will experience in communications on this situation? What are the contexts that affect our ability to control our information flow, and to influence the accuracy of two-way communication?

- Who are the tentative candidates for spokesperson, early on and in the case the situation escalates?
- What are we doing to become and to assure that we remain the reliable, up-to-date source of information and perspective on this situation?
- Who activates our situation (dark) site, and who manages it once it goes public?

- What are our rules in this case on blogging, tweeting, Facebook, LinkedIn, et al? Who follows the social media traffic and conversations, and who prepares entries for our own website?
- Who is responsible for attracting or driving news and other interested people (especially stakeholders) to our site... involving search engine optimization and management?
- Who watches the clock and reminds the team (up to and including the CCO) of deadlines and targets?
- Who keeps the log or record of what happens, what we do, which is identified as the spokesperson, as we do it?
- What expert, legal, technical advice, source, validation do we need?
- So far, are we victim, villain, or something else?
- Do we need to explain why or apologize for anything?
- How does our vision or credo figure into our message?
- How do we show FACE—fast, accurate, consistent, and caring engagement—with all our stakeholders?
- Who on our staff is assigned to think strategically about the perceptions of us by each stakeholder group?
- Are we perceived as accountable, responsible, engaged, available, transparent, thoughtful, possibly heroic (inferred by others not us), dedicated to the best achievable outcome for all concerned, not just ourselves?
- What is our company's BAO in this situation?
- What is our one huge, authentic, and unassailable fact or asset?
- What experiences or crises of other companies are relevant?
- What is our biggest vulnerability, now and ultimately?
- What's the worst-case outcome, in detail, impacting what and whom?
- To what extent is communications the problem, by us or by others?
- How do we make sure that our communication is part of the solution?
- What are our main message points...how do we break this down for relevance for each stakeholder group, each of our business or operating units?

- What are the possible climax scenarios...when the greatest level of tension is likely to be reduced? (Climax is not necessarily what we can control or predict precisely, but it is a possible turning point; so, let's think through some candidate climaxes, because after that, our communication strength and strategies shift.)
- Who on the communications team is in charge of monitoring and keeping the rest of the team informed, 24/7—meaning a posted schedule to rotate this accountability?

Checklist for The Prepared CCO

Before any serious, disruptive condition or crisis occurs, it should be assumed that as CCO, your company has the following necessities for the prepared crisis communicator.

Crisis Contact Directory

This directory includes names, email addresses, phone numbers (home and business wherever practicable) possibly fax numbers, and any other contact enablers you need in a crisis condition, and *they are up to date*.

- Your communications team
- C-suite leaders, CEO, CFO, chief legal officer, and others
- Heads of business units, IT, HR, and everyone else in risk management
- Assistants who support, serve, or schedule each of these leaders
- Any other useful contact information specific to your company.

Crisis Communication Website

When a disruptive condition escalates attention to the enterprise, a corporate crisis-readiness site can be poised to help gain some information flow control. In addition to managing information feeds to ongoing websites, the corporate communication staff needs to set up this standby (sometimes referred to as dark—meaning not accessible to anybody but the CCO, responsible staff, and IT or a technology partner) website.

Attention to the dark site is ongoing. It needs to contain supportable basic facts, data, and key information about the company that could be needed (and will not require having to scramble to assemble) during a critical time. Someone on the communications team should be assigned to keep it current, to test it regularly, and to be prepared to open and maintain it, under the CCO's direction.

Companies are constantly preparing for crisis. Paul Flannigan of Southwest Airlines described his company's pre-crisis work:

> *We're busier when there's nothing going on because we are constantly preparing and altering our contingency plans to address things that could happen. Communicators meet up every month to update those plans. Preapproved statements for various scenarios each have an executive spokesperson attached. We're getting all the buy-in right at the beginning.* (Wilson 2013).

CCO "New Model" Leadership: Pre-Crisis Initiative

Adopt crisis prevention as ongoing vigilance to assure enterprise reach of financial, social, safety, health, and civic responsibility goals. *Tie your effort* to the realities defined by the company's SEC 10-K risk list. *Be proactive with others* in the C-suite to stay aware of any risk elevation. *Build communication influence*: create your own stakeholder perception intelligence systems to plug into the stakeholder systems for early alert: red flags that could grow into crisis situations. *Initiate regular, calm conversations* with C-suite colleagues to assure top-level effort to prevent rumblings from reaching unplanned disruption and crisis levels. *Be prepared*: lead the readiness, appoint people in the communication staff, and prepare online and operational facilities for immediate response to a real crisis.

CHAPTER 12

Crisis Communication Strategies and Execution

In this book, we draw on crisis cases as history. The study of well-documented enterprise crisis outcomes is as important to students of business communication as the study of legal cases is to law students. In both areas of study, however, lessons must be adjusted to incongruent current realities. The game-changing context for us, in studying corporate crisis best practices, is the dynamic impact of communication in the hyperactive social media space. Social-media specialist Shel Israel (2009, Preface), author of *Naked Conversations* and *Twitterville,* charts the growth of the social media tool, Twitter, as leader of a huge context shift. The character-limiting communication device raised the ease of communication receipt and greatly enabled communication output, becoming the most rapidly adopted communication method in history. Twitter zoomed from zero to 10 million users in its first two years.[1] Public opinion and stakeholder conclusions are seriously prominent in casually termed *social conversation.* Chief communication officer (CCO) accountabilities require competent online participation. CCOs know that the erratic, at times irrational, freestyle phenomenon of life in an open society can overwhelm the best-planned, most orderly enterprise crisis communication effort.

This chapter describes best practices in corporate communication, with examples of response and management of crisis interaction by companies (as well as by individuals). We move from the studies and principles of crisis communication to the specifics of preparation and response.

---

[1] In early 2014, Twitter users totaled 645,750,000, with more than 9,000 tweets per second. By the time you read this, these statistics will be so yesterday, probably laughably low.

Two strategies set the stage for CCO leadership in the C-suite and beyond, into operations: ongoing engagement and pre-crisis preparation.

Pre-Crisis: Ongoing Engagement

In noncrisis, day-to-day operations, communicators will monitor a select universe of online ecosystems—customer, competitor, media, and other websites; tweeters, bloggers, social groups, and individuals that are supportive, neutral, or challenging—to inform enterprise management on opportunities to improve relations, sales, and support. Heart of this ongoing engagement (designated "routine" in our crisis anatomy profile) is the company's own website, the one area of corporate communication management that is most assuredly controlled. Website content will keep up with times and needs. In good times, it advocates shared values and builds social capital. It fosters and supports enterprise reputation. Although the control is not so strongly manifested on Facebook, Twitter, and other online channels, these everyday, social-touching activities are monitored and engaged to advance financial and reputational values. This transformational routine strengthens the firm's readiness to deal with crisis challenges.

Pre-crisis Preparation

Pre-crisis preparation involves corporate communication collaboration with marketing, legal, risk management, financial performance, and other enterprise leaders to assure an informed, coordinated response to a disruptive or full-crisis situation. Social media handling, already centralized, will ideally put the CCO (or communication or marketing leaders) in charge of coordination, with specific roles assigned to communication staff. The communication control center (the war room, which we describe in this chapter) requires a sophisticated ability to focus on professional social media interaction, with a detailed plan for monitoring and input.

Crisis simulation sessions can focus enterprise management attention on the reality of crisis and the handling of response. C-suite collaboration and corporate communication leadership, needed when crises occur, are tested. To prepare for the unveiling of the ING Bank of Canada's new name—Tangerine Bank—management hired an outside firm to stage a social media drill. The bank's communication team practiced responding to attack messages—especially Twitter activity—simulated by the consultant firm.[2] In your authors' experience, students in classrooms as well as executives in corporate headquarters always come away from expertly managed, dramatic enactments in crisis drills more aware of the need for corporate attention and discipline in crisis management. When critical disruption occurs, when "damage control" (Dezenhall 2007, 2010) is needed, who must deal with a surge of significance regarding information flow, stakeholder perception, and cultural conditions? You will by now know that our answer is the CCO and the discipline that he and his team engender at the top of the enterprise.

Discipline: Seven-Point Crisis Communication Planning

Stanley Bing (2011), a writer who is engaged in corporate management, writes tongue-in-cheek about C-suite activities. He calls any kind of management "a rare corporate discipline."[3] In the face of this lighthearted despair, based on our experience and with the help of long-time associates in corporate communication, we now get into the detail of crisis management and offer for students of corporate crisis a disciplined seven-point CCO crisis communication plan (Figure 12.1).

1. Prepare a "dark" website

   A company's website is arguably the most controllable factor, the most relied upon and most reliable source, in the panoply of corporate communication. A dark site—that is to say, a private, standby facility that can be opened at the CCO's direction for general access (available pre-public access to frequently test its

---

[2] See: Gellman (2014, B6).

[3] A *Business Week* reviewer (Bing 2011) of Eric Dezenhall's book *Damage Control: The Essential Lessons of Crisis Management* (2011 edition) called it "a mandatory read for any corporate person who is facing a gut-wrenching crisis right now or is likely to one day—which of course means just about everyone." Bing; see Bing's incisive and entertaining books on corporate management behavior.)

Figure 12.1 Crisis communication planning

technical and access qualities)—is a ready repository of information, opinion, photographs, data, fact sheets, and the like that can be useful in the event of a crisis. *It is an ace in the hole that you hope will never have to be played.* On this site, with continuous deliberate attention, the crisis communications team can accumulate accurate, well-supported information that stakeholders will see if negative conditions surround the company. Look in on it privately, frequently. Put someone in charge of keeping this utility-in-waiting up to date. Keep asking, "*what if?*" and post your trust-sustaining positives.

2. Create a stakeholder list

The purpose of corporate communication is to create and sustain stakeholders in the company's plans and delivered values. *Especially during a crisis, the aim, care and trustworthy feeding of information to stakeholders are essential.*

Disruption in a company's plans and value-driving routine—a definition of corporate crisis—can well touch off a relationship crisis, threatening the bonds that connect company and stakeholders. It would be unsettling to others in the C-suite for the communication team to be scrambling for names and numbers when contexts, time, and information content are shifting. Pre-crisis preparation requires maintenance of a current, complete, categorized list of stakeholders and how to reach them: personal, email, telephone, and other connection data.

3. Identify key media or bloggers

An active, standby list of print, broadcast, and online journalists—media, bloggers, tweeters—is another asset in your mastery of crisis communication. *Find, make a list, and follow those who follow your company.* If and when any of those followers, friends, or critics, have good things to say about your company and leaders, capture it and keep it. Put it in a safe place (maybe a corner of the dark site, if it is easy to delete when and if it is not ready for sunlight) for possible use later.

4. Assure situation room "tools"

The crisis communication center is the situation room where the communication team can meet, work, contact, interview, respond to or initiate interviews (with appropriate spokespersons—see point five), and stay engaged purposefully during a crisis. This situation room is most often a conference room, in use normally as a meeting room, that is outfitted with first-rate communication utilities—phones (speaker or personal), whiteboards, TV, computers, or ample (multiple, abundant, high-load) electrical and online connections. An ongoing responsibility for someone in the communication team is the availability, testing, and functioning of the technical tools that corporate communicators and the C-suite will rely on. Arrange outfitting and crisis-priority use of the room with the office administration and technical support people. *And, this is important; it is a room that is taken off the available list for any other use during the high-stress period of focus on the crisis.*[4]

5. Train spokespersons

    A communication team member will be the day-to-day information source for the news media. In addition, almost always, someone at a responsible management level will be needed to deliver *authoritative* messages. Depending on the nature of the crisis, this may be someone at corporate headquarters or at a production, research, sales, or other facility. It is important to identify the candidates during noncrisis, routine times, and provide spokesperson training: Talking point development, presentation skills, styles of communicating consistent with stakeholder or public interests will be part of the training. Corporate communicators customarily engage outside experts to provide the training; it is a good idea for the CCO and her team to go through the exercise first, before exposing other corporate officers to this important exercise.

6. Assign team roles

    Keep crisis consciousness alive within the team. The CCO will need to assign someone to each of the accountabilities in this guide, and put this on your agenda. Review the plan regularly, certainly quarterly, with touch-ups whenever they may be useful—and especially when there are changes in team composition.

7. Integrate with crisis management plans

    The crisis communication plan, the CCO's responsibility, is the enabler of information flow, stakeholder engagement, and supportive culture. This must tie into the overall plan of management to deal with the physical, financial, legal, and other related accountabilities.

---

[4] The room we have called "situation room" or "crisis communication center" has often been referred to colloquially as "the war room." While this short-hand does convey a sense of urgency, it seems to us also to convey some heat, bordering on belligerence. The purpose of corporate management, after all, is a return to mutual values and productive peace. One of the three accountabilities of expert corporate communicators is to positively influence the organization's culture. CCOs' use of language—the most common factor of leadership—drives that influence. CCOs are advised by veterans (going all the way back to Arthur W. Page at AT&T in pre–World War II days) to try to be something of a model of cool competence during a crisis. Bottom line: shy away from talking about "war," which conjures up images of victims and villains, and us versus them.

The focus—or that of the team—must be on assuring that communication planning is directly related to *all* aspects of the corporate crisis management plans. This will require interaction by the CCO and by those who work with the business units, investor relations, and others responsible for mission performance, with an eye on any adjustments needed in the communication plan—for example, stakeholder lists—as an adjunct of change and transformative management leadership.

When It Happens…

With a communication team ready to respond to a disruption that becomes Topic A in the C-suite, the CCO will be among the first to engage. When it is a fast-breaking, unexpected disruption, two actions are typical. The chief communicator becomes a central player in an initial information briefing. Accompanied by a senior member of her team, who is prepared to take notes and provide backup, she meets with other executives, perhaps including the CEO. She asks the strategic who, what, when, why questions. And, depending on what she knows, provides basic information and her plan to learn more and to initiate communication crisis procedures. All concern begins with questions about personal injuries, damages, or worse, if that is a possibility in the known scenario. While this is happening, senior people on the communication team assemble to facilitate a CCO briefing. The logical assembly location may quite possibly be the designated conference room where crisis response guidelines and communication tools are available. Cell phones and text traffic are put to use while waiting for the CCO. Someone is recognized as the room's leader (in effect, highest authority) to facilitate white board planning, and assignments. This home base has been cleared for after-hours access, parking, and building entrance. Crisis response is disciplined (Figure 12.1), competent, compassionate, and highly collaborative.

C-Suite Attitude and Counsel

Describing reality and maintaining optimism—that is, a realistic route to a best achievable outcome—are the hallmarks of competence in leadership communication. In disrupted conditions, the CCO and communication team are the example of professional competence, acting with minimum display of emotion and maximum display of confidence. Nicholas Ashooh (2010), whose C-suite experience included roles as CCO of American Insurance Group and Alcoa, and Gary Sheffer (2013), General Electric's CCO, have held that the chief communicator's imperative asset during a period of disruption must be to listen and adjust to ongoing concern, while maintaining focus on contextual realities. As Arthur W. Page advised in his communication principles: *Remain calm, patient, and good humored*.[5]

Among all the enterprise top players, the CCO is best positioned to discern impact in the stakeholder universe. He is trained (educated, experienced) to be an influential participant in C-suite decisions that build stakeholder support, belief, and advocacy. He is a trustworthy counselor on avoiding to the fullest practicable extent decisions with the potential to raise stakeholder and public backfire. Talking truth to power with confidence is a highly valued function of leading CCOs. It is the "power with" opportunity for a communication expert to view current conditions rationally with the CEO who shares an overall "generalist" perspective. Proof points enable persuasion. The CCO accumulates and has at the ready: current information on stakeholder perceptions, media contexts, political contexts, competition, and other prevailing contexts that enable leadership communication to move toward enterprise BAOs with stakeholder support.

Dealing With an Angry Public

The best crisis plan is crisis avoidance. The next best move is controlling the heat of crisis communication. A public disputes resolution program conducted by MIT and Harvard Business School aims at avoiding contention or crisis escalation. Having participated in the Harvard Negotiation Project and continuing to find pertinent guidance in the project's best-selling leadership book (Fisher and Ury 1981), we recommend these attitudes and actions to facilitate cooler consideration (and possibly warmer reception of your perspective) in real or threatening crisis conditions:

---

[5] See Page Principles and related CCO guidance at www.pagesociety.com

1. acknowledge the concerns of the other side;
2. encourage joint fact-finding;
3. (consider) contingent commitments to minimize impacts (such as compensation);
4. accept responsibility, admit mistakes, share power;
5. act in a trustworthy fashion at all times;
6. focus on building (or sustaining) long-term relationships.

Placing this on the wall of the crisis communication center is recommended by us, as a reminder of a process that has been proved time and again to lower the heat during conflict.

Considering CEO as Crisis Spokesperson

The CEO is the ultimate authority of the enterprise. When he shows up at a crisis site, *it is news.* He is, by his presence, acknowledging the problem and prevailing circumstances. When he talks, he conveys the enterprise position, its understanding of the situation, and its sense of responsibility. The chief executive's language, his personality, his understanding of contexts, and his ability to convey intentions toward resolution—all become part of the process by which stakeholders judge the enterprise.

For these reasons, CCOs must think carefully before counseling the chief executive to become the crisis spokesperson. Contexts need to be considered, importantly including the *ability of authentic spokesmanship.* The fact that the CEO *is* the ultimate authority means that he cannot be easily corrected or nuanced if facts are misstated, promises are inappropriate, or a harried or unprepared executive provides a public comment that undermines the effort to restore stakeholder trust.

An alternative or interim spokesperson—a high-level executive with related responsibilities (*e.g.,* technical or financial accountability) and with spokesperson competence—may be the better first decision as to who "talks for the company." However, the chief executive will need to engage at some point. He may need to get to the scene, and he certainly will need to be ready to engage with stakeholders and authorities early on. Spokesperson training should be a staple in the CCO leadership communication plan. And when the chief executive is skilled, caring, and on his or her game—understanding context, believing in the message content, and mastering the tone of caring and confidence—the CCO has a powerful channel through which to help the company re-connect with shaken stakeholders.

Let us zero in on the drama, the CCO role as communication expert. ABC Company is surprised. An operational disruption has reached crisis proportion. In the C-suite, routine turns into red alert. Questions abound: "What's it all about?" "Who's working on it?" "What's the status now?" The CCO is ready for the inevitable questions: "What do we say, who says it, and when do we say it?" He goes to work, connecting the dots, collecting information, collaborating with C-level peers, enabling his team to do their professional best. It is a disruption that threatens stakeholder relations, the company's reputation, and its performance targets. That is a crisis. The CCO and his team decide this is a case where sooner or later, the chief executive officer will need to be a spokesperson. The course of events has elevated the ultimate-authority necessity of CEOs as crisis spokespersons.

In what now must be considered ancient crisis communication history, CEOs could choose—to their advantage or detriment—to steer clear of the media. Exxon's CEO unavailability to the print-and-broadcast media of the 1980s following the Valdez oil spill has become a used-to-be tale. As we wrote this book in the summer of 2014, Mary T. Barra, chief executive officer of General Motors, joined the ranks of crisis communication leaders early and prominently out front. The enterprise leader generalists—by now you know we mean the CEO and the CCO—are compelled to gear up for an early move to the forefront of a proliferating crisis narrative.

Social fuels the trend. With the immediacy and ease of social communication, the crisis story escalates rapidly in all directions. Transparency takes on such dynamic proportions that, in our view, demands preparation for chief executive exposure out front, communicating authentically on the organization's explanations and intentions, its competence, its compassion, its acceptance of reality, and its basis for hopeful resolutions.

Case Studies: Two Leaders, Authentic Authority

We offer you now two entirely different cases of leaders succeeding as voices of authority. The first is that of a corporate CEO providing an unusually comprehensive, personal and professional perspective, which we found particularly incisive, on the role of a chief executive as chief spokesperson. The CEO frankly reveals lessons he learned in a high-profile crisis. The second case is different in that we depart from our main theme of corporate communication to provide another frank, informing, personal analysis of a respected individual leader, this one in the military, during and following a crisis.

British Petroleum and the Deep Horizon Disaster

In November 2011, a little more than a year after the British Petroleum (BP) crisis disaster in the Gulf of Mexico, BP's CEO Robert Dudley told students at Thunderbird School of Global Management seminar in Arizona that he and his leadership team learned the requirements of crisis response: a serious and realistic recovery plan, optimism that the plan can be achieved, and a thick skin to bear relentless criticism.

As an American who grew up in the Gulf area, Dudley took the reins to lead the international petroleum giant, after the previous CEO, a Briton, failed in his role as crisis spokesperson. A single, poor-communication incident seems to have been his downfall. During a televised interview, the British executive appeared harried and distracted, when the news reporter asked a question about the amount of time the cleanup was taking, the executive acknowledged the difficulty and, in an apparent attempt to identify personally with those afflicted by the crisis, said that he too would "like his life back." The company's board apparently decided to give him that option. He was replaced by another executive officer, the American, Dudley, who thereby became the enterprise spokesperson. We are now able to learn from Dudley's recollections to the class in Arizona, what this CEO and his leadership team learned in a high-profile crisis communication challenge.

One: Collaborative Action Plan

Lesson number one is to develop an achievable action plan centered on affected stakeholders. "You need absolute determination and focus," Dudley said, "the ability to make a plan and stick to it. The way we organized the response across four states was an example of that." With direct involvement with the CEO, BP's leadership communication evaluated stakeholder concerns and expectations in the impacted Gulf states; and organized meetings and press events with local political, civic, and environmental leaders.

In the Thunderbird seminar, Dudley acknowledged that BP came in for considerable heat. "While you need to be sensitive to the feelings that such a crisis engenders, and these feelings will be strong, [so] you need to have a thick skin," said the BP chief executive. "You have to ignore the noise and you can't dwell on the constant public criticism that occurs in such a crisis."

Two: Reality Plus Optimism

Even under fire, Dudley said, "You need a quiet sense of optimism, especially as a leader. That comes from having a clear direction and knowing that you are doing the right thing. As for relationships, on a personal level, you need to accept and appreciate the fact that...crisis, such as this, becomes personal and affects everyone. And in dealing with people in the organization, you have to recognize that everyone is under pressure, especially those managing risk at the frontline." Dudley made the point that the person at the top of the company can set the tone for the company and its intentions, but he cannot do it alone. He said, "It is vital to surround yourself with a committed, positive team—people with diverse experience and viewpoints who aren't afraid to speak up." He emphasized that thoughtful communication is vital, planned or unplanned (perhaps remembering the faux pas communication of his on-the-scene predecessor). Dudley underscored the reality of *engaging* with authorities and political figures; in this case, state government officials on the frontline of the disaster, as well as federal officials who arrived at the scene to evaluate the scope of government help.

His guiding rule as leader was to be careful, caring, and truthful: Denial, said Dudley, "is the worst enemy of effective crisis management." In a very high level of crisis spokesmanship, BP's Dudley participated in a joint news conference on the Gulf Coast with President Barack Obama, who had come to the scene to show his concern and assure federal cooperation and attention to needs created by the explosion and oil spill.

Three: Values Such as Respect

Time pressure is a strong contextual issue, Dudley told the students to find ways to make decisions in the available time—which never feels like enough. He urged reliance on communication principles—treating people with respect even under harried, stressful conditions; working as a team; aiming to do the job as well as it can be done, whatever it might be; and communicating constantly with employees, shareholders, and the public. In the absence of information, Dudley observed, imagination runs wild.

In the high-risk situation of the 2010 crisis, BP's Dudley grasped the value of chief executive as spokesperson, took charge, and handled it with intelligence and emotional competence. He helped recover the leadership communication strength for the company.

Crisis at the Personal Level

How does the company respond to a crisis that is centered on a leader's personal actions? When the personal crisis involving an unexpected, unacceptable situation of a high-level executive becomes the company's crisis, the climax (the place where the negative onslaught, the shouting stops just enough for the communicator to communicate positively) can be—and often is—achieved through the departure of the individual. The board takes action or the executive's attorney's advice, and there is a sudden departure, ideally accompanied by the first positive, post-climax action: the announcement of an early replacement, temporary though it may be.

In cases such as this, the CCO's wheelhouse is fairly quiet. The CCO's job is to get out the news release pretty much as dictated by the corporate lawyers, and to provide virtually no comment thereafter. The C-suite corporate affairs focus is on cleaning up, clearing up, and moving on with as little disruption as practicable. Reassurance is provided in appropriate ways to investors, customers, employees, and other stakeholders. The customary message from the company—although all manner of comment and interpretation may be in play outside—is that one important corporate player is out of the game and that accountabilities are being assumed by another capable player.

But what does the departed executive do? And, sticking to our topic, how does he or she communicate? Is there a leadership communication strategy for a highly publicized, damaging, personal situation, especially if the leader hopes to lead again, somewhere? Drawing on a case highly examined in the public media, old-line and online, and benefitting from candid communication, we can find instruction in the way in which a military leader handled an organizational or personal crisis.

An Example From the Military: General Stanley McChrystal

General Stanley McChrystal was the commander of U.S. troops in Afghanistan in 2010 when a *Rolling Stone* profile portrayed him and his aides as contemptuous of the President. The story, which McChrystal maintains was inaccurate, led him to resign and end his military career.

Patricia Sellers (2013), *Fortune* magazine editor, interviewed the former four-star general, focusing on leading in difficult times. "It's easy to be a leader when things are going well," the interviewer noted. "The true test comes when things fall apart. How do you handle yourself then?"

McChrystal responded: "Well, I decided to myself, that that was an inflection point in my life. And I couldn't change that now. You can't change the past." He took the route counseled by philosophers as far back as ancient Greece: *When men speak ill of you, live so as no one will believe them.* McChrystal told his interviewer: "I was going to try to ... conduct myself every day for the rest of my life in a way that would cause anybody who saw or dealt with me to say, 'That's not congruent with the tone of that report'. So, rather than take on the report directly, I decided to take it on indirectly and just try to disprove it by my conduct."

A leader deciding to "communicate through action" will find it diffi-cult, McChrystal acknowledges: "You pay a big price when you do that. Silence hurts. When you keep your mouth shut and you don't write about it, you don't talk about it … and every day you want to scream." Relying on deeds, not words, he however believes, provides a path to renewed respect and ultimate influence. McChrystal concluded the interview with advice useful for enterprise leaders, who are certain to encounter challenges—whether or not they peak with dismissal of the current leadership role:

> *Get yourself ready to (achieve) what's important to you: What's the core of you? What can't people take away from you? And realize that if you give to other people the opportunity to determine your dignity or your sense of self-worth—if you outsource that to them—they can leave you in a bad place. So you've got to decide.*

After leaving the Army, McChrystal kept his peace, declining inter-views, drawing on his core, reorienting his life. He accepted an adjunct assignment at Yale, teaching a course in what it takes to lead. Within two years, this war-time leader had founded the McChrystal Group consult-ing firm and joined corporate boards, to counsel companies on planning and governing business leadership strategies.

Apologize or Not?

With openness and accountability framing corporate communication, spurred by disclosure laws (such as Sarbanes Oxley, commonly refer-enced as "Sox"), it is somewhat quaint to recall that the "never complain, never explain" cowboy message that John Wayne drawled as Col. Nathan Biddles in "She Wore a Yellow Ribbon" was actually used by a corporate CEO in the 1970s to stonewall the media who were digging into his personal exploits. Today, those with the job of fixing rips in the bonds of stakeholder trust have no time to complain, no option but to explain; and we are at the point where explaining often means apologizing.

Taking responsibility for a serious problem, affecting stakeholders, has almost always risen ultimately to the top of the enterprise, making the chief executive in business (or the candidate in politics) the apologizer.

Writing in a 2003 issue of *Chief Executive Magazine*, Burson Marsteller's Leslie Gaines-Ross (Gaines-Ross 2003) placed apology among the characteristics she saw arising among "a new generation of humbler CEOs." A decade later, however, a wave of leadership apologies in virtually every field—business, politics, sports—turned the humble theme to humbug among critical observers. In 2014, a *New York Times* business writer (Sorkin 2014 B1) teamed with a popular social and business counselor (Dov Seidman) to launch a social media campaign (Twitter hashtag #ApologyWatch) to track the outbreak of apologies and to follow up on post-apology action.

So the leadership questions are the following: Do we apologize? Who does the apologizing? Who are we talking to? And what does our apologizer say? For the CCO, the exercise is a test of truth, proof, and trustworthiness. As always, if apology is the communication action, contexts will shape if not dictate content of the information and tone of its delivery. Contextual trends and realities must be considered. Here are some insights and possible guidelines for corporate communicators:

Weasel-words, half-apologies are entirely ineffective. Apologies have become aggressively direct. Code words, winks, crossed fingers—*I would like to apologize if anyone takes offense … We are aware that some people would not understand …* face-saving equivocation for executive egos, are dropped.

Apologies can have a preemptive advantage. The rule seems to be: the sooner the apology, the better the chance to avoid buildup (especially on social media) of speculation and demand. Without question, the CCO and others at the top of the enterprise need to take responsibility, sustain the service to and connection with stakeholders. Whether such expression appears or is intended as an apology will depend on contexts. The matter of assuming responsibility, acknowledging mistakes, and pledging correction—call it apology or not—is effective in lowering the pressure that builds with authoritative silence. CEOs who have preempted critics on company mistakes (Dudley, BP, in 2010; Barra, GM, in 2014) exemplify the new model of crisis communication within the context of expanding transparency in corporate enterprise.

Apologies are less often the realm of legal counsel. Transparency has led toward abandonment of any C-suite precept that legal liability comes first, translated as not so fast in, and perhaps never, saying you are sorry. The new model assumption that "everybody knows everything" (or thinks they do, and will guess at it, and will socially spread their assumptions) is becoming the rule of play. Even conservative general counsels now understand that *silence may not be golden* when regulators, investors, boards, and a zillion tweeters have access to sources and means of pressuring for admission of guilt. Apologies may be deployed as honest owning up, caring about harm, and possibly (although cases such as BP's in the Gulf disaster and GM in the defective auto issue may ultimately argue the other way) pre-empt legal action and minimize damage awards.

Here is the basic bottom line: apology has become the differentiator between caring and callous company leadership. In business leadership communication, all the analyses of the 2001 collapse of energy-deregulating advocate Enron, one of the 10 largest U.S. companies, center on the fact that the company's leadership and culture obviated the possibility of truth-telling or proof. Allen R. Cohen (2005), of Babson College in Massachusetts, was among those observing that the company was cut no slack, at least in part, because nobody would deliver the expected apology from the top. "If anybody at Enron had said 'We created a culture that backfired on us,' the public would have been more sympathetic," said Cohen.

Examining many crisis cases and the evidence of communication success and failure, we have come to respect the pragmatic and emotionally intelligent value of apology. In our view, for enterprises operating in a democracy, apology is a sort of life-saving device on the deck of the corporate ship. It is serious, once rarely used and now generally expected. For the CCO, the questions are who, when, and how to deploy acceptance, regret, and resolve. The general answer is early enough within the contexts prevailing, and in the form (content, tone) delivering some control by the company of the communication direction. It is what is most often needed in the crisis *climax*, as shown in our crisis anatomy representation. Given the widespread, well-known experience of leaders whose enterprise and personal competence have suffered loss because of negative news and social, online bashing, CCOs are no longer lonely counselors for pre-emptive strategies of C-suite communication. The new strategy of corporate apology may not place humility in the Jim Collins' (2001, 17) model of the Level 5 effective executive leading quietly. Enterprise executives are increasingly ready to outwardly engage in authentic, sustainable relationships with stakeholders where transparency applies to both competent and erring performance. New executives, moving up the corporate ladder, are aware of the rising odds of spotlight reality, where leaders lead performance that respects the stakeholder trust deal, without apology… until necessary to assure sustainable shared returns.[6]

We bring this to a head. When it is time to own up, what is the best example? In our view, the all-time best apology came from a leader in the years of more control and less transparency. It was from Lee Iacocca, chairman and CEO of Chrysler, following the disclosure in 1987 that some of the automobiles offered for sale as new actually had been driven, for testing and other purposes, with the mileage odometer turned off. The company was selling new cars with up to 400 miles on them. Some 60,000 cars were compromised by this.

Iacocca and his communication team hammered out a response. Customers impacted by the factory demo situation would be compensated in the form of extended warrantees. The situation would not recur. Chrysler placed full-page advertisements in newspapers and took to the broadcast outlets with this message, delivering by Iacocca, who was pictured in each advertisement: "We did something to make our customers question their faith in us. These are mistakes we will never make again. Period."

This comes as close as we have seen to the ideal that Nick Smith (2008), the University of New Hampshire professor of philosophy, establishes in his book, *I was wrong: The meanings of apologies*. Smith argues that, while contexts will impact the exact nature of apologizing, the act of taking responsibility ("I was wrong") needs to be personalized and not "collective." As Iacocca demonstrated, the CEO puts his personal credibility on the line. Successful follow-through will require focus and action by others in the company, starting in the C-suite with consistent, strong reliance on leadership communication that is both contrite and compelling.[7]

---

[6] For more on apology, see Coombs, W.T. (2011).

[7] Smith's book is a recommended resource on moral meaning in collective, corporate behavior. Gestures of contrition give rise to further questions about individual and corporate character.

Post-Crisis Analysis: The CCO Role

"What-ifs" pop up in post-crises analytics. What if the workers at the explosion (or the accident or the incident or in the factory) had believed safety and quality trumped speed or efficiency or cost? What if the information flow on conduct and safety was uniformly interactive, two-way, trustworthy, and imperative? What if the mindset in the C-suite had been an unshakable belief in a culture of transparency, trust, caring, and caution? And, to come to the relevance of leadership communication, what if the CCO had been so attuned to the values in the culture—safety, physical, financial, and reputation factors—that he became the C-suite influence that prevented or at least ameliorated the crisis situation?

In his book *Flirting With Disaster* (with the track-stopping subtitle "*Why accidents are rarely accidental*"), Marc Gerstein (2008) recounts his role as "Cassandra" at the C-suite table. (Cassandra, you may recall, was the ruler's daughter endowed with the gift of prophesy but fated never to be believed. The modern dictionary meaning is "one that predicts misfortune or disaster" [Merriam-Webster's Collegiate Dictionary 2003]).

Gerstein tells his Cassandra story in a meeting with peers in a company's leadership. He had put himself on the agenda with what he considered an important topic: avoiding worst-case outcomes. At the table, he handed out hard copies of a memo he had sent to each of them individually. It was an in-depth analysis of market share data and the results of simulation studies that pointed to gloomy future scenarios for the firm. He sought discussion among his peers at the table on the seriousness of the forecast, hoping to generate thought leadership on ways to steer the company away from harm.

Instead, there was restless, resistant body language around the conference table. Finally a team member broke the silence, looking at others, and turned to Gerstein. "Are you positive this could happen?" the team member asked, clearly skeptical. Gerstein says in his book that he was surprised by this reaction. He replied that of course nobody knows the future … but the warnings he had turned up seemed clear to him. His point was to consider the possibilities, conduct a specific and thorough study and if problems are found, try to solve them. Gerstein tried to keep the idea alive, even proposing an outline for a study of cultural conditions.

Gerstein's effort was waved off as a waste of money. His C-suite peers (as well ultimately as members of the company's board) dismissed Gerstein's forecast of a seriously stormy economic outcome. Gerstein was waved off, as was Cassandra in her clairvoyance, and life went on in the company … for a time.

Within 18 months, however, the strength of negative trends took hold. Income sank, hundreds of jobs were lost, and the end came, to use Gerstein's words, with an unwanted and "humiliating merger" with a competitor. In his 2008 book, Gerstein, an MIT Sloan School of Management PhD who taught at Sloan as well as the Columbia Business School, described as "far from unique" his Cassandra-like experience, his C-suite isolation as the only one in management pointing toward potential pre-crisis signals (what we call prodromes or red flags) "until it was too late for anything but damage control."

We provide this unusually candid, insider case as a cautionary tale for the CCO in any enterprise. "I have found the same distorted thinking, errors in decision-making, and self-serving politics at the root of many industrial accidents, product-liability recalls, dangerous drugs, natural disasters, economic catastrophes, and national security blunders," Gerstein (2008, 5) writes in the introduction to his book…

"What-if" thinking is virtually an instinct of the expert communicator. Questions are constantly in mind. What if the CCO ecosystem listening strategy turns up warnings of impending risk of disruption, stakeholder trust, and reputational loss? What happens if the CCO comes to the C-suite table with evidence of issues in the culture and communication range? Will professional CCO instincts be squelched by C-suite peers, or by the CEO's instincts? In a general sense, how does the CCO lead communication on disaster avoidance when others in the C-suite have their own axes to grind? Gerstein's case of C-level intuition trumping his analysis suggests that the CCO take steps to avoid the lonely Cassandra role. Once the CCO detects serious-risk prodromes, through data derived from stakeholder feedback, she might seek external expert analysis to help focus the C-suite team on the evidence in time to execute prevention moves.

Corporate culture and communication related to damage prevention is clearly in the CCO's areas of expertise. The Coast Guard report on blame for the 2010 Gulf oil spill reaffirmed a crisis verity: somewhere in cases such as this, there is almost always the revelation that two organizational factors—company culture and leadership communications—are significant elements in either achieving or failing to achieve corrections in such danger areas as workplace safety and product reliability. In its 288-page study, the Coast Guard said Deepwater Horizon and its owner "had serious safety management system failures and a poor safety culture."[8] In 2014, the external investigator's report on General Motors' defective ignition switch auto crisis similarly bore down on cultural and communication deficiencies.

Obviously, these are deficiencies that knock on the door of the CCO wheelhouse. If we could leave you (as the current or aspiring head of communication in a modern enterprise) with only one point about your relationship with crisis communication it would be this: You will become the go-to person if an unexpected situation suddenly disrupts everything else in the C-suite. When the virtual alarm sounds, you will be expected to provide counsel, coaching, and leadership. You, and highly likely the CEO, will move to the center of C-suite leadership communication. The next chapter is about preparation for such an extraordinary, potentially make-or-break possibility.

CCO "New Model" Leadership:
One Message Exercise

Given the transparency among stakeholders that social media makes possible, CCOs understand that tailoring highly segmented messages for different recipients is not a strategic option. Discuss with your team, and then with others in the C-suite, the three or four consistent messages that can be conveyed in social media and other channels, available to all stakeholders and critics, during calm, disruptive, or crisis communication conditions.

---

[8] (http://www.nytimes.com/2011/04/23/us/23spill.html?_r=3&).

CHAPTER 13

Pre-crisis Intelligence: SEC Risk Factors

Chief communication officers (CCOs) engage the company and its stakeholders through leadership communication. Stakeholder values are underscored. Investors are a critical focus. Signal events such as the quarterly conference call provide benchmark information and commentary by corporate leaders to investors and investment advisers. Alongside this regular flow of information relevant to stakeholders, generated by every U.S. public company, there is an alternative, standing communication resource. This is a year-span report prepared by the company, aimed at the firm's investors, to provide detail on the ways in which investor values could be put at risk. *Annual Report 10-K*, required by the Securities and Exchange Commission (SEC), delineates ways in which external contexts and decisions by management could limit the ability of the enterprise to deliver a return on the investor's dollar.

Although company leaders, importantly including CCOs, work toward transparent, ongoing, two-way communication to maintain positive interest in company-stakeholder deals, the company is required by law to generate a downside perspective. This seeming anomaly is explored in this chapter. We explain origins and purpose of the 10-K *Risk Factors* section, and suggest ways in which the CCO can use company risk factors information to advantage in her overall C-suite communication.[1]

Genesis and Point of the SEC 10-K Report

Let's begin with the origin of government's role in corporate financial communication and the boost given to *corporate transparency* as a com-

---

merce principle. Following economic impact of the American stock market crash in 1929, Wall Street reform became a function of federal government. Controls were placed on the issuing and trading of securities. Sunshine was let into the previous condition of unreported concentration of controlling stock interests in a very few hands. Since enactment of the law in 1934, the federal government's objective, by guidance and force of the SEC, is to have a regulatory hand in U.S. commerce, exercising authority in stocks, bonds, and other securities, to guard against abuse of power, fraud, and secrecy (http://www.sec.gov/about/whatwedo.html). The SEC assumed responsibility for assuring that investors had access to higher levels of company insight. Full disclosure of information became a legal requirement. The SEC was charged, effectively, to enforce corporate transparency.[2]

In the course of defining transparency today, the SEC requires regulated companies to provide shareowners with an annual report (known as Form 10-K) containing a comprehensive overview of the company's business and financial condition, including audited financial statements as well as the specific risk factors that accompany an individual's or group's investment in the company. Issued by the company a few months following the close of the company's fiscal (not necessarily calendar) year,[3] its Form 10-K report is publicly available in the SEC's EDGAR database (http://www.sec.gov/edgar/searchedgar/companysearch.html).

It should be understood that this government-required annual report is distinct from the annual report which a company may publish (or put online) with leaders' messages, photographs, and other material. This

---

[2] More on the history of regulation, see http://www.history.com/topics/securities-and-exchange-commission

[3] Historically, Form 10-K had to be filed with the SEC within 90 days after the end of the company's fiscal year. However, in September 2002, the SEC approved a Final Rule that changed the deadlines for Form 10-K and Form 10-Q for "accelerated filers"—meaning issuers that have a public float of at least $75 million, that have been subject to the Exchange Act's reporting requirements for at least 12 calendar months, that previously have filed at least one annual report, and that are not eligible to file their quarterly and annual reports on Forms 10-QSB and 10-KSB. These shortened deadlines will be phased in over time.

promotional, popularized version (which includes the highly important chief communication officer [CEO] Letter, see Chapter 8) may be combined with the Form 10-K to fulfill what the SEC calls the "annual report to shareholders," which a company must send to its shareholders when it holds an annual meeting to elect directors.[4]

What Can CCOs Learn From 10-Ks—Theirs and Competitors'?

Risk management is an influential aspect of leadership communication, leading us to encourage participation by CCOs in the 10-K process, as counsel to the company's risk management team. There are two important lessons for the CCO in the company's preparation of the 10-K.

1. **Research:** How do C-suite officers identify and rank the potential of risks?
2. **Communication:** How is the information written so that it is easy to understand and it substantiates—and certainly does not undermine—the reader's trust in the company's leadership?

Researching into risk analysis and reporting, gains an important CCO perspective. At first, the downside detail in a company's typical 10-K is so relentless that you wonder how an investor can rationalize investment and belief in the company's success.

Is the risk recitation in the SEC report the same as the drug warnings—dire risks up to and including death that follow the TV advertisements for a drug that is meant to heal and relieve? How can the corporate communicator remain positive and proactive in stakeholder communication if at least some of the stakeholders are reading, every year, this SEC warning list of countless ways that the benefit of stock ownership can be reduced or blown away?

Two Learning Points

First, the disclosure and discussion of risk are validations of management competence. Leadership is about moving forward with company

---

[4] Understand this distinction better by consulting the SEC website http://www .sec.gov/answers/annrep.htm

missions, understanding risks, and navigating through them better than the competition does. The 10-K filing and the *Risk Factors* section of that filing are a display of the company's management strength in identifying and anticipating risks and dealing with them to avoid as much possible the damages of disruption and crisis. With 10-K analyses available, the prospective or active investor can see that company leaders are aware of downside factors. Risk is acknowledged as a fact of innovation and change. As management experts such as Peter Drucker and James Mac-Gregor Burns have proved, transformative leadership means change, and change means risk.

Second, especially for communicators, is the realization that the required SEC process of laying out the specifics of risk is not only a rational, reasonable management practice. It is also an orderly exercise of transparency, the truth that can engender trust among followers and, through sustained leadership communication, result in higher belief in and advocacy of the company, its products, or services.

Excerpts from Company *Form* 10-K Filings

We conclude this chapter with a suggestion for turning the public identification of a company's management risks into an asset in the CCO's interaction with stakeholders and their specific fears. First, however, let us examine the communication contexts, content, and tone or style that are common in the annual report filed with the SEC.

Following is a small sample of the millions of words fed to the SEC by thousands of investor-owned companies in past years.[5]

Apple

Among the risk factors in Apple's 10-K in 2011, the company delivered this warning about depending on the people running the company

---

[5] The authors wish to emphasize that these samples are arbitrary and do not present any weight of significance that the company itself places on the selected sentences. A.1 sections typically comprise many pages in the 10-K filings, with companies covering 20 or more specific risk areas. For complete information on these and other companies, interested readers are urged to go to the SEC sources.

(http://investor.apple.com/secfiling.cfm?filingID=1193125-11-282113&
CIK=320193):

> Much of the Company's future success depends on the continued
> availability and service of key personnel, including its CEO, its
> executive team and highly skilled employees. Experienced person-
> nel in the technology industry are in high demand and compe-
> tition for their talents is intense, especially in the Silicon Valley,
> where most of the Company's key personnel are located.

Procter & Gamble

Procter & Gamble's 10-K for the year ended in June 2012 identified
risks inherent in global manufacturing, which could negatively impact
P&G's business results (http://www.sec.gov/Archives/edgar/data/80424/
000008042412000063/fy2012financialstatementsf.htm):

> In the manufacturing and general overhead areas, we need to
> maintain key manufacturing and supply arrangements, including
> any key sole supplier and sole manufacturing plant arrangements,
> to achieve our targets on cost. While we have business continuity
> and contingency plans for key manufacturing sites and the supply
> of raw materials, significant disruption of manufacturing, such
> as labor disputes, loss or impairment of key manufacturing sites,
> natural disasters, acts of war or terrorism, and other external fac-
> tors over which we have no control, could interrupt product sup-
> ply and, if not remedied, have an adverse impact on our business.

Ford Motor Company

Ford Motor's FY2011 10-K contemplated the risk of lower-than-antici-
pated market acceptance of new or existing products (http://www.sec.gov/
Archives/edgar/data/37996/000115752311001210/a6622311.htm):

> Although we conduct extensive market research before launching
> new or refreshed vehicles, many factors both within and outside

of our control affect the success of new or existing products in the marketplace. Offering highly desirable vehicles that customers want and value can mitigate the risks of increasing price competition and declining demand, but vehicles that are perceived to be less desirable (whether in terms of price, quality, styling, safety, overall value, fuel efficiency, or other attributes) can exacerbate these risks. For example, if a new model were to experience quality issues at the time of launch, the vehicle's perceived quality could be affected even after the issues had been corrected, resulting in lower sales volumes, market share, and profitability.

Wal-Mart Stores, Inc.

In its fiscal year 2006 report to the SEC, Wal-Mart was warning investors through its 10-K that, "we may face impediments to our expansion in the United States, including conversions of Discount Stores into Supercenters, which could adversely affect our financial performance." Details on this risk followed on the SEC site (http://www.sec.gov/Archives/edgar/data/104169/000119312506066792/d10k.htm):

> The growth in the net sales and operating net income of our Wal-Mart Stores segment and our SAM'S CLUB segment depends to a substantial degree on our expansion programs. Our expansion strategy depends upon our ability to execute our retail concepts successfully in new markets within the United States and upon our ability to increase the number of stores in markets in which we currently have operations. Our ability to open additional Supercenters, Discount Stores, Neighborhood Markets and SAM'S CLUBs and to convert existing Discount Stores into Supercenters depends in large measure upon our ability to locate, hire and retain qualified personnel and to acquire new store sites on acceptable terms. Local land use and other regulations restricting the construction of buildings of the type in which we operate our various formats, as well as local community action opposed to the location of specific stores at specific sites, may affect our ability to open new stores and clubs, to convert Discount Stores into

Supercenters or to relocate or expand existing units. Increased real estate, construction and development costs could limit our growth opportunities and our ability to convert our Discount Stores into Supercenters. If we are unable to open new Supercenters, Discount Stores, Neighborhood Markets or SAM'S CLUBs or continue to convert Discount Stores into Supercenters, our financial performance could be adversely affected. In addition, if consumers in the markets into which we expand are not receptive to our retail concepts, our financial performance could be adversely affected.

This random sample of a few *10-K Risk Factors* reports (which you, the reader, can easily update and study those of other companies online) indicates the wide extent to which today's public companies are an open book not only to investors, but to any inquiring journalists, politicians, advocacy groups, communities, or anyone else. The possible negatives of this transparency are countered by the continuing flow of corporate communication, describing conditions—progress, effort, and adjustment to current contexts—that determine corporate values. In addition, many companies produce their own annual reports. The company's investors, employees, customers, and others—as well as competitors, the media, and prospective stakeholders—can glean information of value from the company's professionally designed, often colorful annual report, containing the chairman's letter, descriptions, and photographs of operations and leaders, products, and services. Corporate communicators participate, and are commonly responsible for, this report's content and production. One further note: some companies incorporate the SEC report, including the risk-factor section, usually in a separate, distinctive typeface, into their annual reports.

Using Risk Disclosure as a Communication Asset

This chapter has focused on the annual report required (along with other reports, e.g., the quarterly *10-Q*)[6] by the SEC. How can CCOs use the *10-K Risk Factors* report as a communication asset tool? Following is a

---

[6] To find out about other SEC forms and reporting requirements, see http://www.sec.gov/edgar.shtml

suggested path to an aid in executing the CCO's role in stakeholder perception management.

Step One: Create a Risk Factors Checklist

The purpose is to provide the CCO and team members with a short-form reminder of the vulnerabilities that management has reported. Prepare as brief as practicable a numbered risk factors list based on the company's risk factors paragraphs. This could be signals or key words (e.g., environmental, labor relations, defects, supply shortages, global) taken from each of the *Item 1.A Risk Factors* paragraphs. More simply, the checklist could be the summary sentence that many companies use as the heading for each of the risk-factor descriptions. The checklist can be a reference in forming corporate communication strategies, and it will be particularly useful in stakeholder perception intelligence: how and where to aim your listening channels, and how to better review and evaluate feedback intelligence.

Step Two: Identify Vulnerable Stakeholders

The purpose here is to help communication focus on stakeholders and its accountability in stakeholder perception management. Think through the categories of stakeholders most vulnerable in each of the risk exposure categories of risk exposure identified in the 10-K. Add these to each of the numbered items on your Crisis Factors Checklist. If practicable, rank the stakeholder groups by order of direct impact by the identified risk.

Step Three: Specify Vulnerability Values

Here, the purpose is to align the risks identified by the company with the fear values of identified vulnerable stakeholders. The 10-K risks viewed by the company (*e.g.*, product quality failure) may be predominantly risks to the company's investor values (*e.g.*, loss of sales and revenue, resulting in lower financial results). The same risk areas may be perceived differently by noninvestor stakeholders (*e.g.*, product owners or users, who are adversely impacted at a personal health, safety, job, or choice level). Using risk research findings on how individuals perceive threat at a personal level, CCOs will benefit by advancing the effort toward matching up risk and all stakeholder vulnerabilities.

We underscore this point: adding to the checklist of risk factors the best estimation of stakeholder (including noninvestor) fear factors should be an asset in strategies for informed pre-crisis perception, as well as the content and tone of proactive, ongoing leadership communication.

Bringing Risk Factors into the Reality of "Fear Factors"

Corporate involvement in risk and crisis communication starts with understanding stakeholder perception of risks and their specific fears.

In a Georgetown University lecture on crisis communication, Honeywell Vice President Thomas Buckmaster (2014) urged corporate communicators to bring the company response to crises down to the level of personal perceived threats. "Crises are human-oriented," Buckmaster said. "The corporate or communication specialist's ability to identify the specific core values that are threatened in a crisis can improve the nature of the response and the communication needed."

Studies by the Richard Wirthlin research firm in the 1980s identified 10 American core-value areas: health, money, relationship to God, family relations, retirement, leisure opportunity, job satisfaction, college education for children, home ownership, and the ability to travel.

Citing the "hazard and outrage" research of Dr. Peter M. Sandman, Rutgers University, Buckmaster said the level of hazard perceived (and the response or level of outrage felt) by people who may be affected by a crisis will determine by their judgment of the risk—and therefore affect the impact of crisis communication. Sandman suggests evaluating risk on criteria such as origin of the hazard (natural or man-made, the individual's volition choice (voluntary or involuntary), immediacy (now or later), and familiarity (it is known or it is new; *e.g.*, the storm that hits a certain coastal area periodically), assumed exposure to the hazard (continuous? occasional?) and the necessity perceived to take action (necessary? a luxury?).

The 10-K risk-warning responsibility for American companies, dating back to the 1930s, continues. For corporate communicators such as

Buckmaster of Honeywell, it becomes one of the contexts that must be accommodated within the scopes of instant 24/7 accessibility and the rising intensity of risk and crisis perception among corporate stakeholders.

CCOs need to be aware of—and if needed help the CFO and investor relations people follow—social media and communication policies. The CCO accountability is continuous engagement in the company's financial communication requirements and its public outflow, collaborating with investor relations, financial, risk, and legal officers. Corporate communication's special strengths to contribute to best achievable outcomes in regulatory requirements and competitive advantages are expert intelligence (stakeholder feedback management, news, and social media inferences) and clear, consistent, and confident leadership communication.

Evolution of ERM

We end this chapter with a short note on Enterprise Risk Management (ERM). ERM has escalated in importance since some risk managers watched helplessly as their businesses melted down. Accenture's 2013 Global Risk Management Study surveyed C-level executives involved in risk management decisions at 44 companies (Teach 2013). The survey revealed (1) direct attention by chief executives, with 98 percent of organizations designating a chief risk officer (CRO); (2) risk management plays a large role in budgeting, investment, and strategy; and (3) ERM is seen as a factor enabling growth and innovation. Chief communication officers are working closely with CROs, chief financial officers, as well as CEOs on ERM.

CCO "New Model" Leadership: Understanding Risk

Examine with your team and others in the C-suite the value of using risk as a way to drive authenticity and trust. Consider posing probable risk questions, suggested by the 10-K risk factors. Think through the downsides of each communication initiative in terms of specific groups of internal and external stakeholders. Before communicating, discuss specific fears and values of each group, determine "what, so what, now what" relevance of information, timing, and delivery method.

CHAPTER 14

Sustainable Business Communication: Financial, Social, and Civic

Leaders of a business enterprise operating in a democracy aim at one existential outcome: doing what is necessary to strategize, execute, and deliver an expressed vision of victory for stakeholders (Figure 14.1).[1] This goal-oriented process can be understood as three critical performance areas: *financial*, *social*, and *civic (with emphasis on government interface)*. In this chapter, we examine the potential role of the chief communication officer (CCO) in these performance areas—we refer to them collectively as *corporate sustainability*—with the end in mind, collaborating with others in the C-suite to add the influence of *sustainable business communication*.

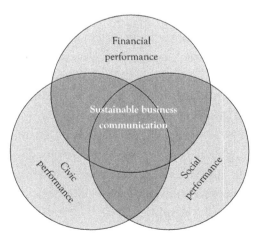

Figure 14.1 CCO accountability

---

[1] Or, as we noted in the example of Steve Jobs and Apple, resetting the vision when conditions do not sustain the reality and hope of achievement.

Financial Performance: Connecting With Investors

The chief executive was contemplative. "It's puzzling," he said to his chief communication officer, looking up from business page clippings and a summary of online comments from financial analysts. "When I floated the idea of buying that other company, a lot of these folks were all for it. Then the lead analyst sounded off, totally opposed to it, and his followers joined in. Then their clients got nervous, and we began to hear 'don't do it, don't do it' from the institutions. That shook up our board. So I had to back off. But it would have been a good deal for everybody, our company, and the other one. It could have been long-term growth for both businesses, if they had understood it better."

Understanding it better is the corporate communicator specialty. A CCO tracks and anticipates stakeholder perceptions. Her "listening stations" are an online ear to the groundswell of investor opinion. She understands the contexts, content, and tone of influential information flow. And her influence in the C-suite aims constantly at a culture of understanding and enabling employees. The CCO's focus on financial performance must be considered the *primary influence* in sustainable corporate communication.

Positioning of a company in the minds of followers (supporters, critics, media) is conditioned by the company's financial performance.[2] A healthy financial performance can create a happy, overall competence image—a *halo*, as Swiss management professor Phil Rosenzweig[3] has defined it in his book, *The Halo Effect* (Rosenzweig 2007)—that makes many other factors look better. If the company is making money ahead of competitors, people including journalists and analysts decide that the company's CEO is highly effective if not brilliant, that the company's products are highly desired by customers, that its suppliers are reliable and supportive, and that its employees are dedicated to ongoing success in an enabled, possibly self-driven or autonomous culture. The halo shines on everything. *Until it doesn't.*

---

[2] We recommend Ries and Trout (1982) for a clear understanding of market positioning and how people remember number one but not number two in competitive categories.

[3] *Phil Rosenzweig* is a Professor at IMD, the International Institute for Management Development, in Lausanne, Switzerland.

Rosenzweig uses the case of Cisco Systems as proof of the halo effect. When, under the leadership of CEO John T. Chambers, the company was highly profitable, and its stock steadily climbed from numbers in the teens to numbers in the fifties and beyond, there was praise all around for Cisco's products, its partners, its leadership, and its culture. Investment advisers recommended the stock and bought it themselves. The media could not say enough good things about the company's formula for fame in competitive enterprise. *Fortune* magazine ran a May 2000 cover story that glowed with praise for the company's chief, its customer focus, and its culture. As Rosenzweig documents, the halo shone bright. Then the clouds came in. Amid a market slide of technology company investments, Cisco's stock fell from its $80 peak to $14. The company's haloed themes of leadership, culture, customer focus, and ability to manage acquisitions followed the plunge of Cisco's financial performance. *Fortune*, as well as other evaluators, now said that the company's prowess had been an illusion.

What does this mean for the CCO? It means working with others in the C-suite to make sure that if a halo for financial performance is conveyed by external evaluators, and especially by high-profile business media, it (1) has the benefit of full knowledge of financial leadership plans and reportable financial facts and (2) does not necessarily imply heavenly performance in any or all other performance areas.

CCO Role: Collaborate With Investor Relations

The mission of investor relations (defined by United States and European organizations) in public companies is to assure an accurate, fair evaluation of the company by external interests (http://hbw.niri.org/Main-Menu-Category/advocate/Regulatory-Positions.aspx).[4] Communication from the company aims at three target audiences:

---

[4] "Investor relations is a strategic management responsibility that integrates finance, communication, marketing, and securities–law compliance to enable the most effective two-way communications between a company, the financial community, and other constituencies, which ultimately contributes to a company's achieving fair valuation. *Investor Relations Society* (United Kingdom): "Investor relations is the communication of information and insight between a company and the investment community. This process enables a full appreciation of the company's business activities, strategy, and prospects, and allows the market to make an informed judgment about the fair value and appropriate ownership of a company."

1. *Investors* (people and groups who buy and sell stock in the company),
2. *Investment analysts* (stock brokers, traders, and counselors who advise those who buy and sell stock), and
3. *Financial media* (followers of markets and companies who write or comment in print, on broadcast media, and online).

Investors, also referred to as shareowners or shareholders, are at or near the top of every company's stakeholder list, perhaps ranking in terms of shared value as above the highly critical levels of employees (although employees may also be shareowners) and customers. The CCO's end-in-mind questions are the following: (1) "How does the company ensure accurate and, in best cases, favorable perceptions in the all-important flow of financial information?" and (2) "Who are the company's external sources of financial information and are the enabling attributes of content, tone, and timing engaged for best achievable outcomes?"

All of this manifests a need for the CCO to be engrained in the investor relations process. And to do that, he will need the knowledge and skills to qualify for collaboration with C-suite influencers in investor relations.[5] The CCO must have, if he wants to be influential at the top of the organization, a deep, current, and probing understanding of the factors that go into the company's financial performance, exactly how that condition is communicated, and ways in which he and his specialty can support and help to guide the treatment and flow of financial information.

CCO collaboration with others in the C-suite on financial performance communication should be (and in our experience, usually is) a natural alliance. After all, the management function of investor relations has its genesis in financial journalism. Early financial communicators in American companies, especially those located in and around New York, were writers who covered financial news. Financial beat reporters were recruited to work in company public relations departments because they knew how to connect with investors, with other financial writers, and with specialists such as stock analysts who influenced public and stockholder opinion. These

---

[5] Your authors express appreciation to a respected counselor and a lecturer in our Georgetown graduate studies, Gene Stevenson, CEO of Macropath, Atlanta, GA, for his guidance and contribution in this discussion of investor relations. (Stevenson, G. 2014, pers. comm.) See also Figure 14.2.

company people spoke the language of Wall Street and business. They were, in the view of evaluators, a trustworthy source. All of this reflected well on the company, its openness, its connection to the needs of the evaluators.

The connective strategy continues. However, roughly since the 1960s, investor relations (IR) has become a specific C-suite art. Public companies have typically assigned responsibility for it to a top officer—often, the chief financial officer (CFO)—or to a qualified senior manager, usually called the IR director or manager, who may or may not be professional public communicators.

However the IR function of investor relations is assigned, the CCO needs a close working relationship; communication harmony starts in the C-suite, with the CCO on the same wavelength with the IR leader. The best achievable outcome is a consistent, carefully planned and executed one-voice investor relations strategy.

Speak With One Voice

CCOs know that communication starts with a listening strategy. Although C-suite leaders listen to uncontrollable information flows (ranging from praise to condemning clamor) about the company from external sources, they seek the controllable: accuracy (at minimum) in the content, context, and tone of the company's messaging.

For most publicly traded companies, a common initiative to provide external investment advisers access to company financial information is a quarterly, phone or web access session. Typically, these sessions are managed and personally opened by the CFO or IR manager, who introduces the CEO and other executives who report on financial results and targets, often providing highlight slides available on web-access screens, and answer questions. Before the call, a huge amount of coordination needs to happen. The CCO and her team work with C-suite executives to determine what will be said by whom, what will be on the slides, what the news release will cover, and preparing participants for the session, anticipating questions, and producing talking points and the news release. One-voice communication on the company's current financial performance requires CCO initiative and compatibility with investor relations.

During the year, the company's voluntary annual report (especially the CEO letter), the required government (SEC) 10-K report, news releases with financial implications are among other essentials of corporate financial influence in which one-voice contexts, content, and tone are generally manageable.

The investor and communication teams will also need to agree on input and coaching related to informal postings to employees, company blogs about the business, road shows, exhibits, senior management speeches or presentations, interviews or conversations by division or country managers to the media or at professional associations—in short, wherever and whenever there is the potential to influence public and shareholder opinion about financial conditions. In a truly coordinated attempt for accuracy and consistent impressions related to investment decisions, the CCO's connectivity and counsel can well extend to review of the CFO's financial presentations, corporate advertising or marketing output that has a financial performance angle.

Worst-case outcomes are contradicting or inadvertent disclosures. An extreme example would be media relations telling a reporter that the company is committed to Project A, whereas the IR person is telling investors that the company has cut spending on Project A and increasing spending on Project B. Mixed messages not only confuse evaluators but they also increase their perception of risk and leadership competence. Financial performance communication can produce halos. It can also, through misconstrued information, produce horns. In our experience, the BAO of financial information flow is achieved through routine, predominantly informal relationships between the CCO and investor relations teams. C-suite alliance is best when team leaders can "walk down the hall, and figure it out." The benefit of communication harmony benefits from periodic team meetings that may also engage corporate marketing, risk management, operating, and business unit communicators, to compare plans, events that touch on investor relations, and messaging.

What is required for the CCO to lead in confirming the one-voice commitment? It starts, as we have emphasized, with a deep dive into company business essentials. The CCO and her team need to understand the dynamics of the business–financial community relationship. CCO immersion in the business means a clear, comfortable relationship with income and balance sheet factors, sales, and markets—in short, everything that affects and expresses how the company makes money, where it stands with regard to income and other financial projections, and what known market, competition, and risk factors pose impact on the company's business status. The CCO's communication team will know that the CCO expects each of them to understand the business, to work for coordinated clarity, and to seek information, regularly access and read financial news, monitor stakeholder communication, and listen certainly for any sign of dissonance among stakeholders and their influencers.

As generalists, with a broad view of company reputational values, corporate communicators are well suited to help determine whether financial information is providing investors and other stakeholders with accurate insight into the company's business. The bottom line on this bottom-line-driven perspective: the company's financial condition must be considered the first among the factors that influence stakeholder views and their decisions. The BAO: influential investor relations engaging communication execution that leads potential and current stakeholders to buy in, to believe, and to become at some level an advocate for the company—its products, its services, and its leadership values (Figure 14.2).

Social Performance: Connecting Through Sustainable Interests

When a company is basking in the glow of a financial halo, is it meaningful to talk about its social performance? Yes, because the financial bottom-line has become inextricably linked to all the other performance factors that influence stakeholder perception and buy-in.

As Batstone (2003), the founding editor of *Business 2.0* magazine, has noted, the public, which includes company stakeholders, not only look at a company's financial or economic position, but they also increasingly look for social sensitivity. They seek answers, or reassurance, to the universal question of human relationships: *"Do you care about me?"* In a book entitled *Saving the Corporate Soul, Business 2.0* editor David Batson goes so far as to connect a range of socially responsible business practices with the belief that a company "has the potential to act with soul when it puts its resources at the service of the people it employs and the public it services."

This is not an isolated perspective. A convincing case for caring capitalism was made before the turn of this century by the editor of *The Green Business* letter. In his book, *Beyond the Bottom Line: Putting Social Respon-*

How can the chief communications officer and the head of investor relations help improve financial performance credibility? An experienced C-suite communicator, Gene Stevenson, CEO of Macropath, Atlanta, GA, suggests six strategies to harmonize management, analyst, and investor understanding.

1. **Manage expectations**—Take steps to assess the financial community's understanding of management's strategy and guidance. The CCO and IR leader can build personal track records of continuously pushing for clear, direct communications from the company, and being disciplined in directly ensuring that investors' understanding of company messages is clear.

2. **Deliver on promises**—Follow-through is crucial, especially in the light of management optimism. When a CEO wants to tell investors about a great new product in the pipeline, the responsibility falls on staff to emphasize how closely the financial community will follow the product's development against the company timeline and budget.

3. **Provide fact-based transparency**—Investors are best served by staff executives who provide the facts and the context surrounding the facts. Investors tend to react negatively to interpretations, not to mention the potential legal risk to the company. So although analysts appreciate the provision of some "color" behind the facts, personal interpretations and opinions are best left out of the discussions.

4. **Know the business**—Know the business or businesses the company is in. Become an expert on the company and the industry, and know the competitive set. Understand what knowledge is not lodged in the communications function; it is important to "know what you don't know."

5. **Offer balanced perspective**—The CCO and IR leader need to be in a position where they can discuss risk as well as opportunity, the downside as well as the upside.

6. **Develop personal relationships**—The CCO and IR leader are alike in facing the need to build personal relationships within their constituencies. Just as critical is the need to monitor feedback from those constituencies on a continuous basis. Personal involvement in the feedback process can result in important knowledge gained.

Figure 14.2 CCO or investor relations: Six collaborative strategies

sibility to Work for Your Business and the World, Joel Makower (1994), a thoughtful lecturer on corporate environmentalism, cited a great number of companies then inextricably linked to social responsibility in terms of creating healthy workplaces, fostering worker empowerment, leading community physical and health development, and taking effective action in public safety and environmental improvement.

Co-author of this book, Bruce Harrison, similarly underscored the practice and value of corporate social and sustainability commitments in previous books: one, following the United Nations 1992 earth summit where the term "sustainable development" was put into corporate commitment terms, and gave rise to sustainability as a modern business responsibility. A second book interpreted the high road of corporate greening in 2008, with its enabling attention to environmental and climate factor improvement.[6]

Collaboration: Corporate Sustainability Officers

In science, the term sustainability explains how biological systems remain diverse and productive over time. Forests and wetlands are examples of sustainable—long-living—biological systems.

In the 21st century, sustainability has become a business management function. Major business schools now provide sustainability training in MBA programs. As of 2005, nearly all of the world's 150 largest companies had a sustainability officer with the rank of vice president or higher. A 2011 study found that the majority of top corporate sustainability executives are two degrees removed from their CEO in the corporate hierarchy, meaning that their boss reports to the CEO.[7]

CCOs in companies with C-level chief sustainability officers (CSOs) have a compatible opportunity for collaboration on the company's social responsibility communications. Joining leadership peers at the corporate

---

[6] Harrison's books are *Going Green: How to Communicate Your Company's Environmental Commitment*, Business One Irwin, Homewood, IL, 1993; and *Corporate Greening 2.0: Create and Communicate Your Company's Climate Change and Sustainability Strategies*, Publishing Works, Exeter, NH, 2008.

[7] See http://en.wikipedia.org/wiki/Chief_sustainability_officer#cite_note-3

sustainability strategy table, corporate communicators are positioned to engage in a process along these lines:

- *Help form the sustainability business case.* Start with ties to financial performance. Chart the course for sustainability that is relevant to the company's strengths. This is a long-term program that will need dedicated resources. Top management and business operations buy-in and encouragement are critical to success. The case for *sustainable communication* is part of the business case.
- *Tie it to governance.* Because top management must get board endorsement and involvement, help connect the plan for sustainable economic performance to the sociopolitical factors. This can be a substantial corporate governance issue. In many companies, outside board members have responded to investor activist inquiries about corporate accountability for risks and opportunities related to relevant issues in other contexts, and will bring important perspectives to bear.
- *Internal alignment.* Internal communication has to achieve workforce involvement and operational accountability. This may be tantamount to a culture change. The flow of information within the company will need to assure that the whole company is aimed at sustainable performance. The CCO can help enunciate a clear definition of corporate sustainability, stated in terms relevant to the company's mission and vision and appealing to its stakeholders and consistent with its values.
- *Stakeholder activism.* Each stakeholder group—investors, employees, customers, suppliers, government—needs to understand, and in the best case be engaged in advocating the company's strategies. Investor and government relations (GR) interactions are particularly important, because the opinions of stakeholders in these arenas can make or break management's resolve.
- *Think ahead.* Do not let short-term mentality limit your future options. Prepare to succeed with the millennium

generation of consumers and other stakeholders, recognizing that any company's sustainability is tied to reasonable expectation of future stakeholder benefit. Some companies are getting involved in school programs and public education about sustainability, participating in the conversation, and possibly shaping the debate.

- *Transparency.* Realize that the company will be evaluated, with or without CCO help. Take charge. Accountability must be documented, and homework shown to outsiders. Prepare to report progress (as well as explain shortfalls) in achieving metrics—such as carbon footprint reductions. Anticipate how your company will back up its promises, manage toward expectations, and get third party evaluations of processes and possibly its products. Invite inspection. The company's sustainability story needs to be stakeholder-relevant and told continuously. The company's website will need to put special emphasis on measurable points of environmental and social responsibility.

- *Maintenance.* Create and use systems for internal and external feedback for continuous improvement in the sustainability program, keeping it relevant to the business and all stakeholders. Work with product stewardship as a sustainability mechanism.

Corporate sustainability means building a business that will last because its financial performance is not handicapped by social and political factors. Communicating strategically, with all the coordination achievable in the company and externally, will help assure that these factors are in the company's favor.

In addition to one-voice, mutual support with your company's sustainability officers or managers, reach out for external collaborators. Explore the options for partnerships with other companies in your business or adjacent businesses, NGOs, external public interest groups, government organizations, customers, and dealers, distributors or retailers. Understand what their needs are and whether the company can work collaboratively toward specific sustainability goals. The CCO needs to research or benchmark each potential collaborator's greening, climate change, and other sustainability commitments.[8] And remember, these potential collaborators, including a growing number of green former antagonists, may already be looking your way.[9]

Case study: sustainability communication

Collaborating with other companies in your business sector can influence sustainability positioning and favor. Patagonia took a leadership role in the apparel and footwear business. Rick Ridgeway, vice president, environmental affairs at Patagonia, helped activate the company's sustainability mission statement ("to make products with no unnecessary harm and use business to inspire and implement solutions to the environmental crisis") and to spread commitment across the business sector. On Ridgeway's watch, the company led in founding the Sustainable Apparel Coalition, which provides a suite of assessment tools to standardize measurement of environmental and social impact from apparel and footwear across product lifecycles and business value chains. Communication is open and the intention of sector effort is transparent: "We've been in business long enough to know that when we can reduce or eliminate harm, other businesses will be eager to follow suit," Patagonia proclaims on its website.[10]

CSOs—Typical Responsibilities

The role of CSOs includes a number of responsibilities that may or may not be associated with the CCO, but will require the CCO's input on communicating company sustainability goals and objectives (MyFuture.com 2013):

---

[8] For more on benchmarking, see Michaelson and Stacks (2014); for a more detailed understanding, see Stacks (2011).

[9] For the current state of corporate sustainability, and careers, see http://myfuture.com/careers/details/chief-sustainability-officers_11-1011.03 And http://en.wikipedia.org/wiki/Chief_sustainability_officer

[10] Information on the Sustainable Apparel Coalition is at http://www.apparelcoalition.org/. Patagonia's Footprint Chronicles˙ (http://www.patagonia.com/us/footprint/) examines Patagonia's life and habits as a company. The goal is to use supply chain transparency to help Patagonia and other companies practice sustainable business. Quote from Patagonia website: "We've been in business long enough to know that when we can reduce or eliminate a harm, other businesses will be eager to follow suit."

- Develop or execute strategies to address issues such as energy use, resource conservation, recycling, pollution reduction, waste elimination, transportation, education, and building design.
- Direct sustainability program operations to ensure compliance with environmental or governmental regulations.
- Monitor and evaluate effectiveness of sustainability programs.
- Develop methodologies to assess the viability or success of sustainability initiatives.
- Develop, or oversee the development of, marketing or outreach media for sustainability projects or events.
- Develop, or oversee the development of, sustainability evaluation or monitoring systems.
- Develop sustainability reports, presentations, or proposals for supplier, employee, academia, media, government, public interest, or other groups.
- Evaluate and approve proposals for sustainability projects, considering factors such as cost effectiveness, technical feasibility, and integration with other initiatives.
- Formulate or implement sustainability campaign or marketing strategies.
- Research environmental sustainability issues, concerns, or stakeholder interests.
- Review sustainability program objectives, progress, or status to ensure compliance with policies, standards, regulations, or laws.
- Supervise employees or volunteers working on sustainability projects.
- Write and distribute financial or environmental impact reports.
- Conduct sustainability- or environment-related risk assessments.
- Create and maintain sustainability program documents, such as schedules and budgets.
- Identify and evaluate pilot projects or programs to enhance the sustainability research agenda.
- Identify educational, training, or other development opportunities for sustainability employees or volunteers.

Civic Performance: Connecting With Government

As we discussed in Chapter 10, doing business in a democracy means recognizing the role of government. Companies incorporated in the United States are both enabled and limited by federal, state, and local authority. The fact and halo effect of corporate leadership can be dimmed by government fines, lawsuits, major recalls, and other levels of presumptive government control. On the other hand, the competitive edge of a company in financial and social benefit terms can be enhanced through government support. These realities—the reality of control and the rationality of hope—add another dimension to the CCOs' relationship with the company's officer and team that handles government relations. In many companies, GR and public relations are interwoven. The formalizing of corporate PR as a watchdog of, and participant in, government affairs was evident as early as the 1920s when Arthur W. Page was advancing the case of the Bell telephone system in its regulatory relationship with government. In the 1950s, business executives were prodded by President Dwight D. Eisenhower to raise the level of enterprise attention to government processes. This led to formation of the Public Affairs Council (first known as the Effective Citizens Organization), which provides GR (or public affairs) officers with guidance and collaborations in political, legislative, and regulatory engagement. Evidencing the close relationship of corporate GR and communication, the Public Affairs Council is represented in the Page Society.[11]

Whether the two C-suite functions (essentially, public relations, and GR) are combined under one (*e.g.*, corporate affairs) officer or are separate but closely coordinated, most civic and political considerations will benefit from the attention of the communicator in her wheelhouse of perception management.

Stakeholder perceivers—customers, investors, employees, neighbors—are sensitized to the company's civic performance *as defined by*

---

[11] The Public Affairs Council, based in Washington, has more than 600 corporations, associations, and consulting firms as members. Douglas Pinkham, PAC president, is a member of the Page Society at this writing. See pac.org

government attention. Government may not be the dominant factor in product manufacturing, but customers as well as critics tilt toward negative perceptions when there are product warnings and recalls. Government may not be the pre-eminent influence on your investors, but when health, safety, and other standards affect the company's bottom line, there are communication requirements related to investors and analysts, critics, and bloggers. And employee questions and interests are stirred by government and political developments. Bringing these cross-functions together occurs in a variety of ways, the CCO is the decisive C-suite player. Through counsel and content, she influences public and employee opinion in leadership speeches, blogs, company hosting of government officials and elected representatives, production of publications, and websites.

Our point is that the CCO is a counselor putting communication strategies, practices, and tools into corporate civic performance. She understands the GR missions at the legislative and regulatory levels and she helps improves the company's odds for success.

In their 2009 book on corporate digital strategies, Paul A. Argenti, professor of corporate communication at the Tuck School of Business, and journalist Courtney M. Barnes, provide extremely useful insights into the wide spectrum of GR interests impacted by social media communication (Argenti and Barnes 2009).

Communicating in Washington

Citicorp of New York once observed in full-page advertisements in Washington newspapers: "Probably no phrase in the English language affords more ambiguity or opportunities for demagoguery than 'the public interest.' Aside from the obvious question of who has the right to speak for the public, there is the still larger problem of just whose interest is being protected, and from whom" (Harrison 1993, 86).

We use this to underscore the point we have repeatedly pushed in this book: *a company succeeds through shared values with stakeholders.* In politics, the CCO's mission and message must connect to public values, in order to get the attention and stir the action of members of Congress, executive branch officials, and others in elected and appointed positions.

Public interest connections are a basic selling point in GR. (While our guidance here is on collaboration in Washington, it is adaptable to state and local situations.[12])

As with a company, Washington is essentially a leadership system run by managers. Washington managers work toward BAOs of their leadership. The first rule of communicating in Washington, or at the state or local level, is to make sure you determine, reach, arm with information the manager of the issue in which the elected or appointed government official has authority.

A respected Washington public relations counselor some years ago (Wittenberg 1989) laid out the "ten commandments of lobbying" in a book warning that the business representative who fumbles the code and culture of the Washington political system risks the loss of his effectiveness.[13] Ernest Wittenberg, who for many years held monthly roundtables of company officials, Senators, and House members, saw the march of business representatives into Washington, seeking help for their companies, as a "parade for democracy." The result can be a victory celebration for the business representative, he said, if she knows the parade route and adopts an appropriate, purposeful demeanor.

As underscored by experienced civic participants such as Wittenberg in Washington, trust and thinking *other*-wise are the basis for influential business or government communication.

Context, content, and *tone* are qualities the CCO can bring to presentations, working with GR. This means the successful business communicator in Washington assures that

1. The case or appeal for action are articulated within the areas of interest, control, or influence of the lawmaker or executive branch and within the timeframe where attention and outcome are achievable.

---

[12] Because both authors have worked in D.C. (Mühlberg as Presidential aide in the White House; Harrison as press secretary to a member of Congress), it should not be a surprise that we use Washington as the venue to explore government relations, with emphasis on communication.

[13] The Wittenberg firm, after 23 years managing high-level government relations for hundreds of business clients, merged with E. Bruce Harrison Company in 1989, the year his book, *How to Win in Washington,* was published by Basil Blackwell, Inc., Cambridge, MA.

2. The presentation is open, honest, and easy to understand, backing up the need for action with facts and figures.

3. And the tone is that of the courteous, helpful collaborator; the focus of all the attention on the message of the moment and the reasons that fulfillment of any request will be a benefit to enterprise, jobs, communities, and other and government outcomes.

CCO "New Model" Leadership: Interactive Sustainability

With the communication, investor, and GR teams, discuss the comprehensive model of company sustainability, involving financial (especially investor), social (including culture and community interests), and civic (political, government stakeholder) implications. Ask "what can we do together that helps individual interests, and enables corporate communication?" (Note, if there is a corporate sustainability function, CCO interaction begins with that individual.) Chart points of collaboration in next quarter, or year.

CHAPTER 15

Continuing the Trustworthy Deal

The successful enterprise creates believers, customers, employment, and investment partners, and, in the best case, advocates for the firm's sustainability. We have in this book promoted the route to enterprise success. Arthur Page at AT&T described it as getting permission from participating publics. Fisher and Ury at Harvard called it "getting to yes." We have summed it up as making deals.

Shared values—win–win commitments—connect the enterprise with its followers as partners in achieving satisfaction and success. These mutual-benefit deals are held together by trust. As the stimulator and binder of the various deals that create company success, communication explains and extends that trust. Trustworthy leadership communication is required to apply the glue of potential deals into every decision and action that is made by every company's management. This puts the chief communication officer (CCO) into an *agent of trust* position.

The CCO is uniquely allied with the chief executive officer in a generalist view. Together they can work to define and harmonize the various elements of *social capital* that bring each class of stakeholders into sustainable deals.

Social capital is the name that historians and anthropologists use to describe the agreed value of forming and sustaining a deal. They have documented the way in which a national society, an ethnic group, a tribe, even a family, agrees on the dominating value of certain traditions and certain items. Forms of money (from shells and beads to distinctive coins and bills, or perhaps bitcoins), rules of inheritance, methods of marriage, acceptability of certain food—these and other totems and practices become the evidence of trust, the honored traditions of cultural acceptance. We can apply this social customization, these deals of culture, to business organizations (Dodd 2012). The *social capital* of free-enterprise business comes in the form of jobs, goods, and money. The company and its employees agree on a value-based relationship: contribution of effort and pay for performance. The company and its customers form agreements on products and services. Company investors and business partners bind together around monetary and economic deals. Trustworthy communication mates people and interests, creating mutual respect for the symbols—or social capital—embedded in the outcomes of shared value deals. Reaching and sustaining the specific social-capital rewards (which is precisely the target of Harvard's dispute resolution and Arthur Page's condition of consent) require the corporation to rely on the co-dependency of deals and trustworthy communication.

Communication brings the accepted social capital into play, defines it, and keeps its trustworthiness active. This is a major factor in placing the CCO at the intersection of deal-making between the company and its stakeholders. James E. Grunig, for many years teaching public relations to students at the University of Maryland, substantiated the equation in his work on "symmetrical communication" recognizing the sender–receiver–sender device for creating trust—which enables the deal. "Instead of thinking of the organization as the source of communication and the publics (stakeholders) as the receiver," observed Grunig, "both are conceived as groups in a transaction"[1] (Newsom et al. 2000).

The process of listening, understanding, and delivering on the desires of each group of stakeholders achieves the goodwill implicit in Grunig's symmetry. If permission and trust are mutually created and sustained through communication, the company gains a favorable reputation. Reinforced over time, this positive linkage yields positive thinking. Corporate reputations can reach the realm of honor, and that is the stimulant for new and long-sustaining relationships.

Broken Deals and Hope

One need not look far to find causes for deals falling apart. Disruptive conditions arise both inside the enterprise and in the contexts surrounding it. News of missteps or misstatements within the company's leadership can shake or break trust-based, value-sharing deals. Corporate communicators have at times been forced to agree with the cartoon sage of the cartoon swamps, Pogo, who somberly observed, "We have met the enemy and it is us." Disruption can come as the result of unintentional information provided by a company official in any of a number of contexts—a media interview, a speech, a phone call with investment analysts, or, in worse cases, such as during crisis conditions (one is reminded of the oil company chief's offhand remark, during the 2010 Gulf of Mexico spill).

External contexts are a more constant challenge to amicable relationships important to the organization's success. The inevitability of uncontrollable contexts, as well as the hope of maintaining deal-sustaining outcomes, has always been the reality of corporate communications. The best laid plans of product introduction are upset by a competing company's product announcement. Rehearsed, accurate, and compelling financial messages run into unexpected market news. Contexts win, in the contests shared with planned content and tone of delivery.

As an example of how long this has been going on in the United States, and to grasp some of the hope in dealing with obstructed deals, we dip once again into the wisdom of Arthur W. Page. In a speech at a public relations course conducted by New York Telephone Company soon after America's Great Depression, Page described the contexts impacting the United States and the Bell System, and the hope that emerged from that devastating reality. "During the last 25 years," said the phone company's thought leader, "we have lived under the 'square deal,' the 'new era,' and the 'new deal.' We have had a couple of panics, one first-class depression, a war, and some minor excitements" (Page 1936).

Shifting contexts laid waste to plans, Page acknowledged. However, as we counsel in this book, the crush of uncontrollable conditions can be followed by controlling the things one can. "During that period," said Page (1936), "the Bell System has grown and become consolidated in position and I think has improved its reputation and standing." He followed with the formula for hope: "If...business is to prosper we have to be sure that it is flexible so that it fits the times and needs of the people it serves." Figure 15.1 provides the Page Principles.

Looking within, flexing, and fitting times and needs: the sages—Pogo and Page—align. The honesty of seeing the enemy as us is almost

Tell the truth. Let the public know what's happening and provide an accurate picture of the company's character, ideals and practices.

Prove it with action. Public perception of an organization is determined 90 percent by what it does and 10 percent by what it says.

Listen to the customer. To serve the company well, understand what the public wants and needs. Keep top decision makers and other employees informed about public reaction to company products, policies and practices.

Manage for tomorrow. Anticipate public reaction and eliminate practices that create difficulties. Generate goodwill.

Conduct public relations as if the whole company depends on it. Corporate relations is a management function. No corporate strategy should be implemented without considering its impact on the public. The public relations professional is a policymaker capable of handling a wide range of corporate communication activities.

Realize a company's true character is expressed by its people. The strongest opinions—good or bad—about a company are shaped by the words and deeds of its employees. As a result, every employee—active or retired—is involved with public relations. It is the responsibility of corporate communications to support each employee's capability and desire to be an honest, knowledgeable ambassador to customers, friends, shareowners and public officials.

Remain calm, patient and good-humored. Lay the groundwork for public relations miracles with consistent and reasoned attention to information and contacts. This may be difficult with today's contentious 24-hour news cycles and endless number of watchdog organizations. But when a crisis arises, remember, cool heads communicate best.

Figure 15.1 The "Page principles"

always, though not guaranteed, to be accompanied by the fact that new starts and staying on course, true to our stakeholders are also us. Reality is hooked to hope. Visionary leaders—take Steve Jobs at Apple as the example—can change a vision from one course toward another. In Jobs' case, the reset vision led toward the best achieved outcome of highly profitable smartphones. Company leaders, having stumbled, can once again earn the permission to proceed, along a restated path of partnership with those with a stake in their success. Honesty, transparency, respect for stakeholder values, and the legal requirements supporting reconnection place great reliance on the connector—the chief communicators in the C-suites, who help the company to extend the reliable handshake of the mutually trusting "we" relationship.

Further encouragement to the CCO going forward: if the company has a base in American values, there is a historic nudge of trust. The collaborative deal-sharing quality seems to be particularly embedded in the American homeland. In his survey of young America, de Tocqueville noted with some astonishment the alacrity with which this country's citizens formed mutual-benefit associations; and Professor Francis Fukuyama at Johns Hopkins University affirmed this affinity for affiliation as a distinctive characteristic of American culture (Fukuyama 1996, 39).

The content of information—put it in motion and call it communication—is the social capital enabler, honoring and applying the glue of the deal. This is how the CCO leads in the C-suite and influences beyond. Communication not only enables the deal, it brings the confidence and the attitude of the deal into the company's culture. Employees understand the commitment to the deal and do their part to keep it active and renewable. The influence can and in our view should be aimed, through collaboration with the CEO and CFO especially, toward the nature of board member communication. BSR, a global nonprofit business network dedicated to sustainability, has underscored the corporate director role in the stakeholder communications process this way: "They have to act like the representatives of owners that they truly are. They have to insist on straight information that does not disguise unpleasant truths. They have to look to the effect of their decisions on the communities where they do business, for the sake of long-term sustainability."[2] In a real sense, every aspect of C-suite leadership depends to some degree on the CCO's aligning values that keep the company–stakeholder deal alive.

---

[1] Professor Grunig, University of Maryland, described four models of PR practice: (1) press agentry/publicity; (2) public information; (3) two-way asymmetric; and (4) two-way symmetric.

[2] See Business for Social Responsibility at http://www.bsr.org/en/about/bsr

Looking Ahead: How CCOs Will Lead

We put this book in front of you as the beginning, not the end, of your exploration and pursuit of victory in the top ranks of enterprise. Wherever you are, we ask you to listen, learn, leverage what you learn and from whom you learn toward the next opportunity, and then leave—in the sense that you move up to the next best achievable outcome (BAO), whether it's in the organization you're in now, or in a new opportunity, the next job (we call this "keeping plan B alive and attractive").

We present this book to readers with our perspective on how the CCO's leadership affects the organization. We draw on lessons learned for a current best-practices summary, and provide our view on what it will take in the near-term future to lead C-suite communication.

During our service as CCOs inside companies and as corporate communication counselors, one extraordinary point has been our major learned lesson: a company is less a conveyer of messages than *a convener of interests*. In every level of corporate leadership, winning or losing rests with the ability to use every communication facility to understand *what others look to the company to create and deliver to them*.

If you are the corporate communicator in a leadership position in a competitive enterprise, you are a force to connect the needs of stakeholders with the company's ability to deliver. This is increasingly complicated, given the fact that the contexts of connectivity constantly change. The dominant contexts—hyperactive social media and data-driven communication targeting—are a huge influence on the logic, content, and tone of connectivity. Disruption, whether planned or accidental, is both a competitive strategy and a communication menace. Influential, value-oriented enterprise connections can prevail only when leadership communicators are able to translate enterprise values into current stakeholder desires. In the technology-enhanced forest of tempting, disruptive connections, the competitive communicator will need to find the route to sustainable deals with the illumination of learned lessons. Here is our perspective, drawing from topics we have discussed in this book, and looking ahead to the probable future role of CCOs.

- The enterprise management process will continue along three proven paths: (1) vision that sets the challenge; (2) teams that connect and engage in strategic missions; and (3) execution toward collaborative, value-adding, stakeholder-building BAOs. Competent communication will continue to enable and energize the entire process.
- At the management level, the corporate CCO will find new uses for a distinctive advantage: *the perspective of a generalist*. While partners in the C-suite are focused on specialties (*e.g.,* financial, operational, human resources, legal performance, enterprise risk), the CCO will range over the field with a comprehensive view shared with one other management leader, the CEO. Using data analytics, new, and old-fashioned methods (*e.g.,* convening people in group or one-to-one discussion), CCOs and CEOs will focus C-suite vision, strategies, and execution on stakeholder interests.
- An escalating CCO influence in corporate success will require (1) advanced strategic management of a current, multichannel, incoming and outgoing, truthful and transparent flow of information; (2) direct- and data-driven interpretation of critical stakeholder perceptions, and (3) practical, ongoing, and personalized contribution to an informed, enabled corporate culture.
- CCOs will continue their role as enterprise physician in the diseases of poor timing and clumsy delivery that at times inflict leadership communication. Awareness of surrounding contexts, and the shaping of communication content and tone will continue to be the antidotes. Apology will still, at times, be the voice of an accountable aftermath. To facilitate healthy communication, CEOs, CFOs, and other C-suite colleagues will at times need the closed-door, "truth-to-power" counsel of CCOs who are competent in convening of interests.
- Already entrenched, the practice of *transformative*, rather than simply transactional, leadership will broaden. Planned disruption will grow as a competitive strategy. A brave new

battle for stakeholder support—indeed, advocacy—will be enabled at least in part by the CCO's grasp of big data to gauge stakeholder expectations, and to engage within the rings of customer preferences and market conditions.

- While leadership traits will always vary with executive leaders, trustworthiness and resourcefulness will sustain reliable leadership communication, outside and inside the enterprise. "Tell the truth and explain the hope" will stand the test of time as the corporate winner's mantra. Meanwhile, when progress is made, the best message of a leader to followers will always be: "Thank you, *you* did it."

- As for the best qualification of the CCO, beyond that of a generalist competent in influential communication, we underscore the *sine qua non* for respect in the C-suite. She must be *a business person, first*. With that respect, the CCO will be welcomed in virtually every C-suite function, including, for example, evaluating risks to financial and operational performance with the help of intelligence gathered in the stakeholder ecosystem. *See the Greg Elliott list in Chapter 4, with business questions every CCO should be able to answer.*

- CCO functionality will advance our perception of *listening* as the source of the river of learning, leveraging, and leading. The future successful CCO will be a listening virtuoso, attuned to the variances of context, expert in the shaping of content, and counselor in message-delivery tone in a world of swirling, 24/7, technology-enabled information, rumor, and facts. As companies accept as principle our *Everybody Knows Everything!* construct (put forth in this book as the spur for planned transparency), corporate leaders will lean into CCO competence to deal with the crowd-sourced flow of innuendo, confrontation, and expectation.

- CCOs will continue to increase their engagement in civic accountabilities, recognizing that in American enterprise, government *is* in the business of business. As these dynamics materialize, CCOs will become a greater advocate for fair, clear, sound, ethical principles that lead in trust-building.[3]

- As enterprise risk management rises as the ubiquitous concern of companies, CCOs will be a major player. The financial value implications of cyber risks will overshadow many of the risk factors routinely reported to investors as required by the SEC, galvanizing the attention of finance chiefs, and affecting not only data security or privacy but also brand or reputation.

In your role and rise as an enterprise communication leader, accept and create new ideas that have potential value in your influence with stakeholders. The early leader of IBM, Thomas Watson, Jr., talked about wild ducks. Watson's point was that if you are in business, dare to follow new ideas (wild ducks) that can give your enterprise a competitive edge, whether it is in products or services or—and this is important to you—it is the way leadership communication connects with stakeholders. The same, tamed, comfortable function won't necessarily fly for you in the arriving future challenges. Wherever you are, construct routes of influence and success as the leader in communication, and embrace change. Major trends and key influencers can be assessed by CCOs by, for example, tracking tweets through cyberspace. In 2014, AT&T's communication staff was monitoring 150 million online sources to measure the sentiment of what was being said about the company and its competitors in real time, according to the company's former CCO and now author-journalist Dick Martin. "Too much of public relations is based on gut feelings or past practices," Martin (2014, 82) observed in a *Conference Board Review* column; "The challenge is to use data—not on the back end of a program in counting clips or measuring outcomes but on the front end in the development of strategies."

CCO leadership now and in the years ahead will evolve from a data substantiated, strategic grasp of contextual communication generated outside and within the enterprise. As key members of participative management, CCOs will excel as the critical "connectors" and "change masters" described by Dr. Rosabeth Moss Kanter of Yale University's School

---

[3] For expert insights and guidance in business ethics, see the EthicalSystems.org site that went online in 2014.

of Management as enabling full-enterprise effort, and producing vanguard enterprises.[4]

In their roles as conveners of interests, CCOs must shine online. Shared value is now, and is certain to be more, heavily influenced by the shifting, wireless sands of shared belief. Potential stakeholders will be persuaded less by passive reception of corporate messages than by the emotional satisfaction that originates in connectivity with like-minded other people. The wavering strength of companies as reliable sources, perceived truth-tellers, or providers of value, has been quantified by a Page Society study.[5] Connectedness, led in the social media by participating corporate communicators, will become the bridge to mutuality and the essential link to trust. The restless search among potential stakeholders for social connectivity is every competitive enterprise's challenge. CCOs are at the front line in this quest for solid ground with stakeholders.

Truth and Behavior Need to Align

This book has emphasized the central role of communication. That emphasis calls to mind the conveying of influential information. We want to make certain that our readers understand that what is said is less important than what is done. Each day in corporate life, leaders need to focus on behavior, their own behavior and that of others in the enterprise. Corporate culture—that is, what people know and how people *act*

---

[4] See Kanter (1984, 2009).

[5] *Building Belief: A New Model for Activating Corporate Character & Authentic Advocacy,* Arthur W. Page Society (2012), shows that 75 percent of people don't believe that companies always tell the truth in advertising; nine out of 10 consumers online trust recommendations from people they know; seven out of 10 trust opinions of unknown users; 68 percent of consumers trust peer recommendations; and 61 percent trust family and friends and customer reviews more than they trust manufacturers, experts, or retailers. When online stakeholders' beliefs are honored and the enterprise pursues in such exercises as crowd-sourcing, *Building Belief* notes, "tremendous advocacy" can result. Read the "new model" news release at http://www.awpagesociety.com/news/arthur-w-page-society-unveils-new-model-for-corporate-communications

within the enterprise—constantly challenges what leaders *say about* the enterprise. John Kotter of Harvard's Business School described it well for us: "Behavior…that is contrary to the vision overwhelms all other forms of communication" (Kotter 1996). A veteran corporate communicator—Bill Nielsen, who headed the function at Johnson & Johnson—reminded students in a 2014 lecture in our Georgetown class that the CCO should communicate only what he holds in his heart to be true. Belief and behavior empower language. Leaders communicate and communicators lead with purpose. To start each day in the realm of leadership communication, a CCO could have no better reminder than this: *to participate effectively in enterprise leadership, what we say must be consistent with what we believe and what we do.*

References

Adler, B. May–June 2013. "Streams of Consciousness." *Columbia Journalism Review*, http://www.cjr.org/cover_story/steams_of_consciousness.php?page=all

Alessandra, A.J., and P.L. Hunsaker. 1993. *Communicating at Work*. New York, NY: Simon & Schuster.

Alinsky, S. 1969. *Reveille for Radicals*. New York, NY: Vintage Books.

Argenti, P., and C. Barnes. 2009. *Digital Strategies for Powerful Corporate Communications*. New York, NY: McGraw-Hill.

Arthur W. Page Society. June 22, 2007. *The Authentic Enterprise, an Arthur W. Page Society Report*. New York, NY: Arthur W. Page Society.

Arthur W. Page Society. 2013. *Corporate Character & Authentic Engagement: An Emerging Model of How Authentic Enterprises Create Sustainable Value and Competitive Advantage*. New York, NY: Arthur W. Page Society, http://www.awpagesociety.com/wp-content/uploads/2013/08/Corporate-Character-2013.pdf

Arthur W. Page Society. n.d. *Page Principles in Action*, http:www.awpagesociety.com

Ashooh, N. March 18, 2010. Lecture on Crisis Communication to Graduate Students at Georgetown University, Washington, D.C.

Augustine, N.R. 1994. *Managing the Crisis You Tried to Prevent*. Boston, MA: Harvard Business School Press.

Augustine, N.R. 2000. "Crisis Management." *Harvard Business Review*. Boston, MA: Harvard Business School Publishing.

Augustine, N.R., and K. Adelman. 1999. *Shakespeare in Charge*. New York, NY: Hyperion Books.

Baldoni, J. October 1, 2012. *Leader Traits Every Great Leader Must Demonstrate*, http://www.forbes.com/sites/johnbaldoni/2012/10/01/three-traits-every-great-leader-must-demonstrate/

Barrett, D.J. 2010. *Leadership Communication*. Irwin, CA: McGraw-Hill.

Barrett, R. February 14, 2013. *Business Analytics Strategy Thrive While Others Survive*, http://www.the-decisionfactor.com/business-analytics-strategy/thrive-while-others-survive-with-epm-and-bi/

Batstone D. 2003. *Saving the Corporate Soul & (Who Knows?) Maybe Your Own: Eight Principles for Creating a Preserving Integrity and Profitability without Selling Out*. San Francisco, CA: Jossey-Bass.

Beilock, S. 2010. *Choke: What the Secrets of the Brain Reveal About Getting it Right When You Have to*. New York, NY: Free Press.

Bennis, W. 1966. *The Leader as Storyteller*. Boston, MA: Harvard Business Review, *http://hbr.org/1996/01/the-leader-as-storyteller/ar/1*

Bennis, W. 1989. *On Becoming a Leader*. Reading, MA: Addison-Wesley.

Bennis, W. 1993. *An Invented Life: Reflections on Leadership and Change*. Reading, MA: Addison-Wesley.

Bennis, W. 1995. *Reinventing Leadership*. New York, NY: William Morrow & Company.

Bertini, M., and J.T. Gourville. June, 2012. "Pricing to Create Shared Value." *Harvard Business Review*.

Beyond Buzz Reputation vs. Character. Winter, 2014. *The Conference Board Review*, http://TCBreview.com/winter-2014/beyond-buzz-reputation-vs-character.html#sthash.75IPKfnz.dpuf

Bing, S. 2011. Review of *Damage Control: The Essential Lessons of Crisis Management*, http://www.amazon.com/Damage-Control-Revised-Updated-Management/dp/1935212249

Block, E. 2004. *Building Trust: Leading CEOs Speak Out: How They Create it, Strengthen it, and Sustain it*. New York, NY: Arthur W. Page Society, http://www.*awpagesociety.com*

Block, E. n.d. *The Legacy of Public Relations Excellence Behind the Name*, http://pagecenter.comm.psu.edu/index.php/about-the-page-center/arthur-w-page-bio

Bolton, R. n.d. "The Conscience of the Company." *Page Turner*, http://www.awpagesociety.com

Boston Consulting Group. 2012. *Improving the Odds: Value Creators Report 2012*. Boston, MA: The Boston Consulting Group

Bowen, S.A. 2010. "An Examination of Applied Ethics and Stakeholder Management on Top Corporate." *Public Relations Journal* 4, pp. 1–19, http://www.prsa.org/SearchResults/download/6D-040101/1012/An_Examination_of_Applied_Ethics_and_Stakeholder_M

Bowen, S.A., B. Rawlins, and T. Martin. 2010. *An Overview of the Public Relations Function*. New York, NY: Business Expert Press.

Bowen, S.A., and D.W. Stacks. 2013. "Toward the Establishment of Ethical Standardization in Public Relations Research, Measurement and Evaluation." *Public Relations Journal* 7, no. 3, pp. 1–28.

Bryant, A. May 19, 2012. "In One Adjective, Please Tell me Who You Are." *New York Times*, p.B2, http://www.nytimes.com/2012/05/20/business/chris-barbin-of-appirio-on-boiling-down-answers.html?ref=todayspaper

Bryant, A. June 18, 2012. "Caution, Please: The Boss's Office is a No-Spin Zone." *New York Times*, p. B2, http://www.nytimes.com/2012/06/17/business/shawn-wilson-of-ushers-new-look-foundation-on-leadership.html

Bryant, A. March 31, 2013. "Want to Know Me? Just Read My User Manual." *New York Times*, http://www.nytimes.com/2013/03/31/business/questbacks-lead-strategist-on-his-user-manual.html?ref=todayspaper&_r=3&;   http://www.questback.com/

Bryant, A. May 18, 2013. "If the Boss Rides a Harley, He Must Be Human." *New York Times*, p.B2, http://www.nytimes.com/2013/05/19/business/harry-herington-of-nic-on-building-trust-in-leaders.html?_r=0

Bryant, A. May 24, 2013. "Three Quick Rules: Be in, Be Real and Be Bold." *New York Times* Business, p. B2, http://www.nytimes.com/2013/05/24/business/brad-garlinghouse-of-yousendit-on-clear-leadership.html?_r=0

Bryant, A. May 27, 2013. "Getting Ahead by Having Answers Instead of Questions." *New York Times*, p. B2, http://www.nytimes.com/2013/05/28/business/getting-ahead-by-having-answers-instead-of-questions.html

Bryant, B. June 4, 2011. "Power? Thanks, but I'd Rather Have Influence, Corner Office." *New York Times*, p. B2.

Buckmaster, T. March 6, 2014. Graduate Lecture, Corporate Crisis Communication Course. Washington, DC: Georgetown University.

Buffett, W. February 22, 2011. "Using Influence to Get Things Done." *Strategy + Business*, http://www.strategy-business.com/article/11104?pg=2 - authors

Burns, J.M. 1979. *Leadership*. New York, NY: HarperCollins.

Capozzi, L., and S.L. Rucci. 2013. *Crisis Management in the Age of Social Media*. New York, NY: Business Expert Press.

CFO Magazine. November, 2013. *The Upside of ERM*, p. 43.

Charan, R. 2001. *What the CEO Wants You to Know: How Your Company Really Works*. New York, NY: Crown Business.

Charan, R. 2012. http://www.ram-charan.com/wp-content/uploads/2012/12/Know-How

Chasan, E. January 22, 2013. *In Early Post-JOBS Act IPR, Truilia CFO Chose Tougher Rules*, http://blogs.wsj.com/cfo/tag/sean-aggarwal/

Ciotti, G. 2013. *The 5 Most Persuasive Words in the English Language*, http://www.copyblogger.com/persuasive-copywriting-words/

Cohen, A.R. February 8, 2005. "How to Stop Passing the Blame Buck, Online Column." *Entrepreneur Magazine*, http://www.entrepreneur.com/article/76294

Collins, J. 2001. *Good to Great: Why Some Companies Make the Leap...and Others Don't*. New York, NY: Harper Business, http://en.wikipedia.org/wiki/Good_to_Great

Collins, J. October 2011. *The 20-Mile March*, http://www.jimcollins.com/books/great-by-choice.html

Collins, J., and M.T. Hansen. 2011. *Great by Choice*. New York, NY: HarperCollins.

Collins, J., and M.T. Hansen. 2011a. "How to Manage Through Chaos." *Fortune*. http://www.jimcollins.com/article_topics/articles/how-to-manage-through-chaos.html

Coombs, W.T. 2011. *Ongoing Crisis Communication: Planning, Managing, and Responding*. 3rd ed. Thousand Oaks, CA: Sage Publications.

Covey, S. 1989. *The 7 Habits of Highly Effective People*. New York, NY: Simon & Shuster.

Covey, S. 2004. *The 8th Habit: From Effectiveness to Greatness*. New York, NY: Simon & Shuster.

Covey, S.R. 1990. *Principle-Centered Leadership*. New York, NY: Simon and Shuster.

Covey, S.R. 1992. *Principle-Centered Leadership*. Fireside Ed. New York, NY: Simon & Schuster.

De Pree, M. 1989. *Leadership is an Art*. New York, NY: Bantam Doubleday Dell.

De Pree, M. 2010. *Leadership is an Art*. New York, NY: Dell.

Dezenhall, E. 2008. *Damage Control*. New York, NY: Penguin Group.

Dezenhall, E., and J. Weber. 2011. *Damage Control: The Essential Lessons of Crisis Management*. Westport, CT: ProspectaPress.

Dodd, M.D. 2012. *A Social Capital Model of Public Relations. Dissertation*. Coral Gables, FL: University of Miami.

Drucker, P. 1954–82. *Practice of Management*. New York, NY: Harper & Row.

Drucker, P. 1973. *Management: Tasks, Responsibilities, Practices*. New York, NY: Harper & Row.

Drucker, P. 1993. *Management: Tasks, Responsibilities, Practices*. New York, NY: HarperCollins.

Drucker, P. 1995. *The End of Economic Man*. Rutgers University, NJ: Transaction Publishers.

Drucker, P. 1996. *The Effective Executive*. New York, NY: HarperCollins.

Dudley, R. November 10, 2011. *Leading in Turbulent Times*, http://www.thunderbird.edu; see doi: http://www.youtube.com/watch?v=RXM51_Rs6lw

Edelman Worldwide. 2014. *The Trust Barometer*, http://www.edelman.com/insights/intellectual-property/2014-edelman-trust-barometer/

Elliot, G. December 3, 2013. Lecture at Georgetown University on Leadership in Communication, Washington, D.C.

Ewin, S. 1996. *PR! A Social History of Spin*. New York, NY: Basic Books.

Farkas, C.M., and S. Wetlaufer. 1996. "The Ways Chief Executive Officers Lead." In *Harvard Business Review on Leadership*. Boston, MA: Harvard Business School Press.

Feinberg, K.R. July 29, 2012. "How to Settle a Dispute, as Told to Spencer Bailey." *The New York Times Magazine*, p. 9.

Fisher, R., and W. Ury. 1981. *Getting to Yes*. New York, NY: Houghton-Mifflan. Penguin Books

Fisher, R., W. Ury, and B. Patton. 2011. *Getting to Yes*. New York, NY: Houghton-Mifflan.

Fiske R. October, 2009. "Today's PR Students Must Learn a Completely New Vocabulary." *PR Week,* http://www.prweekus.com/article/todays-pr-student-learn-completely-new-vocabulary/1270087

Foster, L. 1994. *Hall of Fame Acceptance Speech*, http://www.awpagesociety.com/speeches/1994-hall-of-fame-award-acceptance-speech/

Friedman T. May 19, 2011. "Do You Want the Good News First?" *New York Times, Sunday Review.*

Frosty. August 15, 2008. *Woody Allen Interview: Vicky Cristina Barcelona*, http://collider.com/entertainment/interviews/article.asp/aid/8878/tcid/1/pg/2

Fukuyama, F. 1992. *The End of History and the Last Man*. New York, NY: Free Press.

Fukuyama, F. 1996. *Trust: The Social Virtues and the Creation of Prosperity.* New York, NY: Free Press Paperbacks.

Gaines-Ross, L. May 1, 2003. "It's (Not That) Hard to Say You're Sorry." *Chief Executive.net,* http://chiefexecutive.net/its-ot-that-hard-to-say-youre-sorry

George, B. 1978. *Authentic Leadership: Rediscovering the Secrets to Creating Lasting Value.* San Francisco, CA: Jossey-Bass.

George, B. April 22, 2013. http://www.billgeorge.org/page/true-north

George, B., and P. Sims. 2007. *True North: Discover Your Authentic Leadership.* San Francisco, CA: Jossey-Bass.

Gerstein, M. and M. Ellsberg. 2008. *Flirting with Disaster: Why Accidents are Rarely Accidental.* New York/London: Union Square Press, Sterling Publishing Co.

Goffee, R., and G. Jones. May 2013. Creating the Best Workplace on Earth. *Harvard Business Review,* http://hbr.org/2013/05/creating-the-best-workplace-on-earth/ar/1

Goodman, G. 2011. *Corporate Communication Practices and Trends Study.* New York, NY: Corporate Communication International, www.corporatecomm.org

Graham, L. March 26, 2014. "Social-Media Coaches Spring up to Combat Bad Buzz." *The Wall Street Journal.*

Graham, P. (Ed.). 1955. *Mary Parker Follett: Prophet of Management, a Celebration of Writings from the 1920s.* Boston, MA: Harvard Business Books Press.

Grant A. 2013. *Give and Take: A Revolutionary Approach To Success.* New York, NY: Penguin Book.

Grates, G., K. Burton, and C. Learch. April 2013. *Best-in Class Practices in Employee Communication Through the Lens of 10 Global Leaders,* http://www.instituteforpr.org/orgcomm/best-in-class-practices-in-employee-communication-through-the-lens-of-10-global-leaders/

Griese, N.L. 2001. *Public Relations Pioneer, Patriot.* Tucker, GA: Anvil Publishers.

Grove, A.S. 1996. *Only the Paranoid Survive: How to Exploit the Crisis Points that Challenge Every Company.* New York, NY: Crown Business.

Grove, A.S. 1999. *Only the Paranoid Survive: How to Exploit the Crisis Points that Challenge Every Company.* New York, NY: Doubleday Publishing.

Groysberg, B., and M. Slind. 2012. *Talk, Inc.* Boston, MA: Harvard Business Review Press.

Groysberg, B., and M. Slind. 2012a. "Up and Down: The Promise of Trust-Based Leadership." In *Talk, Inc.* Boston, MA: Harvard Business Review Press.

Grunig, J.E., and T. Hunt. 1974. *Managing Public Relations.* Independence, KY: Centgage.

Halper, B.L., and K. Lubar. 2004. *Leadership Presence.* New York, NY: Penguin Group.

Hamilton, T. July 7, 2012. "Freeh Report Exposes an Unhealthy Culture of Reverence for Big-Time College Sports." *Washington Post,* http://www.washingtonpost.com/sports/colleges/freeh-report-exposes-an-unhealthy-culture-of-reverence-for-big-time-college-sports/2012/07/12/gJQA4GyIgW_story.html

Hammer, M. 2001. *The Agenda.* Troutdale, OR: Crown Business Books.

Harris, S. September 2010. Georgetown University Graduate School Lecture. Washington, DC: Georgetown University.

Harrison, E.B. 2008. *Corporate Greening 2.0: Create and Communicate Your Company's Climate Change and Sustainability Strategies.* Exeter, NH: Publishing Works.

Harrison, E.B. 1993. *Going Green: How to Communicate Your Company's Environmental Commitment.* Homewood, IL: Business One Irwin.

Harrison, E.B. 1999. *Going Green: How to Communicate Your Company's Environmental Commitment.* Burr Ridge, IL: Irwin Professional Publishing.

Harrison, E. B. 2011. *Communicating with the Boss: A No Spin Zone,* http://www.awpagesociety.com/2012/11/communicating-with-the-boss/

Hayward, S.F. 1997. *Churchill on Leadership: Executive Success in the Face of Adversity.* Rocklin, CA: Prima Publishing.

Hilton, A. August 23, 2012. "London Evening Standard." *PRWeek UK.*

Hoffman, B.G. 2012. *Nine Things I Learned from Alan Mulally.* Troutdale, OR: Crown Business, http://changethis.com/jmanifesto/93.01.AmericanIcon/pdf/9301.AmericonIcon.pdf

Immelt, J. 2010. *Growth Starts Here,* http://www.ge.com/ar2010/letter-video1.html

Institute for Public Relations. April 2013. *Best-in-Class Practices in Employee Communication Through the Lens of 10 Global Leaders*, http://www.instituteforpr.org/orgcomm/best-in-class-practices-in-employee-communication-through-the-lens-of-10-global-leaders/

Isaacson, W. 2011. *Steve Jobs.* New York, NY: Simon & Schuster.

Israel, S. 2009. *Twittervill.* New York, NY: Penguin Group.

Kanter, R.M. 1984. *The Change Masters.* New York, NY: Simon & Schuster.

Kanter, R.M. 2009. *Supercorp.* Troutdale, OR: Crown Business.

Katzenbach, J., and D. Smith. 1993. *The Wisdom of Teams.* Boston, MA: Harvard Business School Press.

Kawasaki, G. 2011. *Enchantment: The Art of Changing Hearts, Minds, and Actions.* New York, NY: Penguin Publishing Group.

Kellerman, B. 2008. *Followership: How Followers are Creating Change and Changing Leaders.* Boston, MA: Harvard Business Press.

Kellerman, D. 2010. *Leadership: Essential Selections on Power, Authority, and Influence.* New McGraw-Hill.

Kopecki, D., and H. Son. May 22, 2012. Victory for Dimon as JPMorgan Shareholders Reject CEO-Chairman Split. *Bloomberg*, www.bloomberg.com/news/2013-05-21/Victory for Dimon as JPMorgan Shareholders Reject CEO-Chairman Split

Kotter, J.P. 1996. *Leading Change.* Boston, MA: Harvard Business School Press.

Kouzes, J.M., and B.Z. Posner. 2012. *The Leadership Challenge: How to Make Extraordinary Things Happen in Organizations.* San Francisco, CA: Jossey-Bass.

Kurtzman. J. 1997. *Thought Leaders: Insights on the Future of Business.* San Francisco, CA: Jossey-Bass.

Luntz, F. 2007. *Words That Work: It's Not What You Say, It's What People Hear.* New York, NY: Hyperion Books.

Luntz, F. 2011. *Win: The Key Principles to Take Your Business from Ordinary to Extraordinary.* New York, NY: Hyperion Books.

MacDonald, M. 2012. *Dan Pink.* http://www.letgoandlead.com/2012/07/on-purpose/

Makower, J. 1994. *Beyond the Bottom Line: Putting Social Responsibility to Work for Your Business and the World.* New York, NY: Simon & Shuster.

Martin, D. 2012. *OtherWise: The Wisdom You Need to Succeed in a Diverse and Divisive World.* New York, NY: AMACOM, American Management Association.

Martin, D. 2014. "Mining the Future of PR: It's an Art Yes, But Don't Ignore The Science Behind It." *The Conference Board Review*, Spring.

Martin, T. 2008. *The Authentic Enterprise Provides Basis for Rich Discussion*, http://www.awpagesociety.com/2008/05/the-authentic-enterprise-provides-basis-for rich discussion/

Maslansky, M. November 7, 2013. Leadership in Communication Course, Class Lecture, Georgetown University.

Maslansky, M., S. West, G. DeMoss, and D. Saylor. 2010. *The Language of Trust: Selling Ideas in a World of Skeptics.* New York, NY: Prentice Hall.

Michaelson, D., and D.W. Stacks. 2011. "Standardization in Public Relations Measurement and Evaluation." *Public Relations Journal* 5, pp. 1–22.

Michaelson, D., and D.W. Stacks. 2014. *A Professional and Practitioner's Guide to Public Relations Research, Measurement, and Evaluation.* 2nd ed. New York, NY: Business Expert Press.

Michaelson, D., D.K. Wright, and D.W. Stacks. 2012. Evaluating Efficacy in Public Relations/Corporate Communication Programming: Towards Establishing Standards of Campaign Performance. *Public Relations Journal* 6, 1–25.

Milgram, S. 1974. *Obedience to Authority: An Experimental View.* New York, NY: Harper Collin.

Moore, N., M.L. Hickson, III, and D.W. Stacks. 2014. *Nonverbal Communication: Studies and Applications.* 6th ed. New York, NY: Oxford University Press.

Morsing, M., and D. Oswald. 2008. Novo Nordisk A/S: Integrating Sustainability into Business Practice." *Journal of Business Ethics Education* 5, pp. 193–222.

Moss, R.K. 2009. *Supercorp.* New York, NY: Crown Books.

MS & L Group. September 3, 2010. *Tuning out the Boss and Client*, http://blog.mslgroup.com/tuning-out-the-boss-and-client/

New York State University. October 1, 2009. *Enterprise Risk Management Initiative*, http://erm.ncsu.edu/library/article/balancing-risk-reward/

Newsom, G., J. Turk, and D. Kruckeberg. 2000. *This is PR: The Realities of Public Relations.* Belmont, CA: Wadsworth/Thomson Learning.

Noonan, P. February 6, 2006. "Hit Refresh." *Wall Street Journal*, http://online.wsj.com/news/articles/SB114005840229575522

Novak, M. 1996. *The Future of the Corporation.* Washington, DC: The AEI Press.

O'Rourke, J.S. 2008. *The Truth About Confident Presenting.* Upper Saddle River, NJ: Prentice-Hall.

Op-ed. December 31, 2012. *The New York Times,* http://www.nytimes.com/2012/12/31/opinion/krugman-brewing-up-confusion.html

Page, A.W. December 10, 1936. *Public Relations Today and the Outlook for the Future.* Speech presented at New York Telephone Company, speech number 20 contained in *Words from a Page in history, the Arthur W. page speech collection.* Arthur W. Page Center for Integrity in Public Communication, Pennsylvania State University, http://pagecenter.comm.psu.edu

Page, A.W. 1941. *Bell Telephone System.* New York, NY: Harper and Brothers.

Pandya, M., J. Brown, S. Junnarkar, S. Shell, and S. Warner. December 10, 2004. *Best of the Best: Inside Andy Grove's Leadership at Intel,* http://www.ftpress.com/articles/article.aspx?p=345010

Pandya, M., and R. Shell. 2006. *Lasting Leadership.* Philadelphia, PA: Wharton School Publishing.

Pandya, M., and R. Shell. 2006. *Lasting Leadership.* Upper Saddle River, NJ: Wharton School Publishing, Prentice-Hall.

Peck, M. S. 2003. *The Road Less Traveled: A New Psychology of Love, Traditional Values and Spiritual Growth..* New York, NY: Touchstone Books.

Synge, P.M. 1990. *The Fifth Discipline.* New York, NY: Doubleday Currency.

Peters, T., and R. Waterman. 1982. *In Search of Excellence: Lessons from America's Best-Run Companies.* New York, NY: Grand Central Publishing.

Pew Research Center. 2013. "Digital: As Mobile Grows Rapidly, the Pressures on News Intensify." *The State of the News Media 2013,* http://stateofthemedia.org/2013/digital-as-mobile-grows-rapidly-the-pressures-on-news-intensify/

Pink, D.H. 2009. *Drive: The Surprising Truth About What Motivates Us.* New York, NY: Riverhead Books, Penguin.

Pink, D.H. 2009. *Drive: The Surprising Truth About What Motivates Us.* New York, NY: Riverhead Books, http://www.ted.com/talks/dan_pink_on_motivation.html

Porter, M.E. 1980. *Competitive Strategy: Techniques for Analyzing Industries and Competitors.* New York, NY: Free Press.

Porter. M.E., J.W. Lorsch, and N. Nohria. October 2004. "Seven Surprises for New CEOs." *Harvard Business Review,* http://hbr.org/2004/10/seven-surprises-for-new-ceos/ar/

Powell, C., and T. Koltz. 2012. *It Worked for Me: In Life and Leadership.* New York, NY: Harper.

PR Week. September 1, 2010. *Social Media Survey 2010: The Social Connection,* http://www.prweekus.com/social-media-survey-2010-the-social-connection/article/177511/2/

Provost, T. May 22, 2013. "Regulatory Climate Puts Tech Firms on Edge." *CFO Magazine,* http://ww2.cfo.com/regulation/2013/05/regulatory-climate-has-tech-companies-on-edge/

Reputation Institute. 2008. *What's in a Name?* http://www.reputationinstitute.com/frames/press/India_030803.html

Ries, A., and J. Trout. 1981. *Positioning: The Battle for Your Mind.* New York, NY: McGraw-Hill.

Ries, A., and J. Trout. 1982. *Positioning: The Battle for Your Mind.* New York, NY: Warner Books.

Rosenzweig, P. 2007. *The Halo Effect.* New York, NY: Free Press.

Rottenberg, J. June 2012. "The Real Leadership Lessons of Steve Jobs, Interaction/ Letters to the Editor." *Harvard Business Review*, http://hbr.org/2012/04/the-real-leadership-lessons-of-steve-jobs/ar/1

Safire, W. May 5, 1995. "On Language: Stakeholders Naff? I'm Chuffed." *The New York Times*, http://www.nytimes.com/1996/05/05/magazine/on-language-stakeholders-naff-i-m-chuffed.html

Salonek, T. September 2012. *Leadership as a Conversation: Intentionality*, http://tomsalonek.com/leadership-as-a-conversation-intentionality/

Sarnoff, D., and G. Moore. 1989. *Never be Nervous Again*. New York, NY: Ivy Books.

Scarborough, J. September 17, 2012. *MSNBC Morning Joe show*.

Schrieber, E. April 12, 2013, http://www.linkedin.com/groups?home=&gid=47 46864&trk=anet_ug_hm

Schultz, H. August 9, 2011. *Leading Through Uncertain Times*, http://www.starbucksmelody.com/2011/08/09/message-from-howard-schultz-leading-through-uncertain-times/

Schultz, H. 2012. *Onward: How Starbucks Fought for Its Life Without Losing Its Soul*. Emmaus, PA: Rodale Books.

Scobel, R., and S. Israel. 2006. *Naked Conversations*. New York, NY: John Wiley & Sons.

Scott, B. 2003. *Consulting on the Inside*. Alexandria, VA: American Society for Training & Development.

Seidman, D. 2007. *How: Why HOW We Do Anything Means Everything*. Hoboken, NJ: John Wiley & Sons.

Sellers, P. July 24, 2013. "A General's Advice on Surviving a Setback." *Fortune Money*, http://postcards.blogs.fortune.cnn.com/2013/07/24/a-generals-advice-on-surviving-a-setback/

Shea, G.F. 2002. *Mentoring: How to Develop Successful Mentor Behaviors*. Menlo Park, CA Crisp Publications.

Sheffer, G. February 7, 2013. Lecture to Graduate Students, Georgetown University, Washington, DC.

Smith, N. 2008. *I Was Wrong: The Meanings of Apologies*. New York, NY: Cambridge University Press.

Sorkin, A.R. February 4, 2014. "Too Many Sorry Excuses for Apology." *The New York Times*, p. B1.

St. Louis Elmo, E. 1898. *The AIDA Sales Funnel*," http://www.provenmodels.com/547

Stacks, D.W. 2011. *Primer of Public Relations Research*. 2nd ed. New York, NY: Guilford.

Stacks, D.W. December, 2012. *Using Research to Understand Stakeholder Expectations*, Presentation Given to the Reputation Institute.

Stewart, J.B. July 6, 2013. "Boss's Remark, Employee Deed and Moral Quandary." *New York Times*, http://www.nytimes.com/2013/07/06/business/moral-quandaries-at-mf-global.html?pagewanted=2&_r=0&nl=todaysheadlines&emc=edit_th_20130706

Streitfeld, D., and C. Haughney. August 17, 2013. "Expecting the Unexpected from Jeff Bezos." *The New York Times*, http://www.nytimes.com/2013/08/18/business/expecting-the-unexpected-from-jeff-bezos.html?pagewanted%253Dall

Sudhaman, A. August 28, 2013. "Nokia's Susan Sheehan: Challenger Brand." *The Holmes Report*, http://www.holmesreport.com/people-info/13842/Challenger-Brand.aspx?sthash.iP4lKgwu.mjjo#sthash.iP4lKgwu.3BcfyoBz.dpuf

Surowiecki, J. July, 2012. "Bankers Gone Wild." *New Yorker magazine*, http://www.newyorker.com/talk/financial/2012/07/30/120730ta_talk_surowiecki

Taleb, N.N. 2007, *The Black Swan: The Impact of the Highly Improbable*. New York, NY: Random House.

Teach, E. November 13, 2013. "The Upside of ERM." *CFO Magazine*, http://ww2.cfo.com/risk-management/2013/11/upside-erm/

Wall Street Journal. April 22, 2013. *BCG Releases a Compendium of Winning Moves and Strategies for Leaders to "Own the Future"*, http://online.wsj.com/article/PR-CO-20130422-900015.html

Welch, J. November 11, 2013. "Four Sure-Fire Ways to Motivate Your People and Dinner with You Isn't One of Them." *Business Week*, http://www.linkedin.com/today/post/article/20131104192204-86541065-four-sure-fire-ways-to-motivate-your-people-and-dinner-with-you-isn-t-one-of-them

Wharton School. 2003. *Lasting Leadership: Lessons from the 25 Most Influential Business People of Our Times*, http://knowledge.wharton.upenn.edu/article.cfm?articleid=1054

Wilson, M. February 22, 2013. *How Southwest Airlines Wrangled Four Social Media Crises*, http://www.prdaily.com/crisiscommunications/Articles/13906.aspx

Wittenberg, E. 1998. *How to Win in Washington*. Cambridge, MA: Basil Blackwell, Inc.

Zakaria, F. 2009. *The Post-American World*. New York, NY: W.W. Norton.

Zinsser, W. 1993. *Writing to Learn*. New York, NY: Harper Collins.

Web Links

http://2012annualreport.jnj.com/chairmans-letter

http://businessroundtable.org/uploads/studies reports/downloads/BRT_Principles_of_Corporate_Governance_-2012_Formatted_Final.pdf

http://cdn.exxonmobil.com/~/media/Reports/Summary%20Annual%20Report/2012/news_pub_sar-2012.pdf

http://corporate.ford.com/doc/ar2012-2012%20Annual%20Report.pdf

http://en.wikipedia.org/wiki/Chief_sustainability_officer#cite_note-3

http://h30261.www3.hp.com/phoenix.zhtml?c=71087&p=irol-irhome&jumpid=reg_r1002_usen_c-001_title_r0002

http://h30261.www3.hp.com/phoenix.zhtml?c=71087&p=irol-irhome&jumpid=reg_r1002_usen_c-001_title_r0002

http://hbw.niri.org/Main-Menu-Category/advocate/Regulatory-Positions.aspx

http://investor.apple.com/secfiling.cfm?filingID=1193125-11-282113&CIK=320193

http://myfuture.com/careers/details/chief-sustainability-officers_11-1011.03

http://nysemanual.nyse.com/LCM/Search/default.asp

http://www.apparelcoalition.org/

http://www.awpagesociety.com/

http://www.berkshirehathaway.com/2012ar/2012ar.pdf

http://www.bsr.org/en/about/bsr

http://www.corporatecomm.org/pdf/PRCoalitionPaper_9_11Final.pdf

http://www.edgr.com

http://www.emeraldinsight.com/journals.htm?articleid=1771024

http://www.ethicalsystems.org/

http://www.ge.com/ar2012/#!report=letter-to-shareowners

http://www.ge.com/investor-relations

http://www.haygroup.com/ww/press/details.aspx?id=24434

http://www.history.com/topics/securities-and-exchange-commission

http://www.ibm.com/annualreport/2012/letter-from-the-chairman.html

http://www.intertech.com/Winning-Business/Articles/Tom-Salonek-Big-Biz-Show.aspx

http://www.jnj.com/sites/default/files/pdf/jnj_ourcredo_english_us_8.5x11_cmyk.pdf

http://www.nytimes.com/2011/04/23/us/23spill.html?_r=3&

http://www.patagonia.com/us/footprint/

http://www.sec.gov/answers/annrep.htm

http://www.sec.gov/answers/annrep.htm

http://www.sec.gov/answers/form10k.htm

http://www.sec.gov/Archives/edgar/data/104169/000119312506066792/d10k.htm

http://www.sec.gov/Archives/edgar/data/37996/000115752311001210/a6622311.htm

http://www.sec.gov/Archives/edgar/data/80424/000008042412000063/fy2012financialstatementsf.htm

http://www.sec.gov/edgar.shtml
http://www.sec.gov/edgar/searchedgar/companysearch.html
http://www.successories.com/iquote/author/1895/warren-g-bennis-quotes/1
www.awpagesociety.com/insights/ceo-view

Index

CPSIA information can be obtained at www.ICGtesting.com
Printed in the USA
BVOW08s1650151214

379064BV00007B/14/P

9 781606 498088